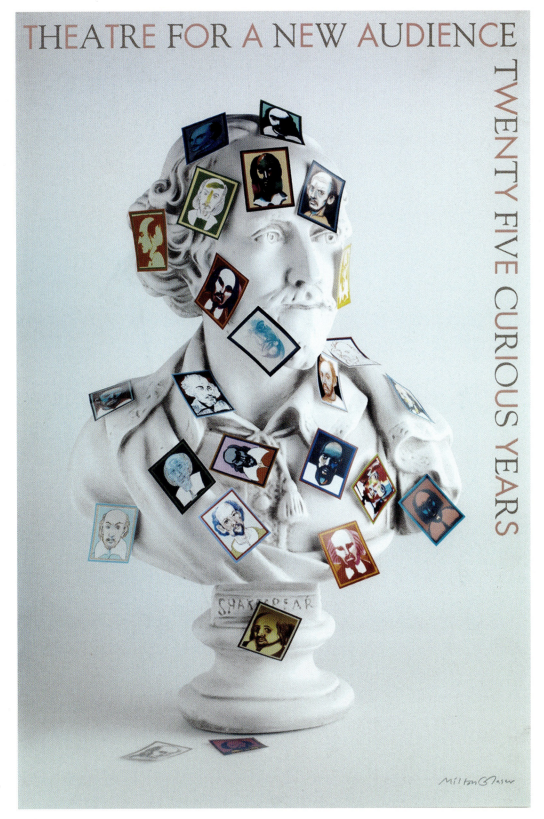

*25 Curious Years*, Theatre for a New Audience, US, 2004. **d:** Milton Glaser, **p:** Matthew Klein

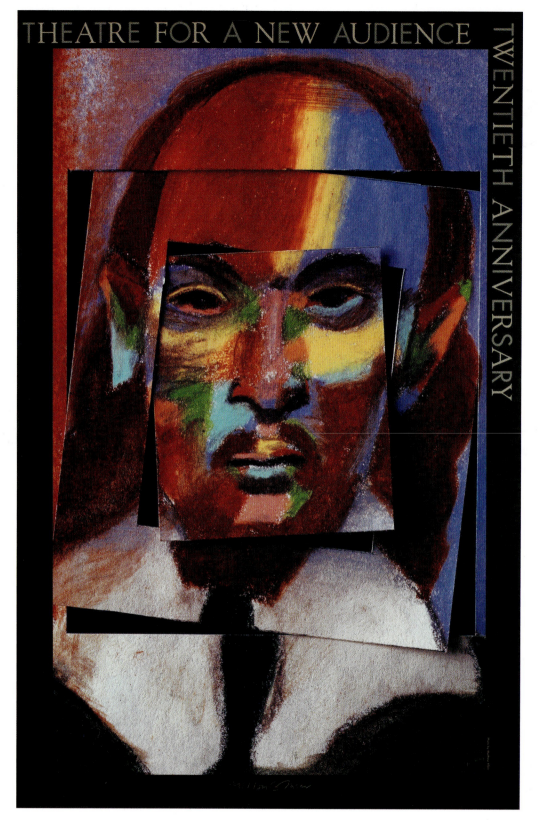

*20th Anniversary*, Theatre for a New Audience, US, 1999. d/ill: Milton Glaser

# PRESENTING SHAKESPEARE

1,100 Posters from Around the World

MIRKO ILIĆ & STEVEN HELLER

PREFACE BY JULIE TAYMOR

Princeton Architectural Press, New York

Published by
Princeton Architectural Press
37 East Seventh Street
New York, New York 10003

Visit our website at www.papress.com.

© 2015 Mirko Ilić and Steven Heller
All rights reserved
Printed and bound in China
18 17 16 15  4 3 2 1  First edition

No part of this book may be used or reproduced in any manner without written permission from the publisher, except in the context of reviews.

Every reasonable attempt has been made to identify owners of copyright. Errors or omissions will be corrected in subsequent editions.

Editor: Sara E. Stemen

Designer: Mirko Ilić

Cover art: left: Twelfth Night, Teatr Dramatyczny im. Jerzego Szaniawskiego, PL, 1980. d: Grzegorz Marszalek (Dydo Poster Collection); right: Rotterdam Toneel, NL, 1959. d: N. Wijnberg; back cover: Free Shakespeare in Central Park, The Public Theater, Delacorte Theater, US, 1993. ad: Jim Russek, d: Rafal Olbinski

Special thanks to: Nicola Bednarek Brower, Janet Behning, Erin Cain, Carina Cha, Andrea Chlad, Tom Cho, Barbara Darko, Benjamin English, Jan Cigliano Hartman, Jan Haux, Lia Hunt, Valerie Kamen, Stephanie Leke, Mia Johnson, Diane Levinson, Jennifer Lippert, Jaime Nelson, Rob Shaeffer, Marielle Suba, Kaymar Thomas, Paul Wagner, Joseph Weston, and Janet Wong of Princeton Architectural Press
—Kevin C. Lippert, publisher

Library of Congress Cataloging-in-Publication Data

Ilić, Mirko, 1956–
Presenting Shakespeare : 1,100 posters from around the world / Mirko Ilić, Steven Heller.
    pages cm
    ISBN 978-1-61689-292-0 (hardback)
    1. Theatrical posters. 2. Shakespeare, William, 1564-1616—Stage history. I. Heller, Steven. II. Title.
    PR3091.I55 2015
    741.6'74—dc23
            2015004930

Dedicated to our leading players, our children:
Zoe Ilić, Ivo Ilić, and Nicolas Heller

We are extremely grateful to the the designers and interns (noted below) at Mirko Ilić Corp. who tirelessly organized and captioned the massive amounts of international material we assembled for this book.

Bethany Ulrich, Claudia Arisso, Daniel Kolb, Evan Pokrandt, Helen Slatvusky, Ivana Vasić, Jenny Jeensun Chae, Jessica Jang, Jessica Yueng, Margethe Harboe, Michelle Quick, Rida Abbasi, Sandra Divković, Shaina Andrews, Yijun Zhu

Thanks also to our friends and colleagues who provided access to private and institutional collections, libraries, museums, and archives. Without their friendship and generosity, this book would not be possible.

Budapest Poster Gallery, Chisholm Larsson Gallery, NYC, Contest Watchers & Goce Mitevski, Georgian State Museum of Theatre, Music, Cinema, and Choreography, Krzystof Dydo & Dydo Poster Collection, Museum Folkwang—Deutsches Plakat Museum, National Theatre (London), Pentagram (New York/London), Philadelphia Shakespeare Theatre, Royal Shakespeare Company, Adnan Omerović, Branko Dursum, Dejan Kršić, Gordana Hrenovica, Misha Beletsky, Patrick Argent, Risa Akita, Rusmir Efendić, Šejla Šehabović, Sofia Babluani, Victoria Honey, Yohey Horoshita, Zijad Mehić

MI + SH

## CAPTION ABBREVIATIONS

ed    Executive Director
cd    Creative Director
ad    Art Director
d     Designer
ill   Illustrator
p     Photographer
art   Artist

## ABBREVIATIONS BY COUNTRY

AL    Albania
AM    Armenia
AR    Argentina
AT    Austria
AU    Australia
BA    Bosnia and Herzegovina
BE    Belgium
BG    Bulgaria
BO    Bolivia
BR    Brazil
CA    Canada
CH    Switzerland
CL    Chile
CN    China
CO    Colombia
CZ    Czech Republic
DE    Germany
DK    Denmark
ES    Spain
FI    Finland
FR    France
GE    Georgia
GR    Greece
HR    Croatia
HU    Hungary
IE    Ireland
IL    Israel
IN    India
IR    Iran
IT    Italy
JP    Japan
LT    Lithuania
LV    Latvia
ME    Montenegro
MK    Macedonia
MX    Mexico
NL    The Netherlands
NZ    New Zealand
PA    Panama
PL    Poland
PR    Puerto Rico
PS    Palestine
PT    Portugal
RO    Romania
RS    Serbia
RU    Russia
SG    Singapore
SI    Slovenia
SK    Slovakia
TR    Turkey
TT    Trinidad and Tobago
UA    Ukraine
UK    United Kingdom
US    United States
UY    Uruguay
ZA    South Africa

...And There's Still Free Shakespeare in Central Park, The Public Theater, Delacorte Theater, US, 1973. d: Susan Frank

*As Y'All Like It*, Saratoga Shakespeare Company, US, 2008. **ad/d:** Tom Rothermel, Erin Rossi

Preface **11**

Introduction **15**

HAMLET **25**

AS YOU LIKE IT **61**

KING LEAR **71**

MUCH ADO ABOUT NOTHING **87**

ROMEO AND JULIET **93**

THE TAMING OF THE SHREW **115**

THE HISTORIES PART I **123** *Richard II; Richard III*

THE HISTORIES PART II **137** *Henry IV 1+2  Henry VI 1*
*Henry V    Henry VIII*
*John*

A MIDSUMMER NIGHT'S DREAM **149**

JULIUS CAESAR **169**

THE COMEDIES **177** *Merry Wives; 2 Gentlemen of V*
*Pericles*
*L. L. Lost   All's well that ends well*

OTHELLO **191**

TWELFTH NIGHT **207**

THE TRAGEDIES **219** *Titus A     A. Cleopatra*
*Coriolanus  Troilus . Cressid"*
*Timon of A*

THE COMEDY OF ERRORS **235**

THE TEMPEST **243**

THE TRAGICOMEDIES **253** *M for measure  2 Noble Kinsmen*
*M of Venice    Winters Tale*
*Cymbeline*

MACBETH **273**

ANTHOLOGIES **301**

Acknowledgments **319**

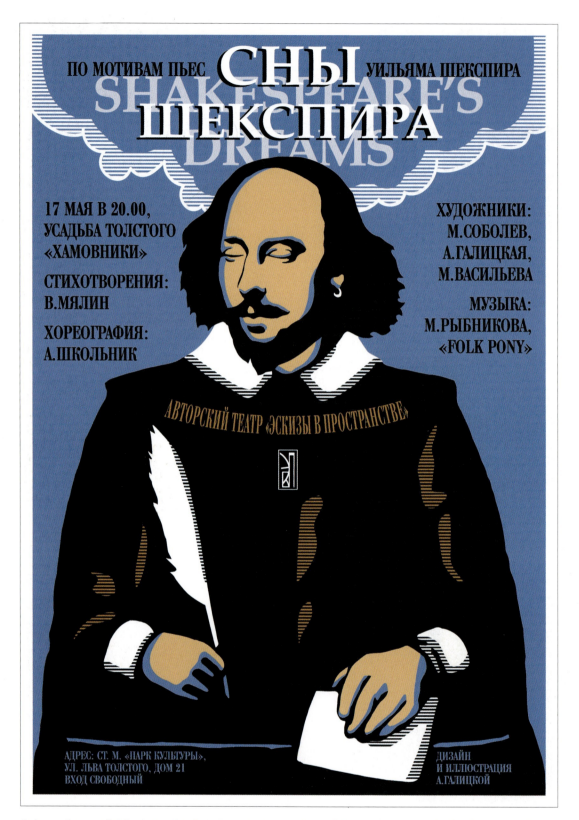

*Shakespeare's Dreams*, "Outlines in Space," Author's Theater, Leo Tolstoy's Khamovniki Memorial Estate, RU, 2014. ad/d: Alexandra Galitskaya

*The Philadelphia Shakespeare Festival*, Philadelphia Shakespeare Theatre, US, 2006. **d:** Mathew McFarren

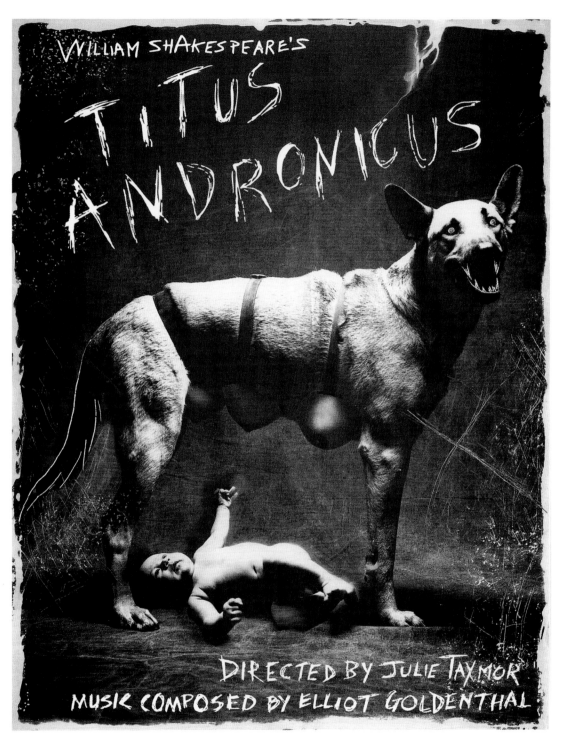

*Titus Andronicus*, Theatre for a New Audience, US, 1994. **ad:** Julie Taymor, **p:** Kenneth Van Sickle

# PREFACE BY JULIE TAYMOR

To create a poster for a Shakespeare play is to tap into its essence and evolve an ideograph, a visual gesture that epitomizes the particular production. Like the director and the stage designer, the poster artist searches for emblematic clues in Shakespeare's poetry, from its fantastical and graphic imagery presented in both word and action and also from the overarching political, psychological, and philosophical themes of the play. The collaboration with the creative team presenting the play—and its particular vision—will naturally contribute to the creation of the artwork as well.

The greatness of a Shakespeare play is its allowance for multiple interpretations, as one can witness from the extreme diversity of the posters within this book. A Midsummer Night's Dream can be conveyed as a light, rollicking romp in the woods for one theater troupe or a dark dialectic on the perils of love, lust, and marriage for another. If well done, both interpretations can work, and the poster for each production will signal what manner of world the audience will be entering. Certain plays contain pervasive, elemental imagery that makes its way into many production posters: the bloodied hand in Macbeth, the skull in Hamlet, a crown of daggers for a multitude of history plays—all are recurring emblems.

### About Titus Andronicus Design

*Romulus and Remus, the mythic twin babes who later founded Rome, were suckled by a she-wolf. And Titus proclaims, "Rome is but a wilderness of tigers...." This hand-scratched, black-and-white photo of a German shepherd suckling an infant suggests the nature of the play. The strapped-on tits were inspired by the work of Joel-Peter Witkin, projecting a sense of playfulness, black humor, and cruelty that is endemic to Shakespeare's vision.*

*National Shakespeare Festival*, **Old Globe Theatre**, US, 1964. **d:** Carl Newman (Museum Folkwang, Deutsches Plakat Museum)

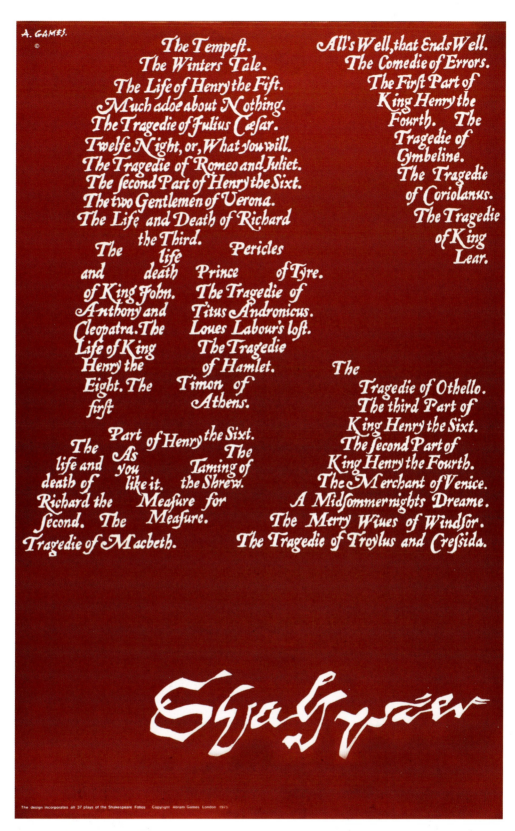

*Shakespeare*, Royal Shakespeare Theatre, UK, 1975. **d**: Abram Games

*Cymbeline Poster Advertisement*, Theatre-Royal, Covent Garden, UK, 1779.

# INTRODUCTION

Four hundred years have passed since death suck'd the honey of his breath. Yet the Bard of Avon's exalted place in the pantheon of theater and poetry—and within the panoply of Western culture—continues, as unshakably monumental as ever. Of course, all thespians worthy of a second curtain call must have at least one Shakespearean performance on their résumé—and all poets must have iambic pentameter coursing through their veins. William Shakespeare is the reason that all the world's a stage and all the men and women are actors. To be truly literate is to wholeheartedly embrace Shakespeare's language. His immortal words speak of the human condition in all its comedic and tragic guises—which is why the seventeenth-century playwright and theatrical critic Ben Jonson proclaimed that Shakespeare "is not of an age but for all time!"

Yet Shakespeare was not known in his own time as the lone star that intensely brightened the sky and bestowed the English language with scores of its most memorable quotations, spoken by the greatest characters in theater. "We now think of William Shakespeare as a unique genius,..." writes Jonathan Bate in *Shakespeare in Art* (Merrell, 2003), "but in his own time, though widely admired, he was but one of a constellation of theatrical stars."

So, what took place during Shakespeare's short lifetime that so enthralled the virgin Queen Elizabeth I and King James I, excited London audiences, and left such an indelible mark on literary legend? Might there have been some artistic alchemy that helped Shakespeare fall into history's arms?

In *Shakespeare in Art* Bate asks a simple question about the prominence of art in the Bard's mythos: "What is the wider cultural story behind the emergence of Shakespearean painting and engraving?" As the authors of the first-ever curated collection of international Shakespearean theatrical posters, we rephrased Bate's query in a way that helped us initiate our own explorations. Could these posters have brought fame to the Bard, or did Shakespeare's work inspire graphic designers to alter the course of poster design?

Bate's scholarly examination of Bardcentric artwork not only attempts to explain the reasons why legions of painters, printmakers, and sculptors chose to depict the scenes and players from Shakespeare's worlds, but why they also evidently opted *not* to visually interpret plays and players by his most significant contemporaries. As early as the seventeenth century, there was no business like Bard business. From hand printing presses to digital LED screens, mass media and communications technology have ensured that Shakespeare as a brand has enjoyed a vastly greater range around the globe than any other playwright living or dead. Audiences were stimulated, in part, by the publication of alluring (and even some less-than-stellar) works of art and design created to commemorate and promote the Shakespeare franchise. This form of sophisticated public relations, which tapped into the art scene before and after Shakespeare's death, might explain how his body of work became so renowned while the others of his generation are less remembered.

**What Fame This Mortal Be**

Life *and* death have been more than kind to William Shakespeare. He was born in Stratford-upon-Avon in 1564 and made his career in London from 1585 through 1592 as an actor, writer, and part owner of the players' repertory called Lord Chamberlain's Men (later renamed King's Men). The regular staging of Shakespearean tragedies, histories, and comedies during his fifty-two years was a successful business, and Will was well paid. Most important, Shakespeare's talents helped him become—as he continues to be—a beacon with unprecedented pop-star recognition. So after his death in 1616, King's Men, the company in which he had retained a profitable share, aggressively resisted all attempts to abridge its exclusive right—or monopoly—to perform the Bard's plays. Although the notion of copyright law did not yet exist, measures to prohibit their publication were scrupulously employed because, Bate notes: "Dissemination in print could have led to rival productions."

Yet despite King's Men's safeguards and prohibitions, in 1619 an unauthorized edition of ten plays was published—although it was only briefly made available to buyers before sales were stopped. Indignant shareholders immediately

*New Theatre Poster Advertisement*, New Theatre, UK, 1831. d: George Robert Gitton

sought and received a quasilegal judgment (akin to a restraining order) that blocked distribution of the rogue publication. King's Men was therefore encouraged to preempt future pirating efforts by publishing an edition of its own in 1623, with the descriptive and lengthy title *Mr. William Shakespeares Comedies, Histories, & Tragedies. Published according to the True Originall* [sic] *Copies*. The volume was printed by Isaac Jaggard, son of printer William Jaggard, and distributed by Edward Blount, with an introductory quotation (or blurb by any other name) by Ben Jonson. Famously referred to as the "First Folio," these historic pages represented half of Shakespeare's known work and helped secure, through its distribution to important patrons and institutions, his absolute reign over the English theater.

In 1660, Oliver Cromwell's repressive religious ban of all theaters and theatrical presentations (and the punitive decrees that branded actors as "rogues") ended when King Charles II was restored to the throne. As part of Charles's more liberal policies, he immediately issued "patents" or licenses for theaters to reopen, after having been shut for almost two decades. A slew of technical alterations influenced the established paradigms of Shakespearean imagery, as evolutions in both printing technology and the art of stagecraft altered the look and feel of Shakespearean visual art. For instance, Christopher Baugh notes in *Shakespeare in Art* that the introduction of moveable scenery during the late seventeenth century impacted the nuanced gestural poses of actors and changed how they physically performed the Bard's speeches on stage. This, in turn, influenced how the characters were rendered by stage artists, which led to new dramatic and comic stereotypes of Shakespearean performers.

Eventually, the widespread availability of Shakespeare's work led to what Bate calls "the cult of Shakespeare" during the 1730s, when restrictions were lifted for inexpensive editions to be published for popular consumption—and the floodgates were opened. In fact, a quarter of all the plays performed on London stages at that time had been penned by Shakespeare. These performances were just one ingredient in the business of theater, involving the concerted efforts of not just producers and other backstage individuals but printers, publishers, illustrators, and painters, who promoted not only Shakespeare's but others' work into the public sphere. Yet Shakespeare's credited works had been the first to appear in quarto editions, which inevitably had helped raise his fame.

Artists and illustrators often reinterpreted the works, liberally adding characters to tableaux and inventing their own distinct backdrops. This surge in illustrations and set design, according to Baugh, ensured the ascendancy of Shakespeare as England's national poet and playwright, resulting in his virtual beatification as the country's theatrical saint.

Shakespearean imagery became a plentiful and fashionable commodity. The eighteenth-century art print market was all aflurry with Shakespearean activity. Sold by subscription, etchings and engravings capturing key details and dramatic moments from *Macbeth*, *Richard III*, and *Hamlet*, among others, further popularized and proselytized for the Bard. In addition, a lively business in theatrical portraits promoted the great and near-great Shakespearean actors of the day and gave currency to the vintage plays and their adaptations.

Artists of the eighteenth and nineteenth centuries who were categorized as painters of historical tableaux could find no better descriptive models for interpreting the past than Shakespeare's scenes of olden times and mythic persons. *Shakespeare in Art* features dozens of "stage painters," including the likes of fantasist Henry Fuseli, spiritualist William Blake, and satirist George Cruikshank, among other talents, whose pictures bolstered the ever-growing Shakespearean legacy. The Victorians, including Pre-Raphaelite painters Sir John Everett Millais and Dante Gabriel Rossetti, applied their romantic and symbolic intensity in equal measure to their depictions of Shakespeare's characters. The Pre-Raphaelite Brotherhood rated the Bard high in their pantheon of "immortals," apparently just one notch under Jesus.

Ultimately, by force of will (so to speak), Shakespeare surpassed his contemporaries as the Western world's dramatist of choice, performed and interpreted by the best and worst of professional players and battalions of amateur thespians. Everyone had a place around Shakespeare's table.

**His Outward Parts**

William Shakespeare may have earned sainthood, but was he real or a phantasm? What did Saint Will *really* look like? The world still does not know for certain. In his day, painters and illustrators were, logically, more focused on rendering the plays than the playwright. And although Shakespeare performed in some of his own plays, no Elizabethan *selfies* exist. It appears he studiously avoided the paparazzi painters as well, leaving large doubts and much speculation as to his physical appearance, hair color, weight, and height. Evidently, only two accepted, "varified" portraits exist, and even these are still debated by scholars as questionable.

Ben Jonson famously wrote: "Reader Looke / Not on his Picture, but his Booke," referring to the most ubiquitous portrait—the black-and-white engraving of Shakespeare by a fifteen-year-old who never met the Bard, Martin

*Silk Playbill*, Royal Lyceum Theatre, UK, 1887. d: W.S. Johnson

Droeshout the Younger, that appears on the title page of the 1623 First Folio. With his Elizabethan collar, generous forehead, and Mona Lisa smile, this is the Shakespeare everyone knows and embraces. Call it the official icon or trade character—the seventeenth-century Pillsbury Doughboy or Mr. Clean—representing the Shakespearean product line and Bard Inc. corporate identity. Whether a true likeness or not, it was pretty well crafted for a lad of fifteen.

A memorial bust of the Bard with similar facial characteristics by Gerard Johnson the Younger resides at the Holy Trinity Church in Stratford-upon-Avon; it may have been made a few years after Shakespeare's 1616 death. The likeness, scholars note, seems to have been approved by his closest relatives, including Shakespeare's widow, Anne Hathaway. Nonetheless, its supposed origins and accuracy are built purely on speculation. A score of other portraits are said to have been made during his lifetime or from memories thereof; many adhere to the Droeshout paradigm (even though the plate for that image went through the press so many times it may have suffered a lot of printing distortions). Others, such as one attributed to Gerard Soest, veer slightly from the common depiction and could be the portrait of a man with similar Shakespearean features, but not the real deal. Yet another, painted in 1603 and assumed to have been rendered by John Sanders, a scenic artist for Shakespeare's theater company, shows the boss at thirty-nine years old, looking away with an uncharacteristically informal tilt of the head. It has long been touted and in turn challenged as the only portrait painted in Shakespeare's lifetime.

For a man who left so many attributed works behind, not to be represented by an unassailable confirmed likeness seems a little odd—and maybe even tragic—but paparazzi artists were in short supply and official portraiture was costly, particularly if one was not a member of the nobility. Of course, Shakespeare came from respectable stock—his father was a successful crafts-businessman and alderman, and his mother came from an affluent farming family. Still, Will was essentially a working boy and not necessarily portrait material until his fame erupted.

Many of history's foremost real and imagined personages owe a debt to the artists who represented them. Where would Caesar be without Roman sculpture? Napoleon without Jacques-Louis David? George Washington without Gilbert Stuart? And God without Michelangelo? All these and scores more iconic visages shape popular recognition and serve other artists as models for homage, parody, and satire, as well as a host of other artistic endeavors—and hijinks. Even given the scarcity of reputable source material, there was (and still is) a prodigious manufacture of busts, reliefs, paintings, and monuments, much of it kitsch by contemporary standards, celebrating Shakespeare's life and myth.

Shakespeare must have had his reasons for refusing to sit for an official portrait, leaving his visage a bit of a mystery (or comic riddle). But he also must have believed that art (and we'll assume visual art as well as poetic art) was essential to *provoke the desire* of his audiences (to paraphrase lines from *Macbeth*, Act II Scene III). "Had not Shakespeare over and over again proclaimed, in his own Sonnets," S. Schoenbaum wrote in *Shakespeare: The Globe & The World*, "the power of his art to eternize his subject?" While this quotation refers to Shakespeare's ability to create timeless-cum-timely human depictions, it can easily be interpreted as a reference to all the visual art that helped imprint Shakespeare so indelibly on the collective consciousness. Those pictures were the banner ads of their day. In fact "banner" is not such a far-fetched word to describe the first postings of Shakespearean nature.

The earliest Shakespearean advertising probably began in 1599 to mark the inauguration of the Globe Theatre in Southwark, London, near the Thames. The Lord Chamberlain's Men raised a flag with Hercules carrying a globe on his shoulders to announce that Shakespeare's *Julius Caesar* was about to open. The same Hercules motif was used over the main entrance with the inscription "*Totus mundus agit histrionem*" (All the world's a stage). The Globe raised flags on its small tower thereafter to signal that plays were being performed. Some showed a symbolic picture, with a simple color-coding system indicating whether a play was comedy (white), tragedy (black), or history (red). White represented light. Black meant death. Red signaled blood.

Theater posters were initiated as well, with street performances often accompanied by paper handbills. The Victoria and Albert (V&A) Museum in London explains on its website how new theatrical events were promoted by processions of the performers themselves, "sometimes accompanied by...vexillators—people carrying banners." Like marchers in those classic nineteenth- and twentieth-century parades announcing that a circus was coming to town, the casts of Shakespearean and other plays signaled a new event by beating drums and playing instruments. Along with this performative promotion, hand-scrawled information was handed out and stuck to posts, "giving rise to the word 'poster,'" notes the V&A history. "But the quickest way of attracting a crowd was by word of mouth, and the sound of the drum and trumpet."

The earliest posters (or playbills) measured about seven by three inches, printed by letterpress on handmade rag paper. According to the V&A, by the end of the 1600s, larger and more expensive typographic posters, or "Great Bills,"

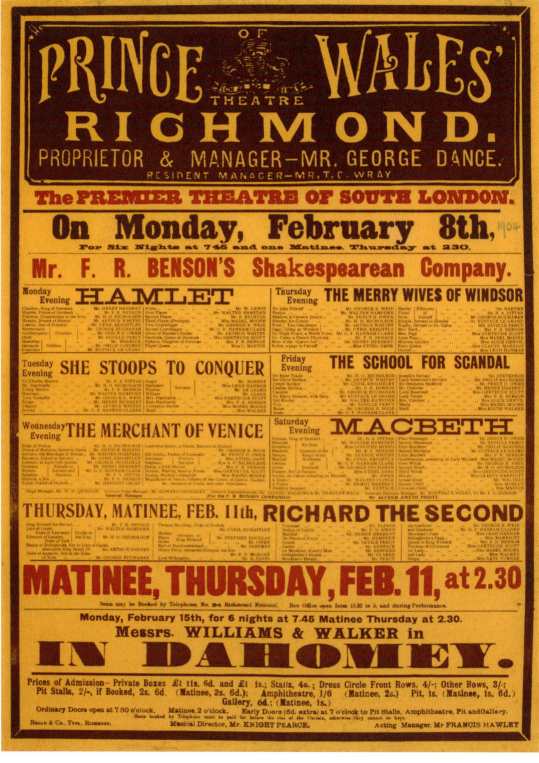

*Prince of Wales Theatre Poster*, Prince of Wales' Theatre Richmond, UK, 1904. d: Broad & Co., Typs.

were also produced, influenced by those of a French theater company that visited London in 1672. They were printed in black and with a more expensive red ink. Eventually, they included the players' names in various sizes according to their roles. The size of type and where it was positioned, known as "billing," became an indication of status.

Dedicated Shakespearean poster printing on paper began inauspiciously, as pictureless sheets crammed with type and with the occasional random or specified engraved printer's ornament. In 1615 the printing house of the stationer and bookseller William Jaggard purchased the venerated printing business of James Roberts, who was the esteemed official printer of the Shakespeare "canon," having been engaged to print a few of the quartos, as well as all of the single-sheet advertising handbills. Jaggard later assumed Roberts's concession that printed all the advertising material for the King's Men company productions. His business became the largest in England, and his son, Isaac Jaggard, helped with much of this theatrical printing work (his name, not the elder Jaggard's, is on the title page of the First Folio). Printed on single sheets of paper typeset with the titles of the plays and casts of performers, the handbills served as promotion, performance program, and souvenir. Now they are rare and fragile artifacts.

Economical printing transformed all theatrical posters. Around 1850 the affordable, widespread use of lithographic printing shifted the standard from black-and-white to color lettering and illustration. Theaters benefited from this chromolithographic revolution, and theater managers realized that long lists of cast members took up too much poster space. (Smaller programs became the venue for players' credits.) In Shakespeare's time, plays changed day after day, whereas by the mid-nineteenth century a single play would be performed for a finite run in one theater, which spawned the necessity for posters promoting that one play. Posters in this book begin more or less at this time of large-scale color printing. Unlike more ephemeral handbills, these were designed to hang during a run of the play and could be more creative in scope, offering richly hued representations of Shakespearean scenes.

As typesetting and printing advanced from hand-operated to steam presses, wood to metal type, quantity and quality increased, until toward the end of the nineteenth century, when a growing profession of French, German, and Italian *affichistes* were creating collectible works of advertising art. The poster had evolved from ephemeral promotion to a platform for iconic imagery that brightened the boulevards and avenues with engaging and entertaining previews of theatrical plots and characters.

## All That Glistens

Shakespearean posters certainly benefited from the art poster movement. However, not all the posters created in the Bard's name glistened. The limits of technology and standards of illustration sometimes got in the way. Even entering the twentieth century, with its better reproduction standards, poster artists could easily fall into the cliché trap. As advertisement a poster has to be clear and concise, but as art the challenge is to communicate efficiently, while inserting a conceptual bonus for the viewer to enjoy.

Rather than solely representational, Shakespeare's imagery can be metaphorical. The incredibly large number of interpretative (as opposed to turgidly literal) posters proves that designers and illustrators have met the creative challenge. Just as some of his plays, including *Hamlet*, *Othello*, *Richard II*, *Merchant of Venice*, and others, have been updated to reflect the social mores or politics of the moment, so too have posters first and foremost promoting the Bard's genius provided opportunities to make statements or push the limits of contemporary prohibitions. During the 1950s through the fall of the Iron Curtain, many such posters were created by Eastern European artists; stymied by government decrees from making overt social or political commentary, they had to master the art of deception. Theater posters in general, and those with Shakespearean themes in particular, such as ones promoting *Richard III* and *Hamlet*, were camo for otherwise critical images.

In compiling *Presenting Shakespeare*, we collected around fifteen hundred Shakespearean theater posters. Not all the posters designed in Shakespeare's name are gold, but enough of them are, and the following selection is a balanced survey of eleven hundred of the historically significant, aesthetically desirable, and conceptually intelligent, produced over nearly two centuries, in many countries and by varied artists, designers, and illustrators. There were certain periods, including during World Wars I and II, when performances were few, if any, and those performed were not heralded in posters or advertisements. Some eras offered more mediocre or cliché-ridden work, which we were duty-bound to edit out. Although our intent has been to reveal the volume of work, it is not at the expense of aesthetic quality. This represents only a partial selection of what is out there, edited from sources all over the globe, representing probably tens of thousands of posters and placards heralding countless performances old and new, good and great. Granted, there is a lot to ponder on the following pages, but as Shakespeare wrote in *As You Like It*: "Can one desire too much of a good thing?"

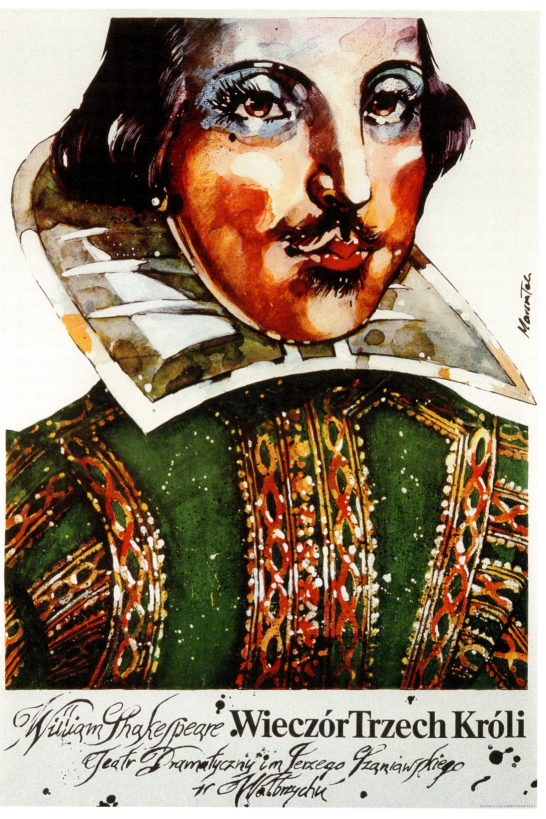

*Twelfth Night*, Teatr Dramatyczny im. Jerzego Szaniawskiego, PL, 1980. **d**: Grzegorz Marszalek (Dydo Poster Collection)

*Measure for Measure*, Lappeenranta City Theatre, FI, 1994. ad/d: Pekka Loiri

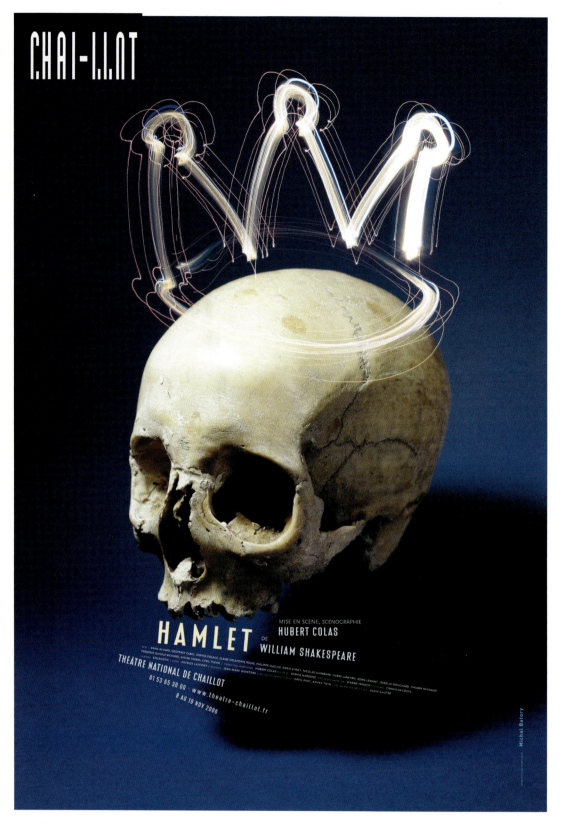

Theatre National de Chaillot, FR, 2006. **ad/p:** Michal Batory

# HAMLET

> O, that this too too solid flesh would melt
> Thaw and resolve itself into a dew!
> Or that the Everlasting had not fix'd
> His canon 'gainst self-slaughter! O God! God!
> How weary, stale, flat and unprofitable,
> Seem to me all the uses of this world!
> Fie on't! ah fie! 'tis an unweeded garden,
> That grows to seed; things rank and gross in nature
> Possess it merely. That it should come to this!
>
> —Hamlet

If *Midsummer Night's Dream* is the most frequently performed of Shakespeare's plays, *Hamlet* may be the most conceptually illustrated of all Shakespeare's tragedies. It certainly offers the poster artist a wealth of mnemonic possibilities—from skull to crown, as well as Hamlet pondering the skull with or without a crown. In some representations the beautiful Ophelia takes her close-up; in others the balcony atop Elsinore castle serves as the primary setting for intrigue; occasionally, a bleeding heart has been used; and then there is the ghost of Hamlet's father, the late King Hamlet, who visits his son at uncomfortable hours of the night.

The now classic pose of Hamlet addressing the skull in his hands was frequently employed by some of the great poster artists of the early twentieth century. Arguably the most simple yet dramatic of them all shows Hamlet in profile, wearing black robes and leggings, standing tall against an empty background and looking intensely into his friend Yorick's eye sockets. It was illustrated by The Beggarstaffs (the pseudonym for English poster makers William Nicholson and James Pryde) and was later in the twentieth century heralded as the epitome of modern minimalism. Just compare it to the intricate realism that was conventional in turn-of-the-century posters such as the one showcasing Robert B. Mantell (page 28).

An intensely tragic Shakespearean tragedy, the story takes on biblical proportions through existential soliloquies about life and melting solid flesh. This further accounts for the veritable ubiquity of the skull. In contemporary posters this venerable prop is not always enough to capture the imagination, so in the twentieth and twenty-first centuries *Hamlet* has inspired more edgy visual approaches.

Hamlet is such a demanding role, with such a singular personality, that producers often demand to see the star's name and/or portrait carry the poster. Indeed, who wouldn't rush to see Jude Law on stage declaiming "Alas, poor Yorick! I knew him, Horatio; a fellow of infinite jest, of most excellent fancy; he hath borne me on his back a thousand times...."?

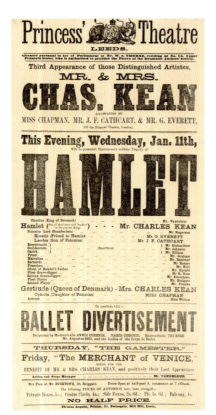
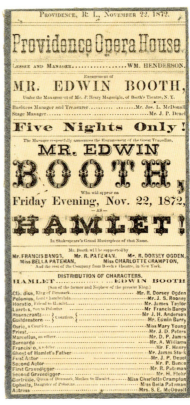

Princess' Theatre, Leeds, UK, 1860. d: n/a
Providence Opera House, US, 1872. d: n/a
Theatre-Royal, UK, 1865. d: n/a
Booth's Theatre, US, 1870. d: H.A. Thomas
Washington Theater, US, 1861. d: n/a

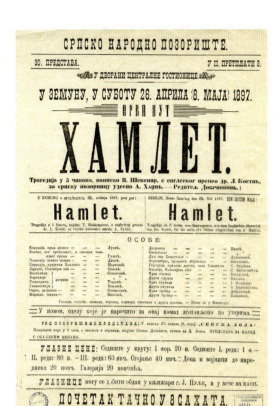

Serbian National Theatre, RS, 1897. d: n/a

Moscow Art Academic Theatre the Second, RU, 1924. d: M.V. Libakov

Georgian Theatre, GE, 1903. ad: Akaki Tsereteli

Habima Theatre, PS, 1947. d: n/a (Eliasaf Robinson Tel Aviv Collection)

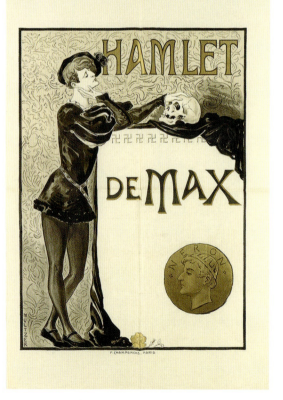

**Theater:** n/a, US, 1890. **d:** The Seer Print

**Theater:** n/a, US, 1884. **d:** W.J. Morgan & Co. Lith., Cleveland, O.

Die Haghespelers Theatre Group, NL, 1915. **d:** Chris Lebeau

**Theater:** n/a, FR, 1910. **d:** Marcel Multzer, Ferdinand Champenois

**Theatre Sarah Bernhardt**, FR, 1899. d: Alphonse Mucha

**Theater:** n/a, UK, 1894. d/ill: J. & W. Beggarstaff (William Nicholson & James Pryde)

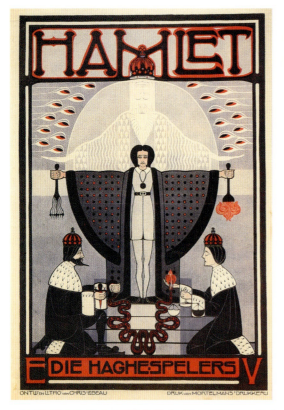
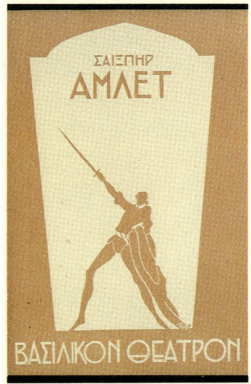
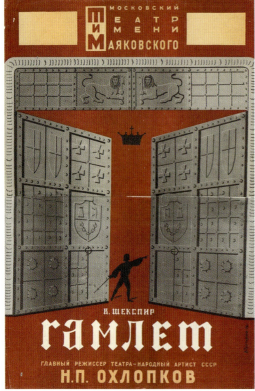

Die Haghespelers Theatre Group, NL, 1914. d: Chris Lebeau

Mayakovsky Moscow Theatre, RU, 1956. d: Tretyakov V., V.F. Ryndin

Theater: n/a, GR, 1937. d: n/a

Theater: n/a, HU, 1964. art: Antal Gunda

30   Presenting Shakespeare

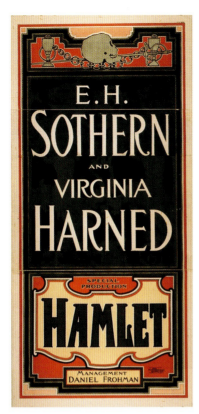
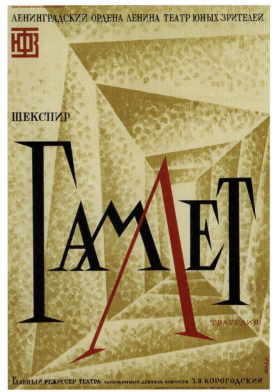

Lyceum Theatre, US, 1900. d: Strobridge & Co. Lith.

Duke's Playhouse, UK, 1983. ad/d/p: John Angus

Lenin Order Leningrad Youth Theater, RU, 1972. d: n/a

Hrvatsko narodno kazaliste Split, HR, 1980. d: Gorki Zuvela

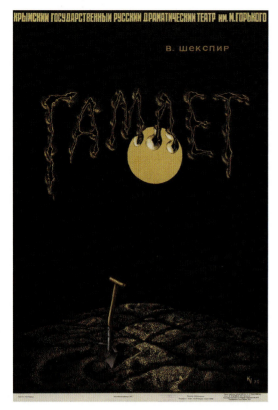
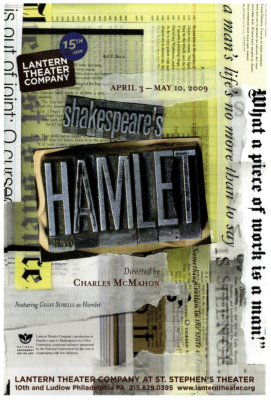
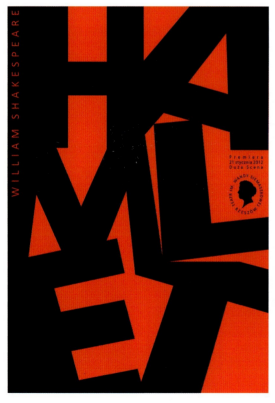
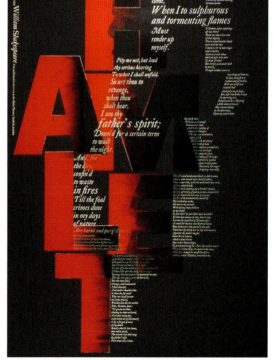

**Gorky State Russian Drama Theater of the Crimea**, UA, 1979.
d: K.N. Cemekov

**Teatr im. Wandy Siemaszkowej**, PL, 2012. ad: Remigiusz Caban,
d: Krysztof Motyka

**Lantern Theater Company**, US, 2009. ad/d: Allan Espiritu

**Globe Theatre**, UK, 2001. ad: Alan Kitching

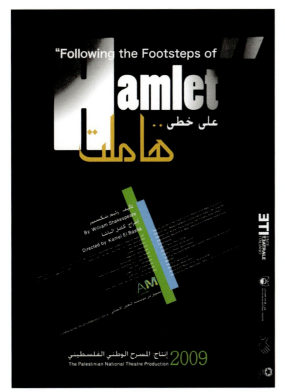

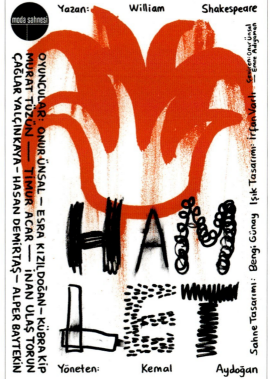

Palestinian National Theatre, PS, 2008. ad/d: Kamel el Basha, p: Akram Safadi

Gogol Center, RU, 2013. ad/d: Peter Bankov

East West Center Sarajevo, BA, 2005. ad/d: Bojan Hadzihalilovic, d: Goran Lizdek

Moda Sahnesi, TR, 2013. d: Cem Dinlenmis

Hamlet 33

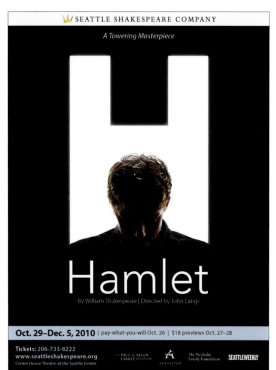

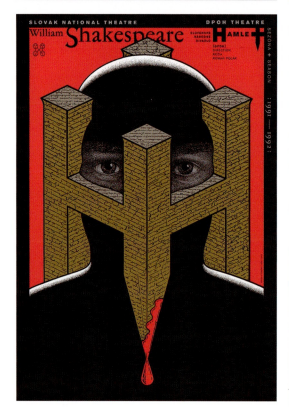
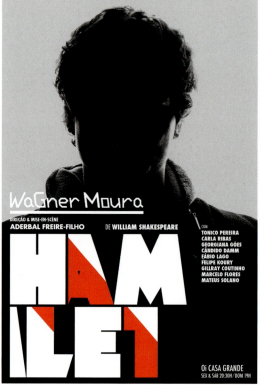

Seattle Shakespeare Company, US, 2010. ad: Jeff Fickes, d: Thea Roe

Slovak National Theatre, SK, 1991. d: Vladoslav Rostoka

Goskontsert Theater, RU, 1984. d: Vitaly Volf

Oi Casa Grande, BR, 2008. ad: Fabio Arruda, Rodrigo Bleque, p: Sandra Delgado

Teatr Ateneum w Warszawie, PL, 1983. d: Wieslaw Rosocha (Dydo Poster Collection)

Les Gemeaux/Scene Nationale-Sceaux, FR, 2009. **ad/d:** Michel Bouvet, **p:** Francis Laharrague

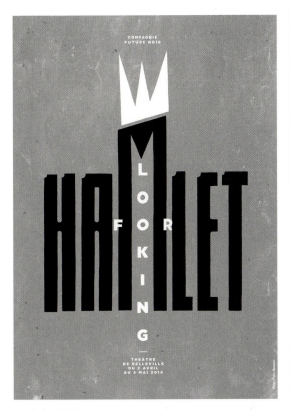

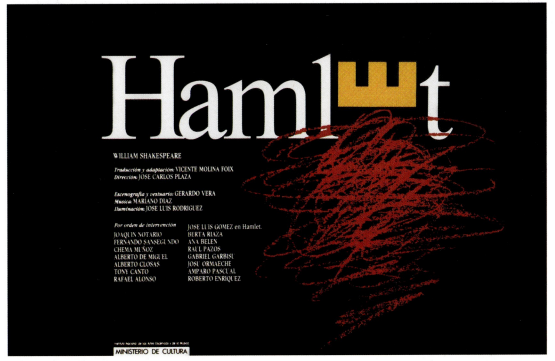

Compagnie Future Noir, Theatre de Belleville, FR, 2014.
ad/d/p: Pierre Jeamneau

Teatro Zifio, CL, 2013. ad/d: Diego Becas Villegas

Centro Dramatico Nacional, ES, 1989. d: Roberto Turegano

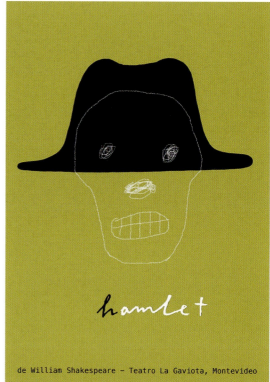
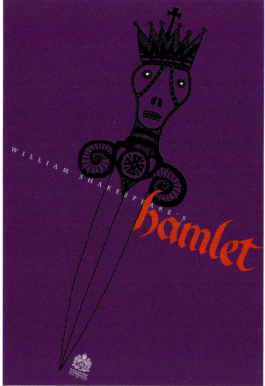

Theaterhaus Dusseldorf, DE, 1998. **ad/d:** Fons Hickmann

Teatro La Gaviota, UY, 1988. **ad/d:** Fidel Sclavo

**Pontificia Universidad Javeriana Cali**, CO, 2014. **ad/d:** Diego Bermudez

**Hamlet Teater**, IR, 2014. **ad:** Masoud Hekmat, **d:** Sadegh Hashemi

Teatr Dramatyczny, PL, 1961. d: Henryk Tomaszewski (Dydo Poster Collection)

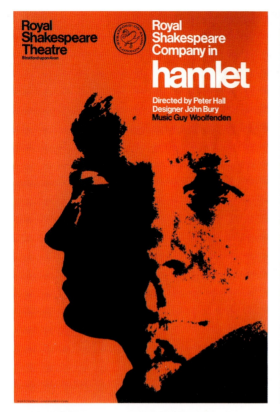

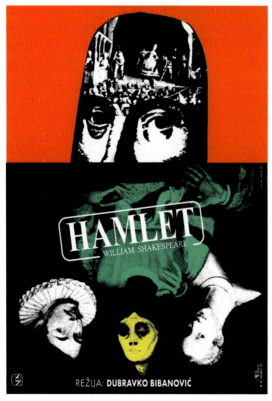

Royal Shakespeare Company, Royal Shakespeare Theatre, UK, 1966.
d: George Mayhew

Narodno pozoriste Sarajevo, BA, 2001. d: Branko Bacanovic

Association Tadaa, US, 2008. ad/d: Yann Legendre

Teatr Dramatyczny im. A. Węgierki, PL, 1983. d: Julian Pałka
(Dydo Poster Collection)

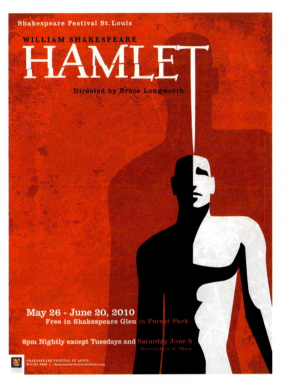

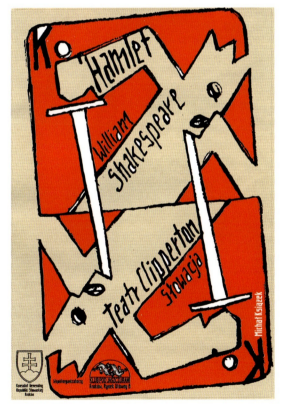

Shakespeare Festival of St. Louis, US, 2010. ad/d/ill: Rich Nelson

Teatr Clipperton, PL, 2004. d: Michal Ksiazek (Dydo Poster Collection)

Zamek Ksiazat Pomorskic, PL, 1978. d: Leszek Zebrowski

Dom Kultury, PL, 2002. d: Monika Starowicz (Dydo Poster Collection)

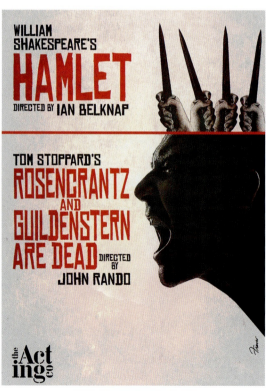

Raamteater, BE, 1986. d: Marcin Mroszczak, p: Aernout Overbeeke (Dydo Poster Collection)

Orkeny Istvan Szinhaz, HU, 2015. d: Levente Bagossy

The Acting Company, US, 2013. ad/d: Frank "Farver" Verlizzo

Theatre Scena STU, PL, 2013. d/p: Katarzyna Zapart

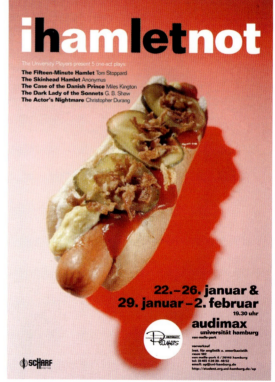

Theatre Nanterre, FR, 2004. **ad:** Lasomatic, **d:** Pamal Bejean, Frederic Bortolotti, Nicolas Ledoux, **p:** Grore Image

University Players, DE, 2012. **ad/d/p:** Ole Friedrich

Matienzo Cultural Center Theatre, IT, 2014. **ad/d:** Marina Tercelan, **p:** Nora Lezano

University Players, DE, 2002. **ad/d/p:** Ole Friedrich

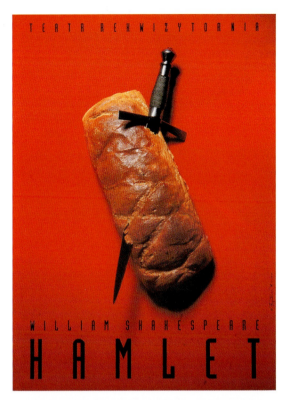

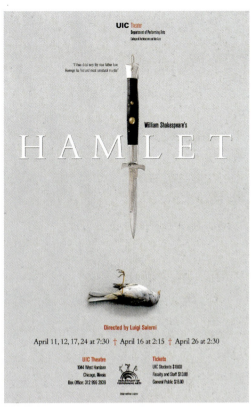

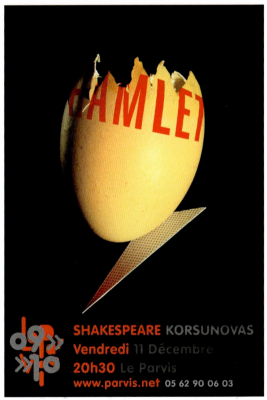

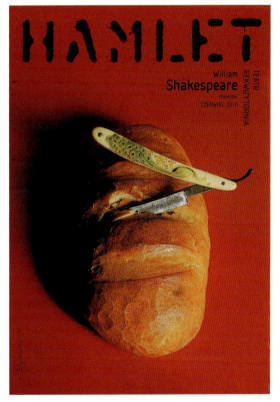

Teatr Rekwizytornia, PL, 2010. d: Tomasz Boguslawski
(Dydo Poster Collection)

Le Parvis, Scene Nationale Tarbes, FR, 2009. ad/d/p: Alain Le Quernec

University of Illinois at Chicago, US, 2008. ad/d/p: Matthew Gaynor

Teatr Rekwizytornia, PL, 2010. d: Tomasz Boguslawski
(Dydo Poster Collection)

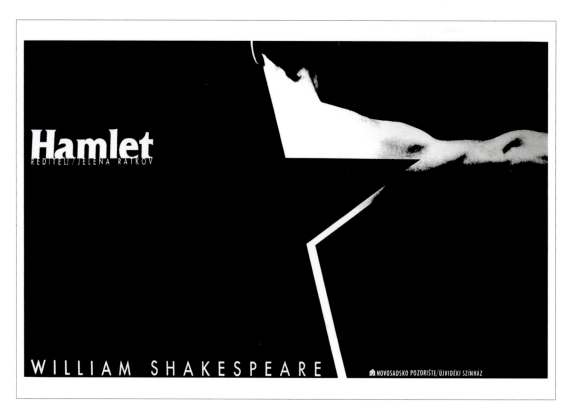

Novosadsko Pozoriste, RS, 1995. ad/d: Atila Kapitanj

Pozoriste Mladih, RS, 2002. ad/d: Atila Kapitanj

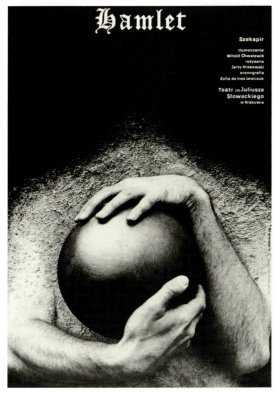
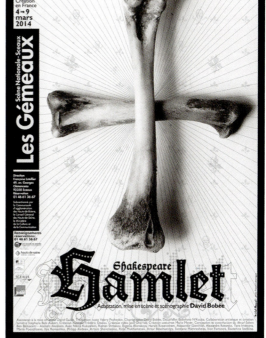

**Teatr Narodowy**, PL, 1971. **d**: Andrzej Krauze, Marcin Mroszczak
(Dydo Poster Collection)

**Teatr im. Juliusza Slowackiego**, PL, 1978. **d**: Mieczyslaw Gorowski
(Dydo Poster Collection)

**Royal Shakespeare Company**, Royal Shakespeare Theatre, UK, 2013.
**d**: Royal Shakespeare Company, **p**: Enrico Sechelli (Millennium Images)

**Les Gemeaux/Scene Nationale-Sceaux**, FR, 2009. **ad/d**: Michel Bouvet,
**p**: Francis Laharrague

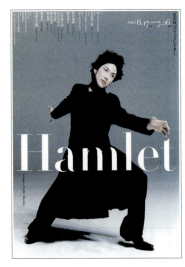

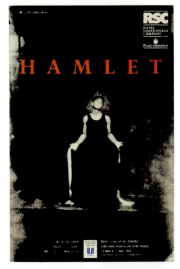
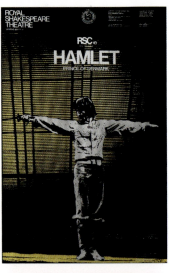
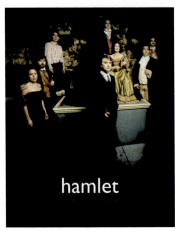

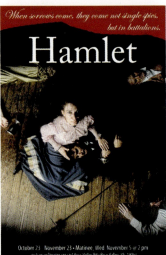

Setagaya Public Theatre, JP, 2003.
ad/d: Tatsuya Ariyama, p: Yasuhide Kuge

Shakespeare & Company, US, 2011.
d/p: Kevin Sprague

Hedgerow Theatre, US, 2014.
ad/d/p: Kyle Cassidy

Kaspar Theatre, CZ, 2005. ad: Ales Najbrt, (Studio Najbrt), p: Adam Holy

Royal Shakespeare Company,
Royal Shakespeare Theatre, UK, 1993.
d: Douglas Brothers

Hedgerow Theatre, US, 2014.
ad/d/p: Kyle Cassidy

Royal Shakespeare Company,
The Courtyard Theatre, UK, 2008.
ad/d: Andy Williams, p: Jillian Edelstein

Royal Shakespeare Company,
Royal Shakespeare Theatre, UK, 1970.
ad: George Mayhew, d: Royal Shakespeare Company, p: Donald Cooper

Hedgerow Theatre, US, 2014.
ad/d/p: Kyle Cassidy

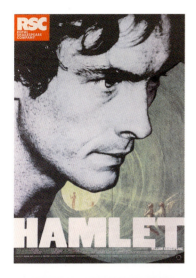
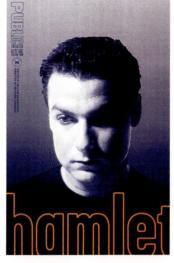
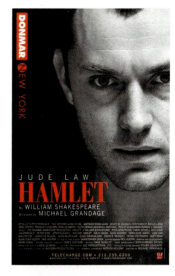
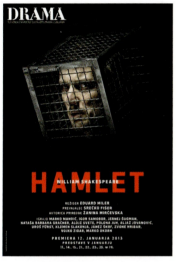
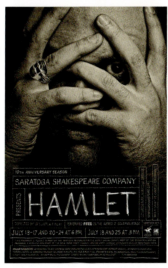

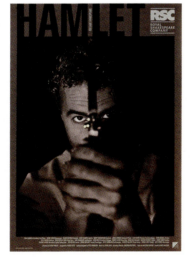

Royal Shakespeare Company,
Royal Shakespeare Theatre, UK, 2004.
d: Andy Williams, p: Andy Cleverley,
art: Hieronymus Bosch

Slovensko narodno gledalisce Drama
Ljubljana, SI, 2013. ad/d: Danijela Grgic,
p: Peter Uhan

Shakespeare & Company, US, 2006.
d: Adam Rothberg, p: Kevin Sprague

The Public Theater, US, 1999.
ad/d: Paula Scher (Pentagram)

Saratoga Shakespeare Company,
Congress Park, US, 2010.
ad/d: Tom Rothermel, p: Eric Sahrmann

Royal Shakespeare Company,
Royal Shakespeare Theatre, UK, 2001.
d: Andy Williams, p: Alistair Thain

Broadhurst Theatre, US, 2009.
ad: Vinny Sainato, p: Hugo Glendinning

Mini Teater, SI, 2009. ad: Robert Waltl,
d: Maja Gspan, p: Marko Mandic Archive

The Lyttelton Theatre, National Theatre, UK,
1976. d: Richard Bird, Michael Mayhew,
p: Anthony Crickmay (Collection of Chisholm
Larsson Gallery, NYC)

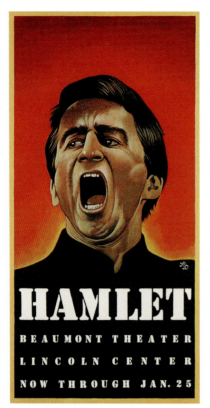
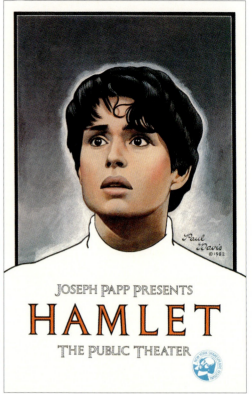
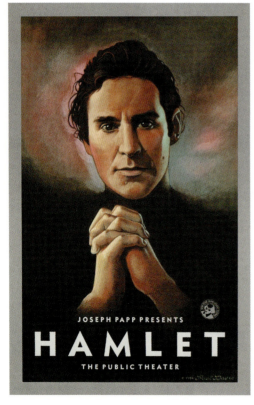
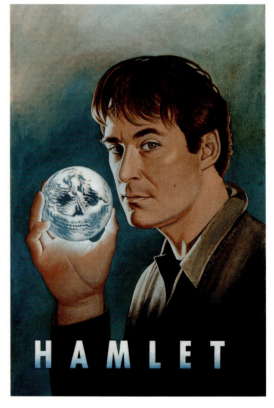

Vivian Beaumont Theater, Lincoln Center, US, 1975.
ad/d: Reinhold Schwenk, d/ill: Paul Davis

The Public Theater, US, 1986. ad/d/ill: Paul Davis

The Public Theater, US, 1982. ad/d/ill: Paul Davis

The Public Theater, US, 1990. ad/d/ill: Paul Davis

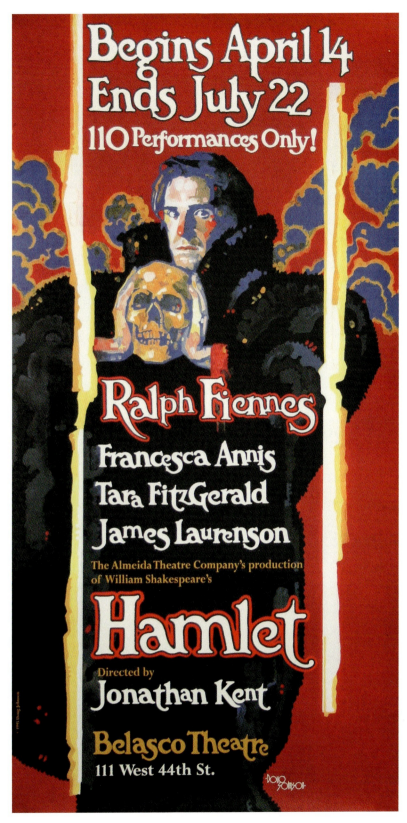

Belasco Theatre, US, 1995. **d:** Dovo Sonnson (Collection of Chisholm Larsson Gallery, NYC)

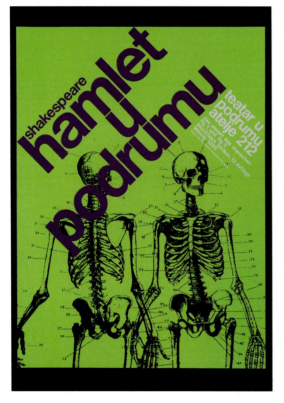

**Teatr Dramatyczny m. st. Warszawy**, PL, 1980. **d:** Jerzy Czerniawski
(Dydo Poster Collection)

**Teatar u podrumu Atelje 212**, RS, 1971. **d:** Slobodan Masic

**Barka Sunhaz**, HU, 2005. **d:** Istvan Orosz

**Setagaya Public Theatre**, JP, 2004. **ad:** Kiyoaki Ichikawa, **d:** Kaori Sato,
**ill:** 100% Orange

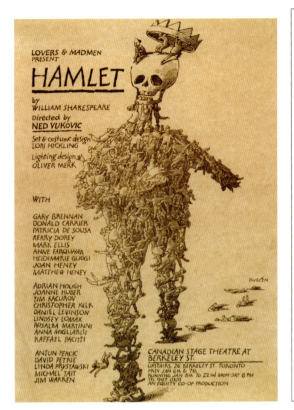

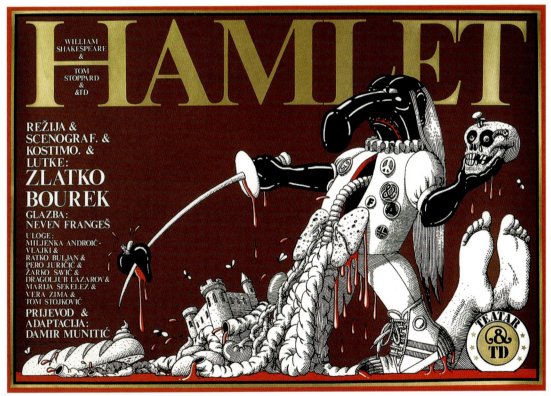

Canadian Stage Theatre at Berkeley St., CA, n/a. **d:** Dusan Petricic

Cotuit Center for the Arts, US, 1997. **d/ill:** Edward Gorey

Teatar &TD, HR, 1981. **d/ill:** Mirko Ilic

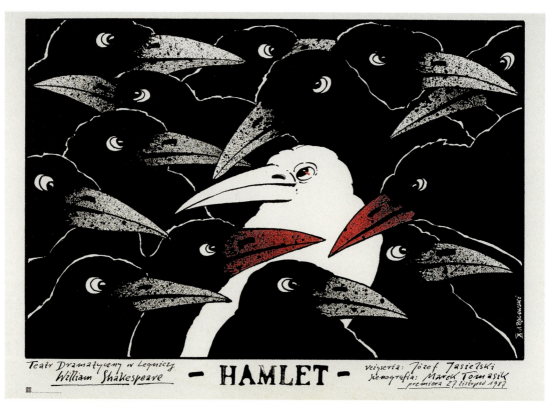

Teatr Dramatyczny w Legnicy, PL, 1987. ad/d: Andrzej Pagowski (Dydo Poster Collection)

Teatr Nowy w Poznaniu, PL, 2006. d: Jerzy Czerniawski (Dydo Poster Collection)

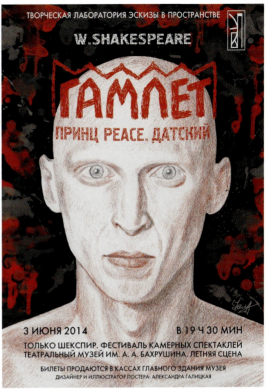

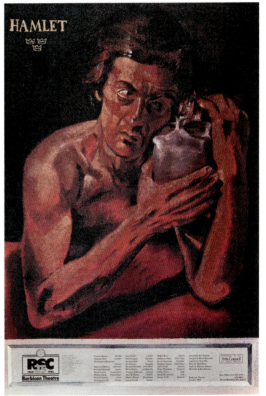

**Teatr Wybrzeze**, PL, 1996. **d:** Wieslaw Rosocha
(Dydo Poster Collection)

**Teatr Ochoty**, PL, 1985. **ad/d:** Andrzej Pagowski
(Dydo Poster Collection)

**Bakhrushin State Central Theatre Museum**, RU, 2014.
**ad:** Outlines in Space, Authors Theater, **d:** Alexandra Galitskaya

**Royal Shakespeare Company, Barbican Theatre**, UK, 1985.
**d:** The Drawing Room, **art:** Philip Core

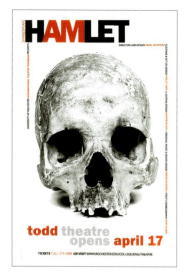
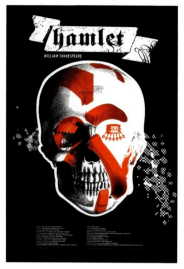
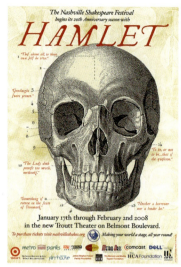

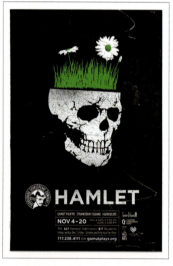
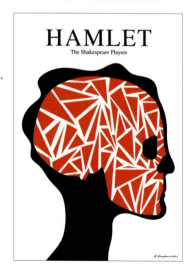
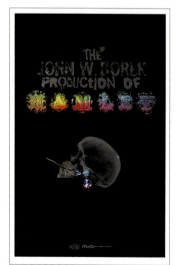
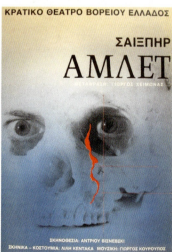

**University of Rochester (International Theatre Program)**, US, 2003. ad/d/p: Nigel Maister

**Little Green Pig**, US, 2014. ad: Jaybird O'Berski, d: Randy Skidmore

**The Shakespeare Players**, DE, 2012. d: Filip Kujawski

**Knjazevsko-srpski teatar Kragujevac**, RS, 2010. ad/d/p: Ivan Misic

**Centro Dramatico Nacional, Teatro Maria Guerrero**, ES, 2008. ad/d: Isidro Ferrer

**The MJCCC Theater**, US, 2014. d: Louie Podlaski

**Nashville Shakespeare Festival, Troutt Theater**, US, 2008. ad/d: Tracy Leigh Ratliff

**Harrisburg Shakespeare Company at Gamut Theatre Group, Gamut Classic Theatre**, US, 2011. ad/d: Rob Smith

**The National Theatre of Northern Greece**, GR, 1988. d: Andrew Visnevski, Lili Kendaka

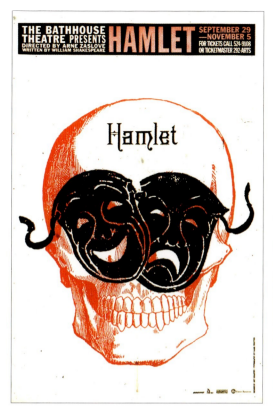
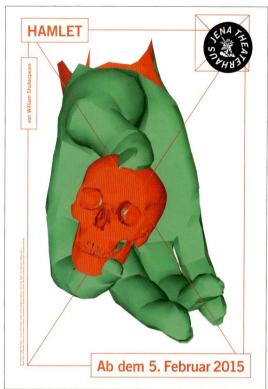

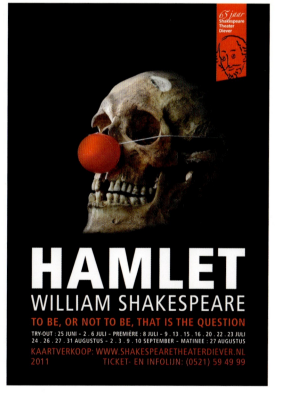

Bathhouse Theatre, US, 1989. d: Art Chantry

Teatr im. Juliusza Osterwy, PL, 1974. d: Leonard Konopelski

Theaterhaus Jena, DE, 2015. ad/d: David Eckes, Paul Steinmann

Shakespeare Theater Diever, NL, 2012. ad: Jack Nieborg, d: Pamlien Schutter, p: Korn Tummerman

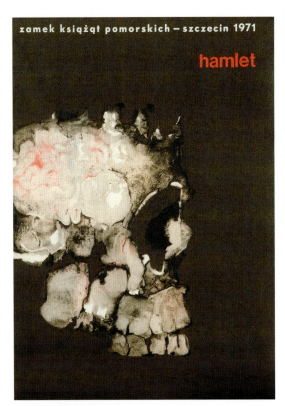
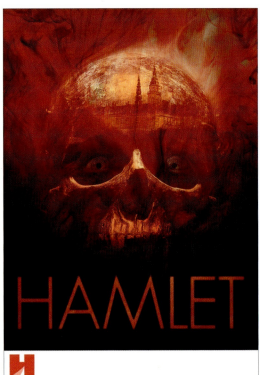

Zamek Ksiazat Pomorskich, PL, 1971. d: Jerzy Kolacz
(Dydo Poster Collection)

Hartford Stage Company, Hartford Stage, US, 2014.
ad/d: Taylor Goodell Benedum

Krakowski Teatr Scena STU, PL, 2012. d: Leszek Wisniewski (Dydo Poster Collection)

# HAMLET
## WILLIAM SHAKESPEARE

**RSC** — ROYAL SHAKESPEARE COMPANY

NATIONAL TOUR

rsc.org.uk

Supported using public funding by ARTS COUNCIL ENGLAND

## 'Revenge his FOUL and most UNNATURAL MURDER...'

**COMPANY INCLUDES**
PAAPA ESSIEDU

**DIRECTOR**
SIMON GODWIN

**DESIGNER**
PAUL WILLS

**LIGHTING**
PAUL ANDERSON

**MUSIC**
SOLA AKINGBOLA

**MUSIC ASSOCIATE**
JON NICHOLLS

**SOUND**
CHRISTOPHER SHUTT

**MOVEMENT**
MBULELO NDABENI

**FIGHTS**
KEV McCURDY

The Royal Shakespeare Company takes Shakespeare's searing tragedy of murder and revenge on national tour in 2018.

A student is called home from university to find his life turned upside down. He had the world at his feet, but now everything has changed. Who can be trusted, who can be believed?

Sent by the ghost of his father to avenge his brutal death, Hamlet's mission to expose the truth is a perilous journey of madness, murder and lost love. What will ultimately become of a young man sent to kill?

Following a critically acclaimed run in Stratford-upon-Avon in 2016, rising star Paapa Essiedu plays the title role in a riveting and contemporary take on *Hamlet*.

'A new star is born'
TELEGRAPH

MAIL ON SUNDAY

INDEPENDENT    OBSERVER    SU

The RSC Acting Companies are generously supported by THE G

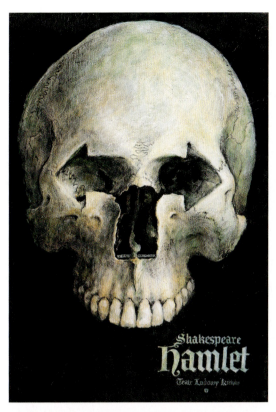
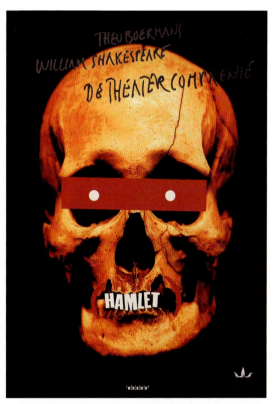

**Teatr Ludowy Krakow**, PL, 2005. **ad:** Krzysztof Dydo,
**d:** Wieslaw Grzegorczyk (Dydo Poster Collection)

**De Theatercompagnie**, NL, 2002. **ad/d/p:** Anthon Beeke

**Teatr Ateneum**, PL, 1975. **d:** Jerzy Czerniawski (Dydo Poster Collection)

Teatr Narodowy, PL, 1976. **ad/d**: Franciszek Starowieyski (Dydo Poster Collection)

# AS YOU LIKE IT

*All the world's a stage,*
*And all the men and women merely players:*
*They have their exits and their entrances;*
*And one man in his time plays many parts,*
*His acts being seven ages. At first the infant,*
*Mewling and puking in the nurse's arms.*
*And then the whining school-boy, with his satchel*
*And shining morning face, creeping like snail*
*Unwillingly to school. And then the lover,*
*Sighing like furnace, with a woeful ballad*
*Made to his mistress' eyebrow. Then a soldier,*
*Full of strange oaths and bearded like the pard,*
*Jealous in honour, sudden and quick in quarrel,*
*Seeking the bubble reputation*
*Even in the cannon's mouth.*

—Jacques

Set in a duchy in France, *As You Like It* takes place largely in the Forest of Arden. Duke Frederick has exiled his brother, Duke Senior, and usurped his titles and lands. But he has allowed Senior's daughter, Rosalind, the best friend of Frederick's own daughter, Celia, to remain in court. That is, until Orlando, who is deeply in love with Rosalind (and also in exile), is forced further into hiding by his brother, Oliver. Orlando flees to the forest with Rosalind, who is disguised as a young man named Ganymede, and she takes along the jester, Touchstone. Also in tow is Celia, disguised as a pauper, now called Aliena. In the forest they engage with other sundry characters, including a shepherdess named Phebe.

Phebe, who is loved by Silvius, is in love with Ganymede (aka Rosalind), who is not the least bit interested in Phebe. Touchstone has also fallen in love with the dim-witted Audrey, who he is compelled to marry to keep away her other suitor, William. The soap opera continues with Orlando promising to marry Rosalind. Oliver, another heir to nobility, meets and falls for Aliena (Celia). In the end, all the characters pair off and marry, and Frederick, who has had a change of heart, returns the duchy to its rightful heirs.

Looking at the following posters one might never know that some of Shakespeare's most oft-quoted lines, including the first line of the passage above, were spoken in *As You Like It*. These famous speeches are left for the players, while poster designers have more often employed symbols of love, often against a woodland backdrop, including the literal image from the play of pinned-up love poems on trees. In an early chromolithographic poster the actress Elizabeth Kennedy, who played Rosalind in 1903, is shown as the primary image (page 62). The character of Rosalind is reprised in contemporary posters, too. Sometimes a portrait of the Bard himself is the sole visual element, suggesting that some designers have found it difficult to select the most illuminating symbol for this comedy about love.

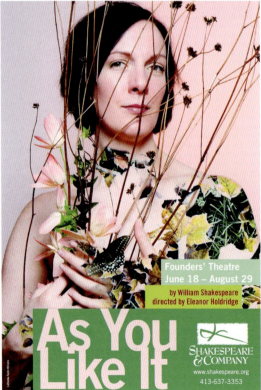

Theater: n/a, US, 1903. d: The Strobridge Litho. Co., p: Bushnell

Shakespeare & Company, US, 2004. d: Mary Garnish, p: Kevin Sprague

Sarajevo National Theater, BA, 1986. ad/d: Branko Bacanovic

The Public Theater, US, 2013. ad/d: Paula Scher (Pentagram)

Teatr im. Stefana Jaracza w Lodzi, PL, 1981. ad/d: Andrzej Pagowski (Dydo Poster Collection)

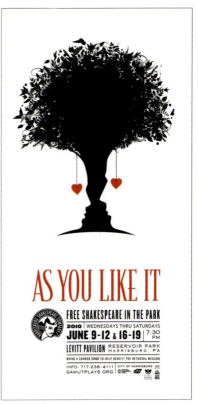
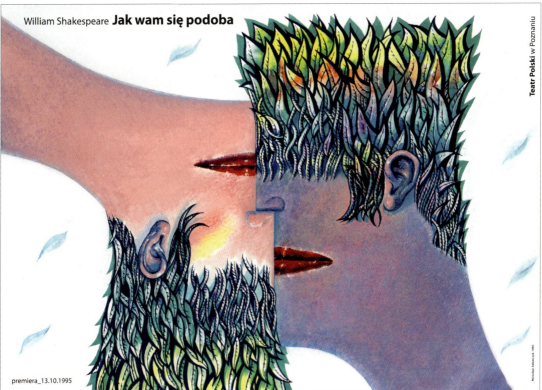

University of Michigan Matthaei Botanical Gardens and Nichols Arboretum, US, 2014. ad/d: David Zinn

Harrisburg Shakespeare Company at Gamut Theatre Group, US, 2010. ad/d: Rob Smith

Teatr Polski w Poznaniu, PL, 1995. ad/d: Miroslaw Adamczyk

Arena Group, FI, 2011. ad/d: Pekka Loiri

Shakespeare Company Berlin, DE, 2014. ad: Christian Leonard, d: Elitza Nanova, p: Susanne Schleyer

Owl Spot, JP, 2010. ad: Kiyoaki Ichikawa, d: Kaori Sato, ill: 100% Orange

Shakespearean Youth Theatre, US, 2010. ad/d: Steven Verdoorn

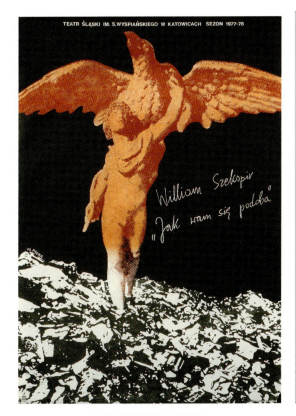
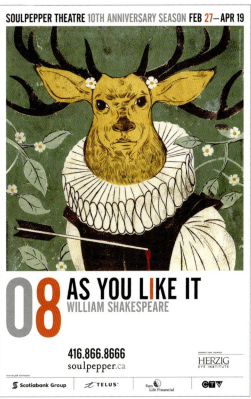
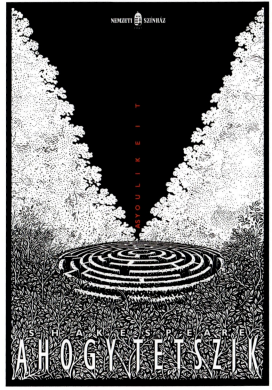

**Teatr Slaski**, PL, 1977. **d:** Mariusz Palka (Dydo Poster Collection)

**Nemzeti Szinhaz Budapesten**, HU, 2014. **d:** Istvan Orosz

**Soulpepper Theatre Company**, CA, 2008. **d:** Anthony Swaneveled, ill: Edel Rodriguez

**The Shakespeare Theatre of New Jersey**, US, 2013. **ad:** Scott McKowen, Christina Poddubiuk, **d/ill:** Scott McKowen

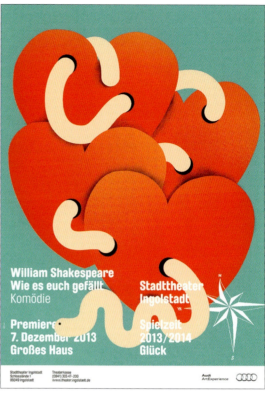
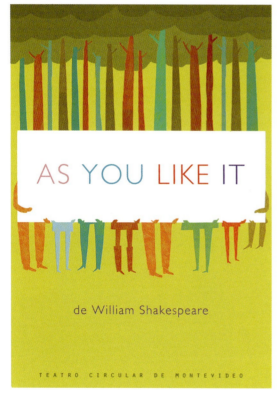

Jugoslovensko dramsko pozoriste, RS, 2010. ad/d: Slavimir Stojanovic

Teatro Circular de Montevideo, UY, 1986. ad/d: Fidel Sclavo

Stadttheater Ingolstadt, DE, 2013. ad/d: Sascha Lobe, d: Ina Bauer

Royal Shakespeare Company, Aldwych Theatre, UK, 1966.
d: George Mayhew

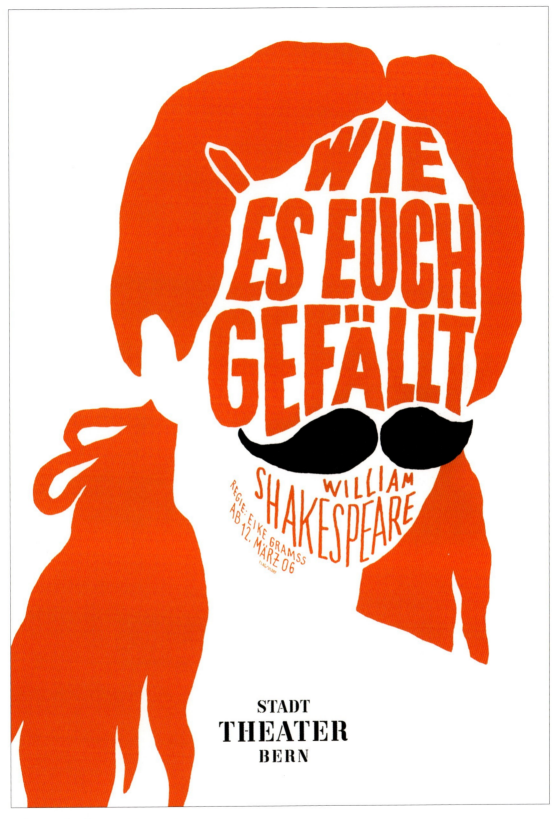

Stadttheater Bern, CH, 2006. ad/d: Flag Aubry, Broquard

Stadtische Buehnen Osnabruck, DE, 1981. art: Jerzy Czerniawski (Dydo Poster Collection)

# KING LEAR

*Life and death! I am ashamed*
*That thou hast power to shake my manhood thus,*
*That these hot tears which break from me perforce*
*Should make thee worth them. Blasts and fogs upon thee!*
*Th' untented woundings of a father's curse*
*Pierce every sense about thee! Old fond eyes,*
*Beweep this cause again, I'll pluck ye out.*

—King Lear

There is little brightness found in the popular dysfunctional family tragedy Shakespeare called *The Tragedy of King Lear* (although a later alternative ending after the Restoration provides a happier ending). The play is about chaos and madness and the realization that man is truly insignificant and unable to alter his fate in the universe. The plot revolves around two wicked sisters with insatiable hunger for power and how this dissolves the order that King Lear has brought to his domain. Insanity is Lear's destiny, since it is he who is the target of his family's betrayal from all greedy sides.

Lear wrongly believes that his favorite daughter, the virtuous Cordelia, is disloyal for not professing her undying love to him. So he banishes her from his kingdom without any property. In Lear's blindness to the fact that her decision not to take her deserved part of his realm was an act of love (as was her decision to reconcile with him later on), tragedy strikes. Meanwhile Cordelia's sisters, Goneril and Regan, are as rabid a pair as ever walked on stage, suggesting that the cause of all Lear's misery is his inability to make the right life decisions. There is little joy to be had in the fact that Lear eventually is able to see the truth about Cordelia. Her forgiveness notwithstanding, they are both taken to prison, where Cordelia meets the end of a rope.

Poster designers often focus on Lear's crown to symbolize a kind of powerless power. It can also be seen as a restraint that binds his head and mind. A portrait or caricature of a tormented, bedeviled, and defeated Lear is often the main image of these posters. Occasionally, though, the daughters bear the metaphorical visual load. But the conceptual theme that is most employed is rooted in metaphorical and physical blindness: Lear is often portrayed with red eyes. In fact, using his plucked-out eyes proves to be a very effective—and memorable—graphic conceit

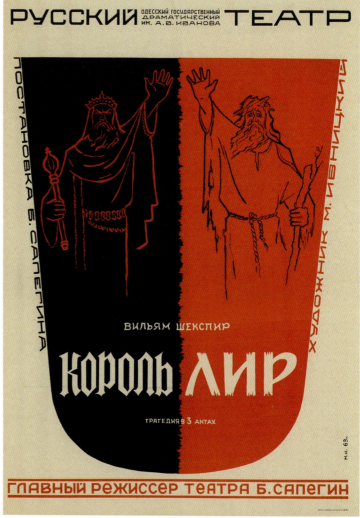

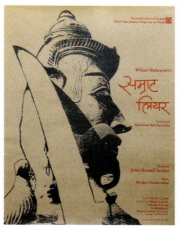

Pancevo Serbian Singing Society, RS, 1871. d: n/a

Narodno pozoriste u Sarajevu, BA, 1954. d: n/a

Theater Instituut Nederland, NL, 1954. d: n/a

A.V. Ivanov Odessa State Drama Russian Theater, UA, 1963. d: M.I.

National School of Drama, IN, 1997. ad/d/p: Parthiv Shah

The National Shakespeare Company, US, 1970. d/ill: David Stone Martin

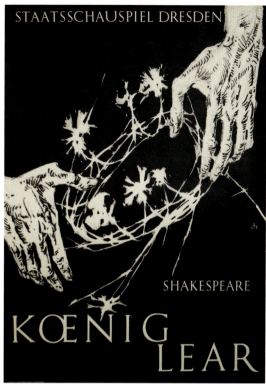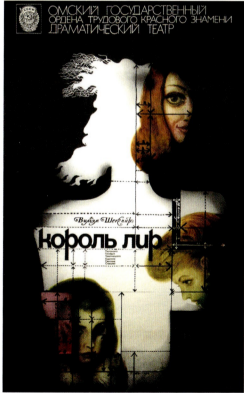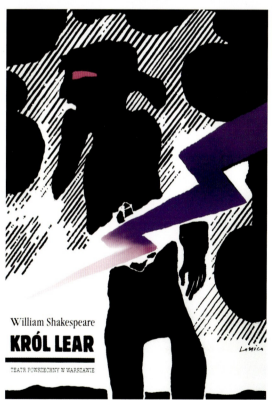

Rustaveli Theatre, GE, 1966. ad: Mikhail Tumanishvili

Omsk State Drama Theater, RU, 1982. d: Vitaly Volf

Staatsschauspiel Dresden, DE, 1960. d: n/a

Teatr Powszechny w Warszawie, PL, n/a. d: Jan Lenica
(Dydo Poster Collection)

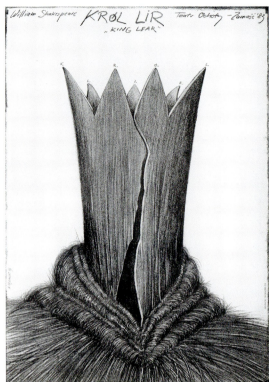

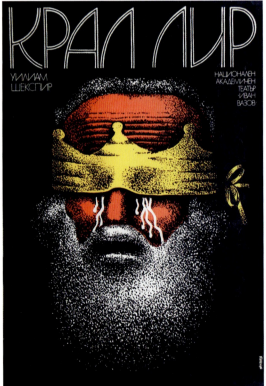

Veszprem Petofi Szinhaz, HU, 1999. d: Istvan Orosz

Teatr Nowy w Lodzi, PL, 2000. d/p: Rafal Oubinski

Teatr Ochoty, PL, 1983. d: Andrzej Pagowski (Dydo Poster Collection)

Ivan Vazov National Theatre, BG, n/a. d: Ognian Funev

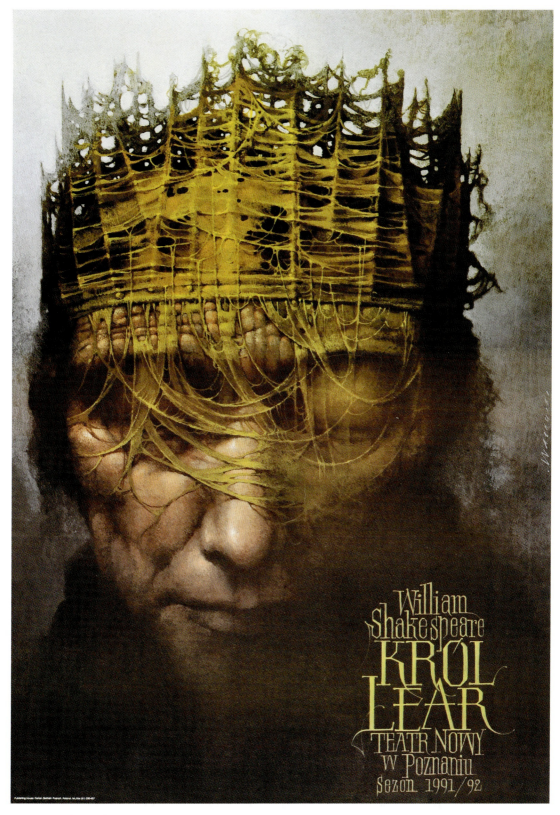

**Teatr Nowy w Poznaniu**, PL, 1991. **d**: Wieslaw Walkuski (Dydo Poster Collection)

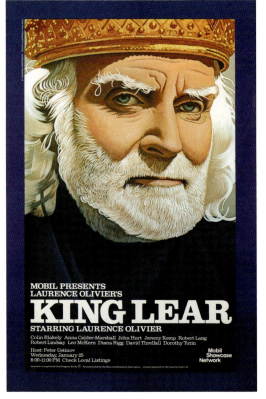

Teatr Wspolczesny Szczecin, PL, 1997. d: Leszek Zebrowski

Lincoln Center Theater, US, 2004. ad: Jim Russek, d: James McMullan

Mobil Masterpiece Theatre, US, 1984. d/ill: Paul Davis

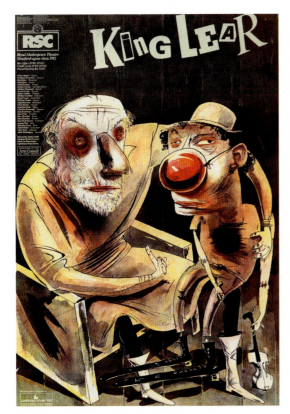

Royal Shakespeare Company, Royal Shakespeare Theatre, UK, 1982.
d: The Drawing Room, ill: Ian Pollock

Teatr Powszechny w Radomiu, PL, 2000. d: Stasys Eidrigevicius

University of Michigan, US, 1994. d: Jan Sawka (Dydo Poster Collection)

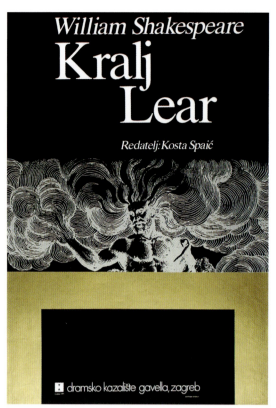
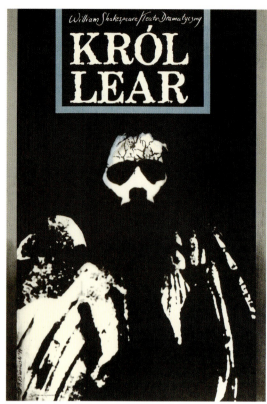
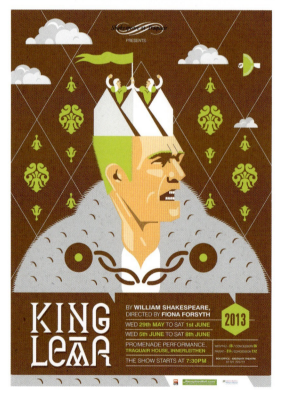

Dramsko kazaliste Gavella, HR, 1985. **d:** Ivan Picelj

Shakespeare at Traquair Theatre, UK, 2013. **d:** Michal Stachowiak

Teatr Dramatyczny, PL, 1977. **d:** Andrzej Klimowski

Teatro Zifio, CL, 2013. **ad/d:** Diego Becas Villegas

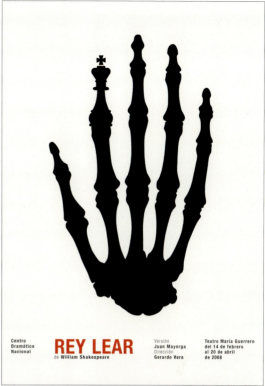

Association Tadaaa, US, 2008. ad/d: Yann Legendre

Centro Dramatico Nacional, Teatro Maria Guerrero, ES, 2008. ad/d: Isidro Ferrer

Serbian National Theatre, RS, 1989. ad/d: New Collectivism

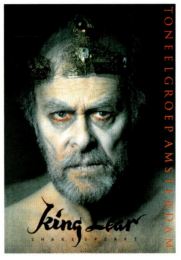
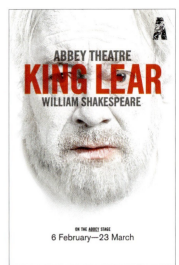
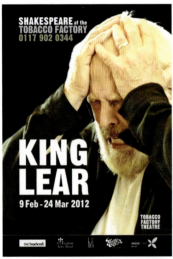
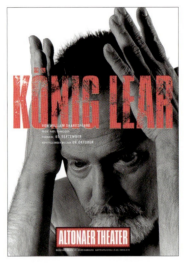
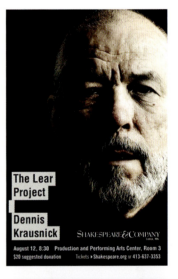
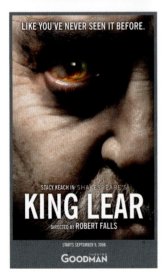
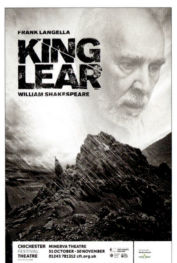

Synetic Theater (Rustaveli Theatre), GE, 2012.
ad: Paata Ciqurishvili

The Tobacco Factory, UK, 2012.
d: Alpha Charlie Design, p: Graham Burke

Goodman Theatre, US, 2006.
ad/d: Kelly Rickert, p: Brian Warling

Toneelgroep Amsterdam, NL, 1989.
ad/d/p: Anthon Beeke

Altonaer Theater, DE, 1998. ad: Ole Friedrich

Chichester Festival Theatre, UK, 2013.
ad/d: Shaun Webb Design, p: Jay Brooks

Abbey Theatre, The National Theatre of Ireland, IE, 2013. ad: Ciarán ÓGaora, d: Stephen Ledwidge, p: Anthony Woods

Shakespeare & Company, US, 2008.
d/p: Kevin Sprague

Theatre Calgary, CA, 2015. ad: Christina Poddubiuk, d: Scott McKowen, p: David Cooper

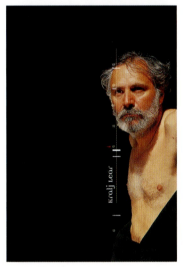
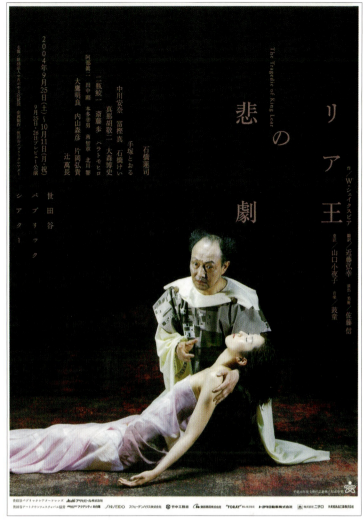
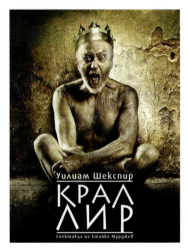

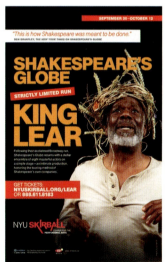

The Stratford National Theatre of Canada, Koninklijke Schowburg, NL, 1973. d: n/a

Ulysses Theatre, HR, 2001. ad/d: Eduard Cehovin, p: Damjan Kocijancic

Plovdiv Drama Theater, BG, 2012. d/p: Georgi Vachev

Setagaya Public Theatre, JP, 2004. ad: Tatsuya Ariyama, p: Yasuhide Kuge

Za-Koenji Public Theatre 1, JP, 2014. ad: J.A. Seazer, d: Keita Kobayashi, p: Ritsuko Kanbayashi

New York University Skirball Center, US, 2014. ad/d: Kristina Deckert, p: Ellie Kurttz

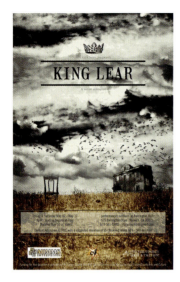

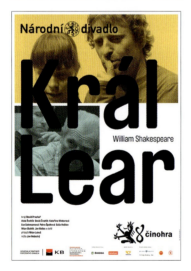
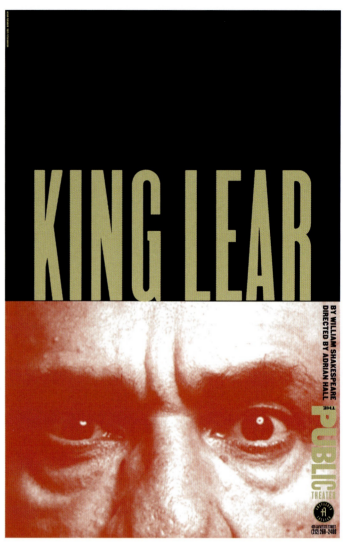
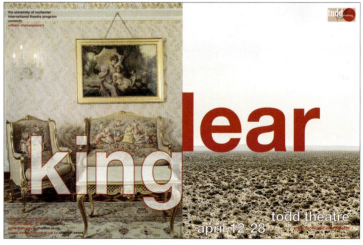

Barrington Hall, US, 2014. **d:** Erica Cruz

Royal Shakespeare Company,
Royal Shakespeare Theatre, UK, 1976.
**d:** Ginni Gillam, Mark Polkinghorne,
**p:** Toyne Newton

**Narodni divadlo**, CZ, 2011. **ad:** Bohumil Vasak
(Studio Najbrt)

The Public Theater, US, 1995. **ad/d:** Paula Scher (Pentagram)

University of Rochester International Theatre Program, Todd Theatre, US, 2007.
**ad/d:** Nigel Master

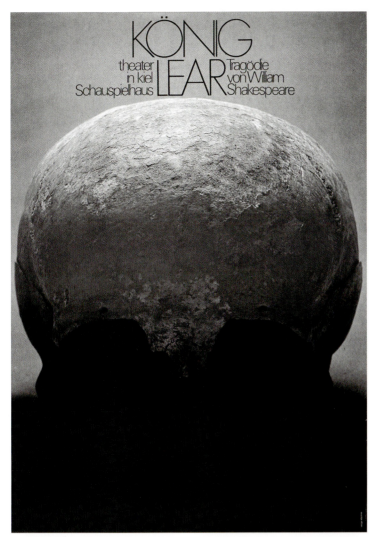
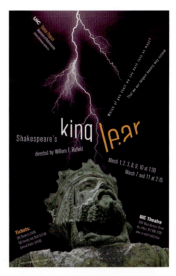

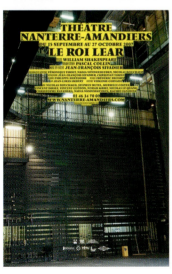
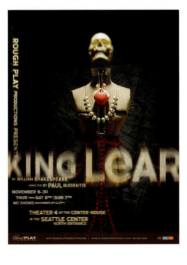

**Theater in kiel Schauspielhaus**, DE, 1974. **d:** Holger Matthies (Museum Folkwang, Deutsches Plakat Museum)

**Theatre Nanterre-Amandiers**, FR, 2007. **ad:** Labomatic, **d:** Frederic Bortolotti, Nicolas Ledoux, **d/p:** Pascal Bejean, **p:** Florence Lebert

**Rough Play Productions**, US, 2010. **d/p:** Ross Hogin

**University of Illinois at Chicago**, US, 2007. **ad/d/p:** Matthew Gaynor

**Denver Center Theatre Company**, US, 2007. **ad/d/ill:** Scott McKowen

**Rustaveli Theatre**, GE, n/a. **ad:** Robert Sturua

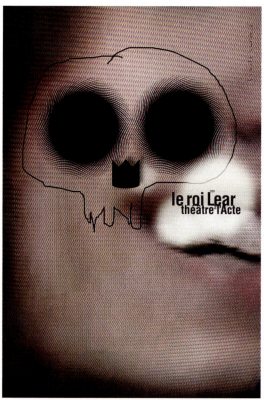

**Collective Shakespeare**, BR, 2013. ad/d: Thiago Andre Seifert, p: Ana Cristina

**Theatre de la Renaissance**, FR, 2008. ad/d/p: Cedric Gatillon

**Theatre² l'Acte**, FR, 2007. ad/d/p: Curchod

**Teatr Rekwizytornina**, PL, 2013. d: Tomasz Boguslawski (Dydo Poster Collection)

Krawkowski Teatr Scena Stu, PL, 2013. d/p: Katarzyna Zapart

Lenin Komsomol State Youth Theater of Latvian SSR, LV, 1979. d: Maris Argalis

# MUCH ADO ABOUT NOTHING

*O Hero, what a Hero hadst thou been,*
*If half thy outward graces had been placed*
*About thy thoughts and counsels of thy heart!*
*But fare thee well, most foul, most fair! Farewell,*
*Thou pure impiety and impious purity!*
*For thee I'll lock up all the gates of love,*
*And on my eyelids shall conjecture hang,*
*To turn all beauty into thoughts of harm,*
*And never shall it more be gracious.*

—Claudio

The most noteworthy plot development in *Much Ado About Nothing* is not that it is, as one critic noted, "studded with dastardly deception, trickery and treachery, bungling buffoonery and witty wisecracks!" but that no one is killed or maimed by the end of this comedy of love lost and found. Moreover, the ending leaves the audience smiling, which accounts for the cleverly benign posters that announce the funniest of the Bard's comedies.

Benign is not a criticism. The poster images simply eschew the usual Shakespearean conflicts. But there is still a common thread: love, which has its own distinctive codes and language (and baggage). In *Much Ado* all the trite and novel symbols for love apply.

Claudio falls hard in love for Hero, the daughter of Leonato. They decide to be married. Yet a week before the wedding the pair play a game on their two friends, the witty Beatrice (Leonato's niece) and the equally clever Benedick (Claudio's noble friend), to get them to stop their incessant bickering and fall in love with each other. The intervention works—Beatrice and Benedick fall secretly in love.

The plot, however, thickens. Benedick's friend, the troublemaker Don John, recruits his smarmy companion Borachio to make love to Margaret, Hero's servant, as she stands at Hero's window. Don John convinces Claudio to watch from a distance. Predictably, he mistakes Margaret for Hero, then rebukes her for lechery and then leaves her at the altar on their wedding day. Hero is humiliated, and her family sends her away, telling all that she died of grief. (In fact, she is hiding until redemption time.) Fortunately, two night watchmen overhear Borachio bragging about his deed, and he is arrested. Hero is, therefore, proven innocent, but Claudio, who believes she is dead, is punished for his unfair accusations. Leonato demands that Claudio tell everybody in the city that his daughter was not to blame, and as further comic penance, Claudio is to marry Leonato's "niece"—who looks exactly like Hero. At the church ceremony, a masked Hero reveals herself to Claudio, who is joyful, putting an exclamation point on the reverie.

Posters for *Much Ado* show love represented by crossed cupid arrows, devilish cupids, candles with hearts as flames, and the obvious mask motif.

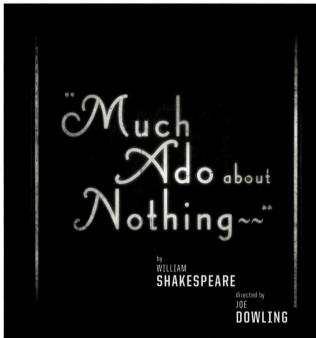

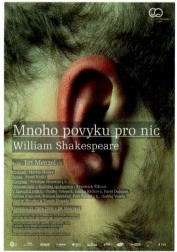

**Guthrie Theater**, US, 2011. **ad:** Vinny Sainato (SpotCo), **d:** Nicky Lindeman, Ester Wu (SpotCo)

**Jeugdtheater Diever**, NE, 2014.
**ad:** Grytha Uisser, **d:** Paulien Schutten,
**p:** shutterstock.com

**Teatar Komedija**, MK, 2014.
**ad:** Andrej Cvetanovski, **d:** Sergej Svetozarev

**Shakespeare & Company**, US, 2003.
**d:** Mary Garnish, **p:** Kevin Sprague

**Royal Shakespeare Company,
Royal Shakespeare Theatre**, UK, 1988.
**d:** Chris Frampton, **p:** Joffe

**Jihoceske divadlo**, CZ, 2009. **ad:** Michal Lang,
**d:** Robert V. Novak, **p:** Ivan Pinkava

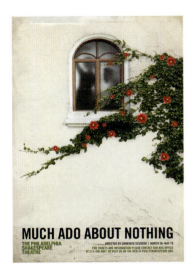
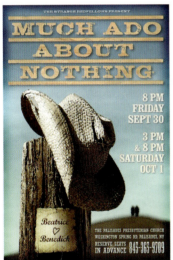

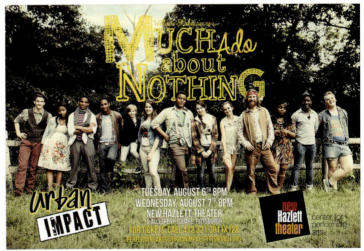

The Philadelphia Shakespeare Theatre, US, 2013. d: n/a

The Strange Bedfellows, US, 2011. ad/d: David Green (Brightgreen Design)

Libanon on Stage, Charity Theatre of the Order of Malta, DE, 2010. ad/d/p: Alexander von Lengerke

Portland Community College, US, 2014. ad: Cece Cutsforth, d/p: Anthony Catalan

New Hazlett Theater, US, 2013. ad/d: Eric Anderson, p: Rebecca Chiapelli

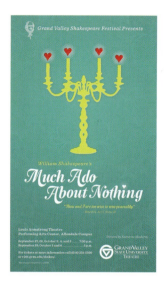
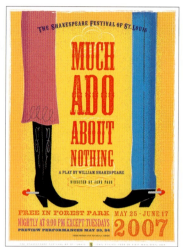

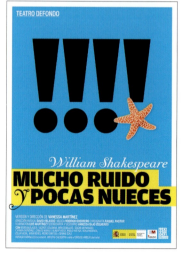
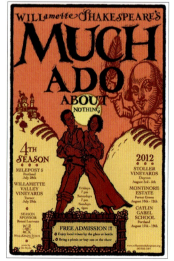

**Louis Armstrong Theatre**, US, 2013.
ad: Nancy Crittenden

**Royal Shakespeare Company, Royal Shakespeare Theatre**, UK, 1982.
ad/d: John David Lloyd, Jim Northover,
d: Martyn Hey (Lloyd Northover)

**University of Michigan Matthaei Botanical Gardens and Nichols Arboretum**, US, 2012.
ad/d: David Zinn

**Shakespeare Festival of St. Louis**, US, 2007. ad/d/ill: Rich Nelson

**Landestheater Tubingen**, DE, 2008.
d: Kena Pfluger

**Teatro Defondo**, ES, 2008.
ad: Diego Areso Nieva

**Teatro da Cornucopia**, PT, 1990.
ad/d: Cristina Reis, ad: Luis Miguel Cintra

**Teatr Klasyczny**, PL, 1968.
d: Waldemar Swierzy (Dydo Poster Collection)

**Willamette Shakespeare**, US, 2012.
ad/d/ill: Dee Boyles

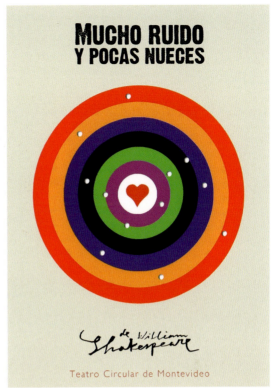
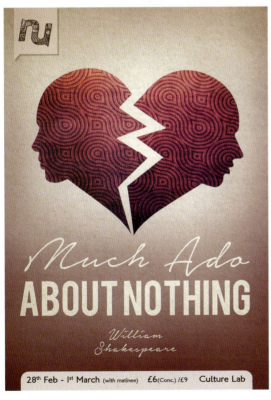

Teatr Wybrzeze Gdansk, PL, 2008. ad/d: Lex Drewinski

Newcastle University Theatre Society, 2015, UK.
ad/d/p: Luke W. Robson, d: Chloe Marquand

Teatro Circular de Montevideo, UY, 1990. ad/d: Fidel Sclavo

The Bradfordians Dramatic Society, UK, 2012. ad/d: Marc Bessant

Sopocka Scena Off de Bicz, PL, 2008. d: Leszek Zebrowski

# ROMEO AND JULIET

*She hath, and in that sparing makes huge waste,*
*For beauty starved with her severity,*
*Cuts beauty off from all posterity.*
*She is too fair, too wise, wisely too fair,*
*To merit bliss by making me despair:*
*She hath forsworn to love, and in that vow*
*Do I live dead that live to tell it now.*

—Romeo

Whether it is the plot line of the musical *West Side Story* or lyrics from the Reflections' doo-wop song *(Just Like) Romeo and Juliet*, the tragedy of these two star-crossed lovers has had a profound influence on a wide swath of popular culture. The term *star-crossed lovers* itself, describing a doomed romance, was first spoken in the prologue of Shakespeare's play. And how many times has some version of "parting is such sweet sorrow" or "a rose by any other name would smell as sweet" been uttered in passing as a simple tic of vernacular speech? Sweet sorrow, indeed!

The language of *Romeo and Juliet*'s poster art has been fairly consistent, translating the original dialogue into the graphic idioms of each era. Harkening back to the earliest pictorial posters is, of course, the image of the two lovers in fond romantic embrace. This theme has evolved considerably from the classic poses to more inventive contemporary studio photographs featuring interracial and same-gender couples. Then there is the heart image. Since the play is a heartbreaker, the heart is torn in two (and often bleeding), sometimes including depictions of the lovers. Then there is that famous rose by any other name, used as a key symbolic element. But it is the dagger that has gained the most prominence over the years.

It is that final, indeed requisite, Shakespearean death scene that focuses the audience on the dagger. Romeo sees Juliet's apparently lifeless body. Deciding not to go on living, Romeo swallows a vial of poison. Juliet awakens, sees Romeo has committed suicide, and tries to kill herself by kissing him, hoping there is enough poison on his lips to have some residual effect. Realizing this is in vain, Juliet stabs herself, inflicting the mortal wound with Romeo's own dagger.

The scene stabs at everyone's heart. But one of the cleverest poster ideas does not rely on the standard symbols—rather, it is the front page of an Italian newspaper, with the headline "Romeo and Juliet," with a few blood splatters on the page for emphasis (page 103).

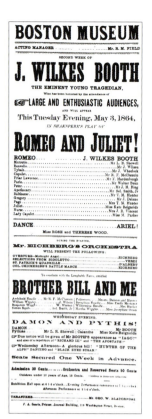
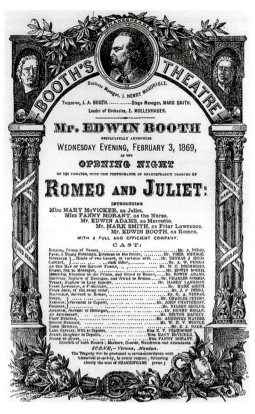

Boston Museum, US, 1864. d: n/a

Booth's Theatre, US, 1869. d: n/a

Euclid Avenue Opera House, US, 1875. d: n/a

Boston Museum, US, 1881. d: n/a

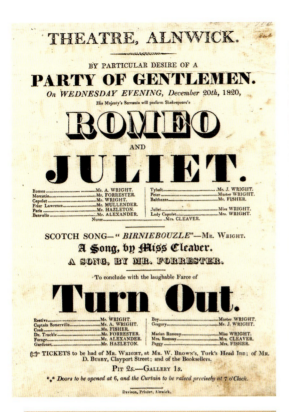

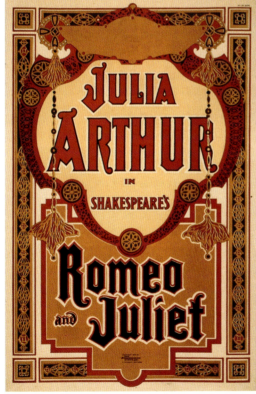

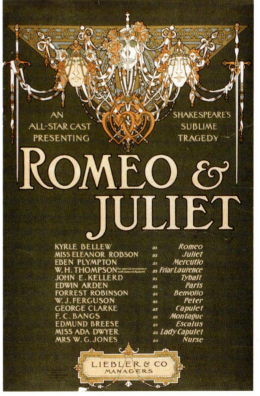

Theater Alnwick, US, 1820. d: n/a

Theater: n/a, US, 1899. d: Strobridge & Co. Lith.

Srpsko Narodno pozoriste, RS, 1876. d: n/a

Theater: n/a, US, 1903. d: Strobridge Litho Co.

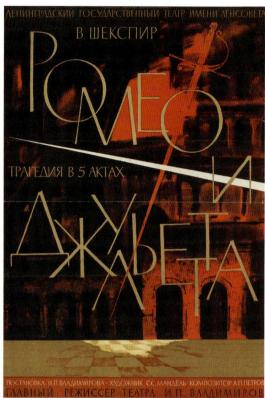

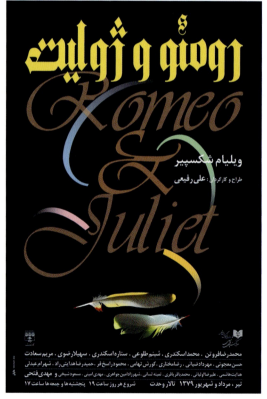

Moscow Drama Theatre, RU, 1948. d: n/a

Moscow Theatre of Mimicry and Gesture, RU, 1985. d: I. Shumilov

Lensovet Theatre, RU, 1964. d: S.S. Mandel

Dramatic Arts Centre, Ministry of Culture, IR, 2000.
ad/d/p: Ebrahim Haghighi (Alliance Graphique International)

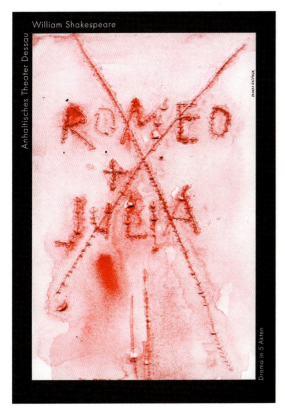
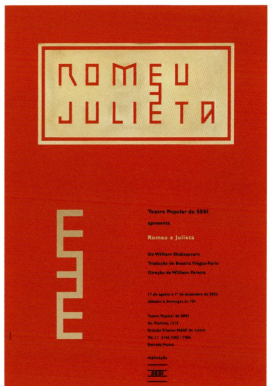

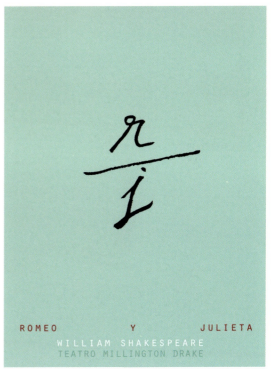

Anhaltisches Theater Dessau, DE, 2010. d: Erhard Gruttner (Museum Folkwang, Deutsches Plakat Museum)

Clube Estefania Theatre, Festival Temps d'Image, PT, 2014. ad/d: Pedro Nora

Teatro Popular do SESI, BR, 2002. ad/d: Guto Lacaz

Teatro Millington Drake, AR, 1995. ad/d: Fidel Sclavo

Penn State Pavilion Theatre, US, 1994. ad/d: Lanny Sommese

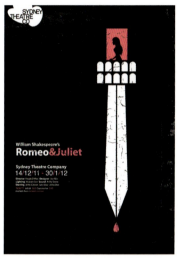
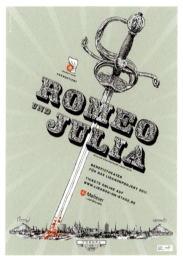

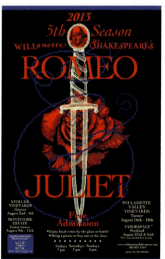

La Casa de Claypole, AR, 2013.
ad/d/p: Max Rompo, ad: Pontenpie

Sydney Theatre Company, AU, 2011.
d: Will Conley

Shakespeare & Company, US, 2009.
d/p: Kevin Sprague

The Shakespeare Players, DE, 2013.
d: Filip Kujawski

Libanon on Stage, Charity Theatre of the Order of Malta, DE, 2011.
ad/d: Alexander von Lengerke

Theater: n/a, DE, n/a. d: n/a

Shakespeare Festival of St. Louis, US, 2001.
ad/d/ill: Rich Nelson

Art University of Semnan, IR, 2010.
ad/d: Mohammad Hossein Ghiasvand

Willamette Shakespeare, US, 2013.
ad/d/ill: Dee Boyles

Romeo and Juliet 99

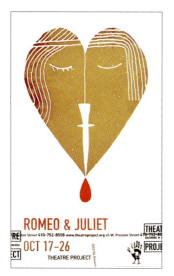
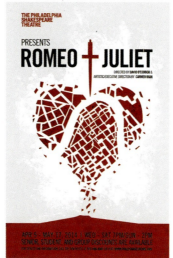
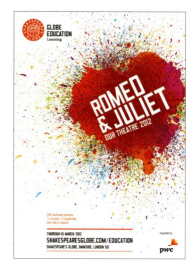

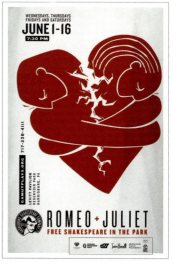

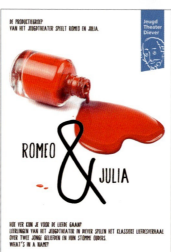

**Baltimore Theatre Project**, US, 2003.
**ad/d:** David Plunkert

**Harold Clurman Theatre**, US, 1980.
**d:** Jan Sawka (Dydo Poster Collection)

**Teatar Joakim Vujic**, RS, 2005.
**ad/d:** Slobodan Stetic

**The Philadelphia Shakespeare Theatre**, US, 2014. **d:** n/a

**Teatr im. Wandy Siemaszkowej**, PL, 2013.
**ad:** Remigiusz Caban, **d:** Krzysztof Motyka

**Jeugdtheater Diever**, NL, 2013.
**ad:** Grytha Visser, **d:** Paulien Schutten,
**p:** Shutterstock

**Shakespeare's Globe**, UK, 2012. **ad/d:** Embrace

**Harrisburg Shakespeare Company at Gamut Theatre Group**, US, 2012. **ad/d:** Rob Smith

**Teatr na Woli**, PL, 2003. **d:** Roslaw Szaybo
(Dydo Poster Collection)

100  Presenting Shakespeare

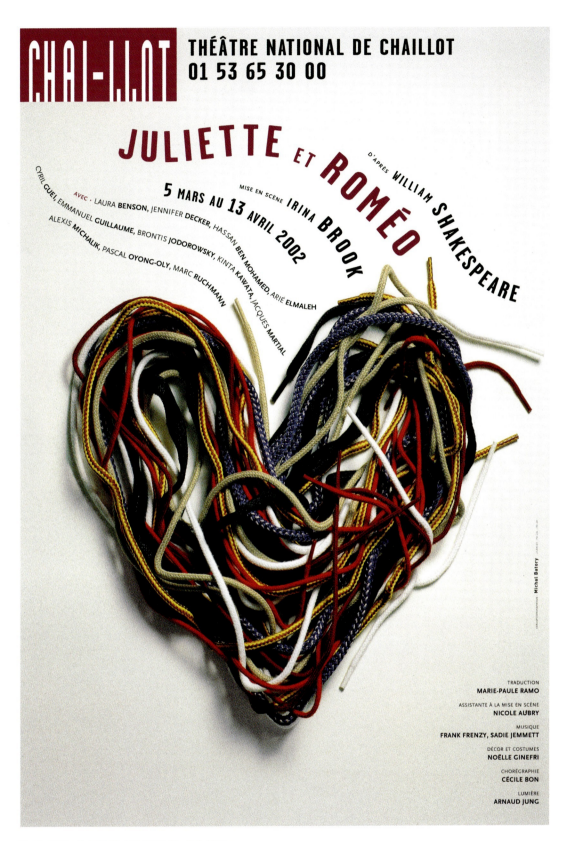

Theatre National de Chaillot, FR, 2002. d/p: Michal Batory

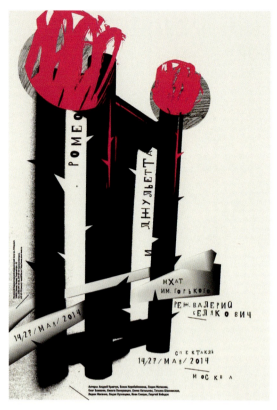

Gogol Center, RU, 2014. ad/d: Peter Bankov

Theater: n/a, PL, 2005. d: Sebastian Kubica (Dydo Poster Collection)

Gogol Center, RU, 2014. ad/d: Peter Bankov

Teatr Slaski im. Stanislawa Wyspianskiego, PL, 2000.
d: Roman Kalarus (Dydo Poster Collection)

102  Presenting Shakespeare

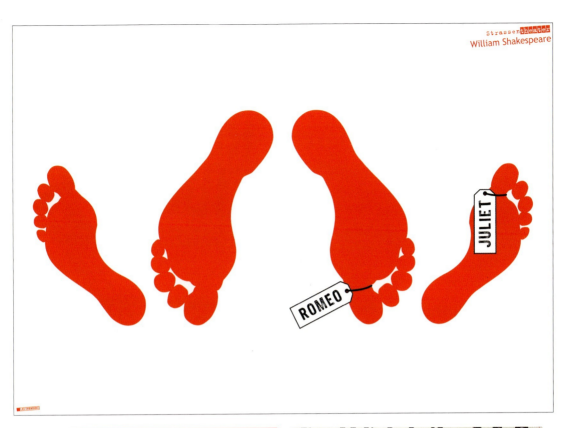

Strassentheater, DE, 2007. ad/d: Lex Drewinski

Production Workshop, Brown University, US, 2013. d: Jonathan Key

Royal Shakespeare Company, Royal Shakespeare Theatre, UK, 1986.
ad/d: John David Lloyd, Jim Northover (Lloyd Northover)

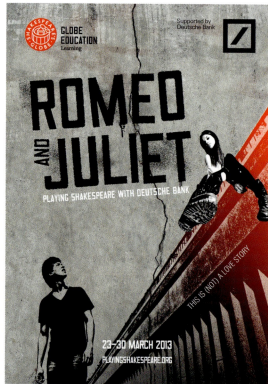
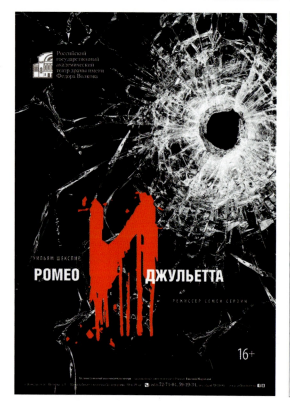
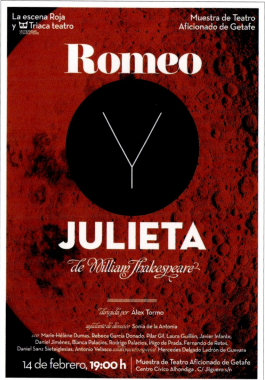

Teatr Powszechny w Radomiu, PL, 2009. d: Justyna Czerniakowska (Dydo Poster Collection)

The Russian State Academic Drama Theater Named After Fyodor Volkov, RU, 2014. d: Yekaterina Belova

Shakespeare's Globe, UK, 2013. ad: Adrian Hastings (Premm Design), d: Premm Design

Triaca Teatro, ES, 2009. ad: Diego Areso Nieva

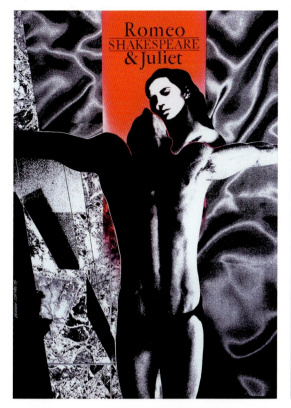
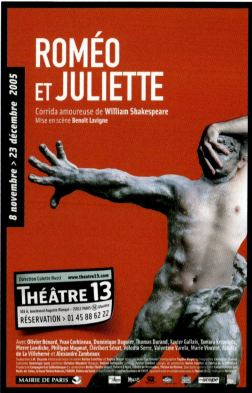

DESA, PL, 1989. **d:** Roslaw Szaybo (Dydo Poster Collection)

Teatr Wspotczesny Wroclaw, PL, 1978. **d:** A. Klimowski

Theatre 13, FR, 2005. **ad/d/p:** Cedric Gatillon

Romeo and Juliet 105

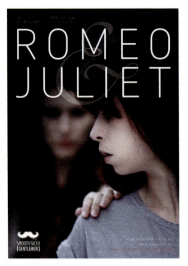
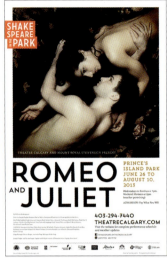

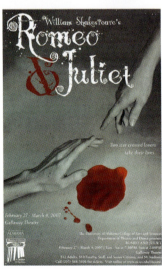

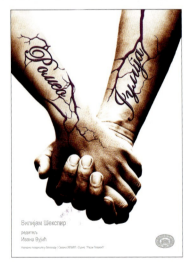

**Dimas Bueno e Tatiane Iovanovitchi**, BR, 2009.
ad/d: Marcos Minini, p: Daniel Sorrentino

**Camden Fringe**, Lion and Unicorn Theatre,
UK, 2010. ad: Paula Benson,
d: Velenzia Spearpoint, p: Ezra Spearpoint

**University of Alabama Theatre and Dance,
Marian Gallaway Theatre**, US, 2007. d: n/a

**Smooth Faced Gentlemen**, UK, 2012.
ad: Haz Al-Shaater, d: Brother Brother,
Yaz & Haz Al-Shaater, p: Haz Al-Shaater

**Nagaoaka Design Fair**, JP, 2012. ad/d: Tetsuro Minorikawa

**University Players**, Audimax, DE, 2003.
ad/d/p: Ole Friedrich

**Theatre Calgary**, CA, 2013.
ad: Christina Poddubiuk, d: Scott McKowen,
p: David Cooper

**National Theatre in Belgrade**, RS, 2006.
d: Jovan Tarbuk

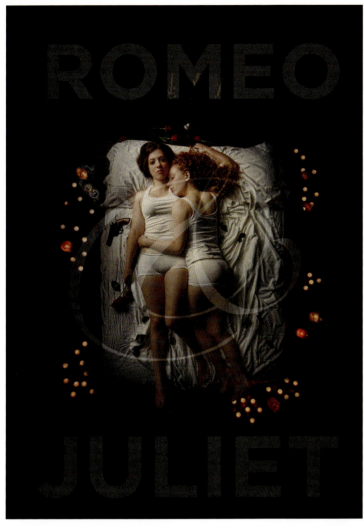

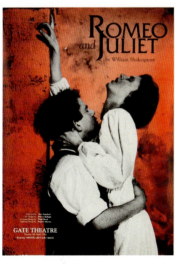

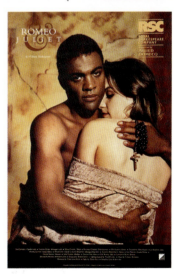

Curio Theatre, US, 2013. ad/d/p: Kyle Cassidy

Dublin Gate Theatre, IE, 1991. d: n/a

The Lisbon Players Theatre, PT, 2011. ad/d/p: Chase Valentin

Royal Shakespeare Company, Royal Shakespeare Theatre, UK, 1991. d: Pentagram, p: Douglas Brothers

International Theatre Festival MESS, BA, 2002. ad/d: Bojan Hadzihalilovic, Sejla Kameric, p: Dejan Vekic

Royal Shakespeare Company, Swan Theatre, UK, 1998. d: Clare Booth, p: Paul Rider

**Teatr Jednego Znaku**, PL, 1978. **d**: Marian Nowinski (Dydo Poster Collection)

**Teatr Polski w Szczecinie**, PL, 2011. **d**: Leszek Zebrowski (Dydo Poster Collection)

**Teatr Rozmaitosci**, PL, 1983. **d:** Marian Nowinski
(Dydo Poster Collection)

**Theatre La Chamaill**, FR, 1982. **d:** Mieczyslaw Gorowski
(Dydo Poster Collection)

**Teatr im. Stefana Jaracza**, PL, 2002. **d:** Wieslaw Walkuski (Dydo Poster Collection)

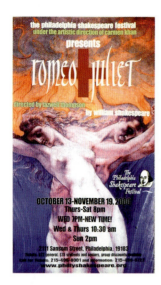

**The Philadelphia Shakespeare Theatre**, US, 2000. d: n/a

**Teatr im A. Sewruka**, PL, 2013.
d: Leszek Zebrowski

**Teatr Polski w Szczecinie**, PL, 1980.
d: Grzegorz Marszalek
(Dydo Poster Collection)

**Teatr Domu Wojska Polskiego**, PL, 1956. d: Andrzej Sadowski (Dydo Poster Collection)

**Teatr Narodowy, scena Teatr Maly**, PL, 1981.
d: Roslaw Szaybo (Dydo Poster Collection)

**San Jose Youth Shakespeare, Historic Hoover Theatre**, US, 2013. d: Karen Macauley

110  Presenting Shakespeare

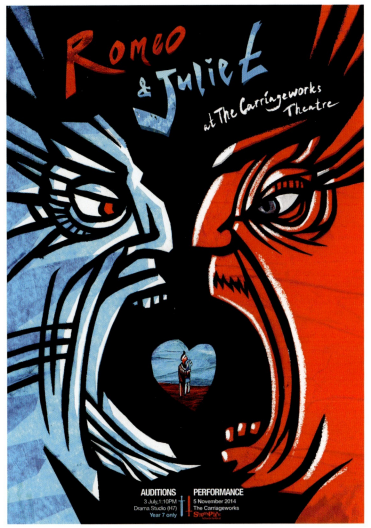
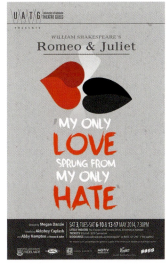
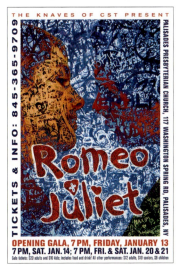
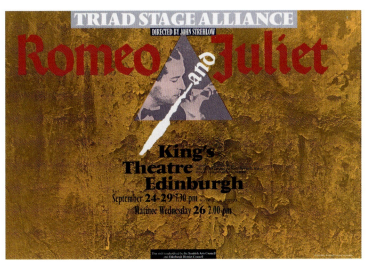

St. Mary's Menston Catholic School, The Carriageworks Theatre, UK, 2014.
ad: Derek Yates, d: Tatiana Alisova

Triad Stage Alliance, UK, 1984. ad/d/p: Hans Bockting

University of Adelaide Theatre Guild, AU, 2014. ad: Jim McGuinness, Keith McEwan
d: Jim McGuinness

Children's Shakespeare Theatre, US, 2012.
ad/d: David Green (Brightgreen Design),
p: Chris Carroll

Theatergesellschaft Willisau, CH, 1982.
ad/d: Niklaus Troxler

Teatr Nowy w Poznaniu, PL, 2005. d: Jerzy Czerniawski (Dydo Poster Collection)

Teatr Ochoty, PL, 1985. d: Andrzej Pągowski (Dydo Poster Collection)

Theatre La Chamaill, FR, 1982. d: Mieczyslaw Gorowski (Dydo Poster Collection)

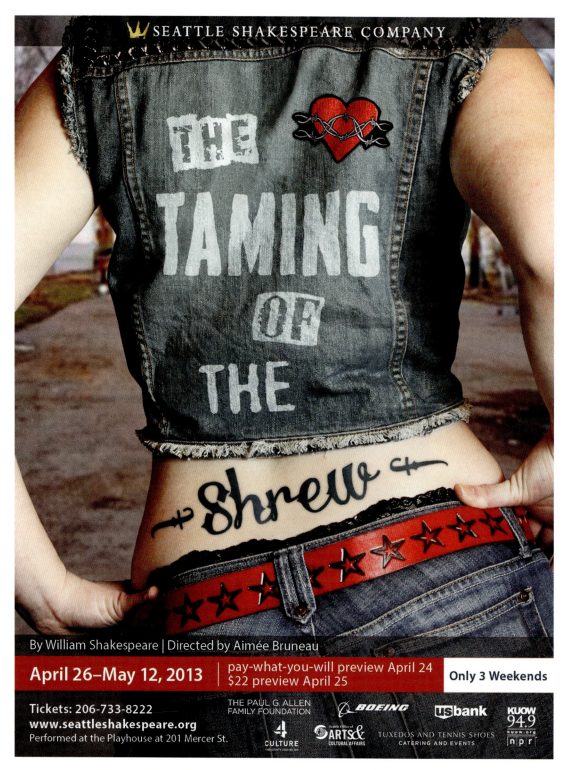

Seattle Shakespeare Company, US, 2013. ad: Jeff Fickes, d: Thea Roe, p: John Ulman

# THE TAMING OF THE SHREW

*No shame but mine: I must, forsooth, be forced*
*To give my hand opposed against my heart*
*Unto a mad-brain rudesby full of spleen;*
*Who woo'd in haste and means to wed at leisure.*
*I told you, I, he was a frantic fool,*
*Hiding his bitter jests in blunt behavior:*
*And, to be noted for a merry man,*
*He'll woo a thousand, 'point the day of marriage,*
*Make feasts, invite friends, and proclaim the banns;*
*Yet never means to wed where he hath woo'd.*
*Now must the world point at poor Katharina,*
*And say, "Lo, there is mad Petruchio's wife,*
*If it would please him come and marry her!"*
—Katharina

This is either one of Shakespeare's most misogynistic or pro-woman comedies, depending on where one sits.

Katharina, the shrew of the title, is not only a nasty, argumentative female, she is an obstacle to the marriage between her younger sister, Bianca, and her suitor, Lucentio. Bianca is prevented by their father from marrying before Katharina does. But Katharina's foul personality makes her undateable, no less marriageable, until she is betrothed to Petruchio. He has decided to take a wife with money, sight unseen, and proceeds to tame the shrew through enhanced interrogation means, including sleep and food deprivation. Ultimately, Katharina succumbs, and she and Petruchio are happy. The twist comes when, after marrying Lucentio, Bianca becomes the rebellious shrew.

The images representing this play fall into two main categories: showing the shrew imprisoned or in some kind of real or symbolic bondage—with the accoutrements thereof—or portraying the shrew as misanthropic, like some kind of fire-breathing beast. There is also a subset depicting male/female conflict, as in the posters of a boxing match. Whatever the conceit, an echo of violence and domination underscores all these posters.

Srpsko Narodno pozoriste, RS, 1869. d: n/a

Department of Culture of the Leningrad City Executive Committee, Lensoviet Leningrad State Theater, RU, 1971. d: Viktor Kundyshev

Georgian Theatre, GE, 1903. ad: Akaki Tsereteli

Ordzhonikidze Novokuzntesk State Drama Theater, RU, 1977. d: n/a

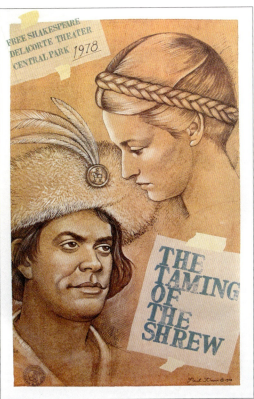

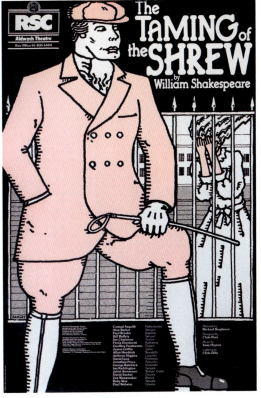

Westfalisches Landestheater, DE, 1961. d: n/a
(Museum Folkwang, Deutsches Plakat Museum)

Royal Shakespeare Company, Royal Shakespeare Theatre, UK, 1982.
d: Tim Allen, ill: Alan Morison

The Public Theater, Delacorte Theater, US, 1978. d: Paul Davis

Royal Shakespeare Company, Royal Shakespeare Theatre and
Aldwych Theatre, UK, 1978. ill: Farley

The Taming of the Shrew   117

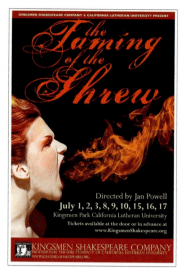
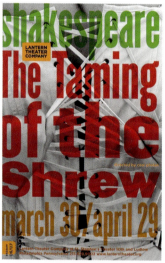

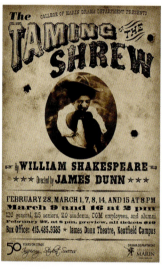
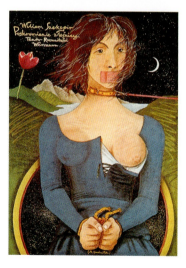

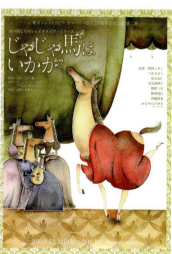

Oyun Atoleysi, TR, 2006. ad: Haluk Bilginer, d: Iskender Kardaslar

Lantern Theater Company, US, 2007. ad/d: Allan Espiritu, d/p: Lucy Price

Teatr Rozmaitosci, PL, 1976. ad/d: Andrzej Dudzinski

Royal Shakespeare Company, Swan Theatre, UK, 2008. ad/d: Andy Williams, p: Jillian Edelstein Ulman

University Players, DE, 2011. ad/d/p: Ole Friedrich

Wiener Lustspielhaus, AT, 2010. ad: Richard Donhauser, Rainer Kumpfhuber

Kingsmen Shakespeare Company, US, 2011. ad: Michael Adams, d: Cary Hanson

College of Marin Drama Department, James Dunn Theatre, US, 2014. d: Roger W. Dormann

Tokyo Shakespeare Company, Iwato Theatre, JP, 2010. ad: Kaoru Edo, d: Masami Tajiri, ill: Tomoko Kawaichi

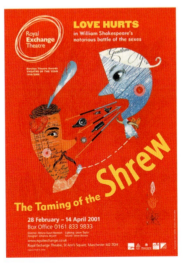

Hrvatsko narodno kazaliste Split, HR, 1983. d: Boris Bucan

Box Hill High School, AU, 2012.
ad: Toby Wilking, Sebastian White,
d/p: Sebastian White

Manchester Royal Exchange Theatre, UK,
2001. ad/d: Ian Vickers, d: Thea Roe,
ill: Sara Fanelli

Teatr Jednego Znaku, PL, 1987.
d: Marian Nowinski (Dydo Poster Collection)

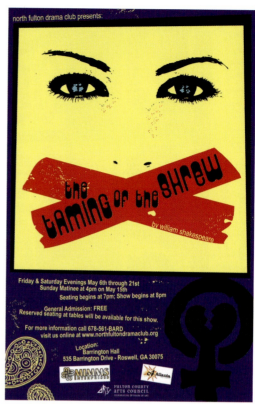
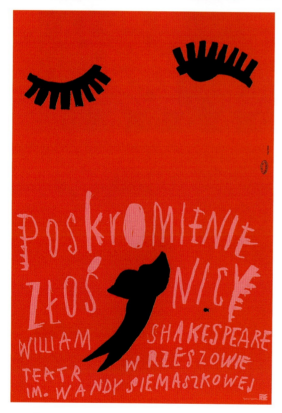
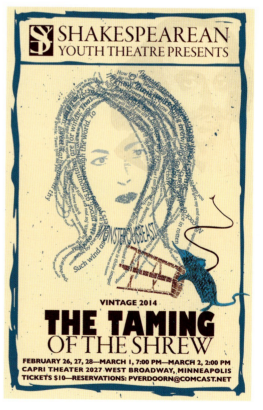

Youth Theatre, BG, n/a. d: Dimitar Tasev

Teatr w Rzeszowie, PL, 2006. ad/d: Lech Majewski

North Fulton Drama Club, US, 2011. ad/d: Erica Cruz

Shakespearean Youth Theatre, Capri Theater, US, 2014. ad/d: Steven Verdoorn

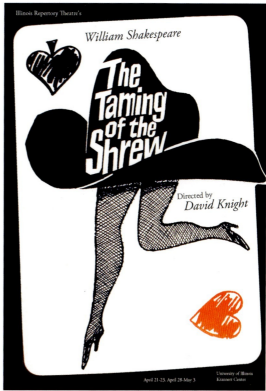
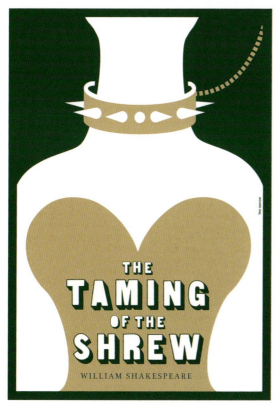
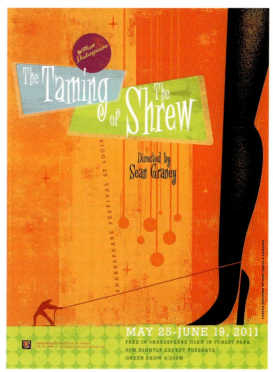

**Teatr Rekwizytornia**, PL, 2010. **d:** Tomasz Boguslawski
(Dydo Poster Collection)

**Association Tadaa**, FR, 2008. **ad/d:** Yann Legendre

**Illinois Repertory Theatre**, US, 1986. **ad/d:** Roman Duszek

**Shakespeare Festival of St. Louis**, US, 2011. **ad/d/ill:** Rich Nelson

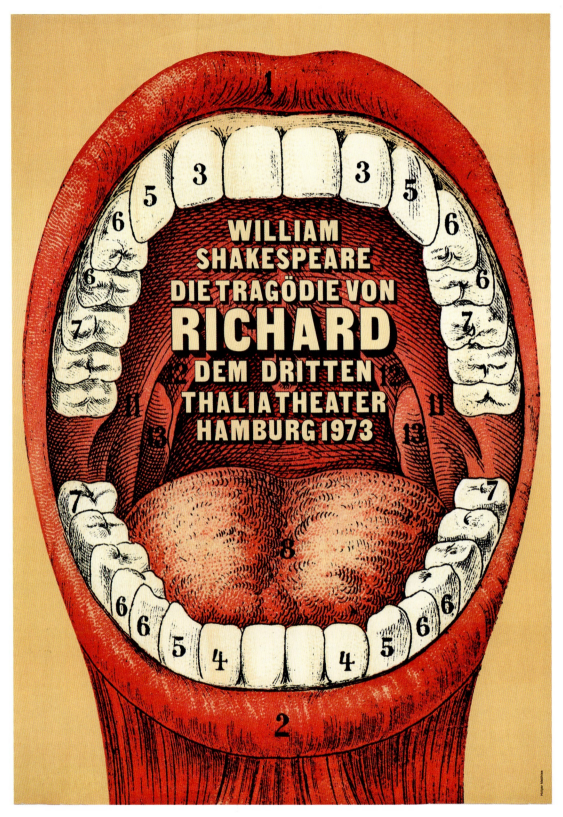

Thalia Theater Hamburg, DE, 1973. d: Holger Matthies (Museum Folkwang, Deutsches Plakat Museum)

# THE HISTORIES PART I

### Richard II
"Deep malice makes too deep incision; Forget, forgive; conclude and be agreed," says Richard II in this portrait of the fall from grace of the last king of the house of Plantagenet. He receives his reward for a criminal reign of war with Ireland, taxing commoners and fining nobles for crimes committed by their ancestors.

### Richard III
"Now is the winter of our discontent," says power-hungry Richard (duke of Gloucester), who conspires to usurp the throne from his brother and murders everybody in his way in order to wear the sharp-pointed crown. Then he finds that the bard has other plans as payback for his ignoble deeds.

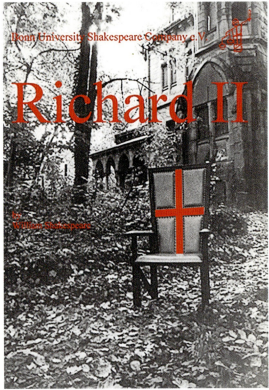
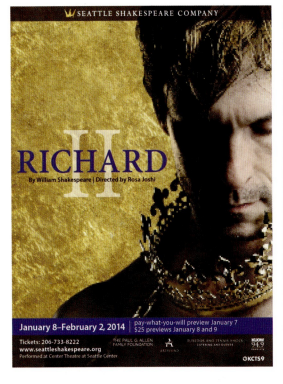

Royal Shakespeare Company, Royal Shakespeare Theatre and Barbican Theatre, UK, 2013. ad/d: Andy Williams, p: Jillian Edelstein

Seattle Shakespeare Company, US, 2014. ad: Jeff Fickes, d: Thea Roe, p: John Ulman

Bonn University Shakespeare Company, DE, 1993. d: n/a

New York Shakespeare Festival, The Public Theater, Delacorte Theater, US, 1987. ad/d/p: Paul Davis

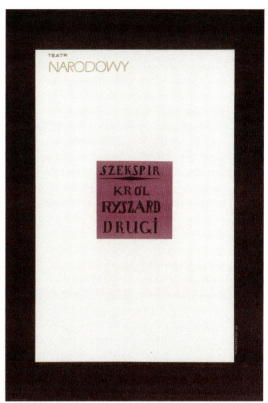
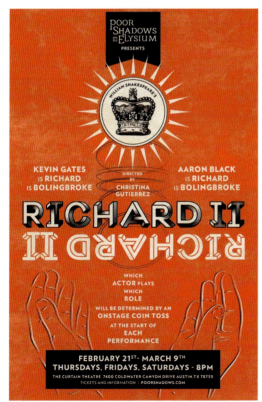

Les Gemeaux/Scene Nationale-Sceaux, FR, 2011.
ad/d: Michel Bouvet, p: Francis Laharrague

The Curtain Theatre, US, 2012. d: Jennymarie Jemison

Teatr Narodowy, PL, 1964. d: Henryk Tomaszewski
(Dydo Poster Colleciton)

The National Theatre at the Old Vic, UK, 1972. cd: Ken Briggs,
ad: Laurence Olivier

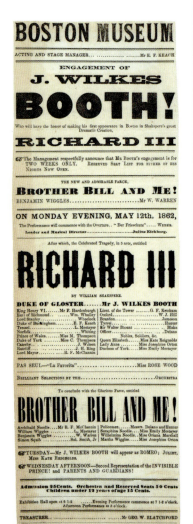
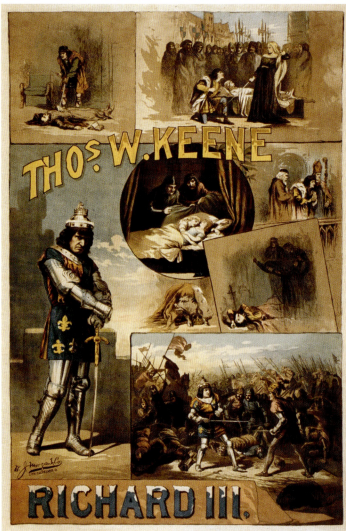
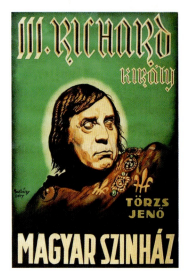

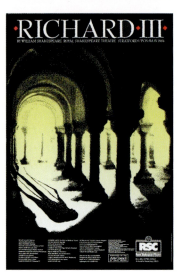

**Boston Museum**, US, 1862.
d: W.J. Morgan & Co. Lith.

**Magyar Szinhaz**, HU, 1937. d: Matskassy Gyula

**Theater: n/a**, US, 1884. d: W.J. Morgan & Co. Lith.

**University of Wisconsin-Milwaukee Fine Arts Theatre**, US, 1984. d: n/a

**Royal Shakespeare Company, Royal Shakespeare Theatre**, UK, 1984.
ad/d: John David Lloyd (Lloyd Northover),
d: Jim Northover (Lloyd Northover)

Teatret Moellen, DK, 2001. ad/d/p: Gitte Kath

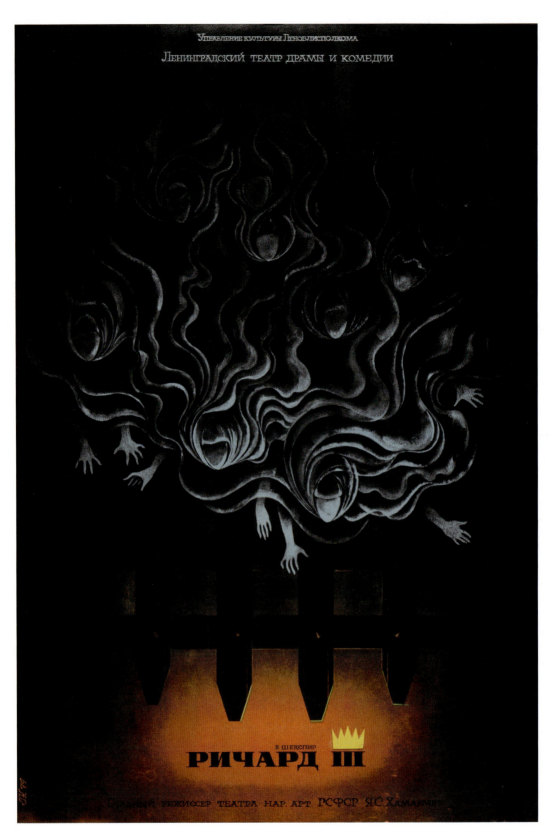

Leningrad Drama and Comedy Theater, RU, 1980. d: Galina Korbut

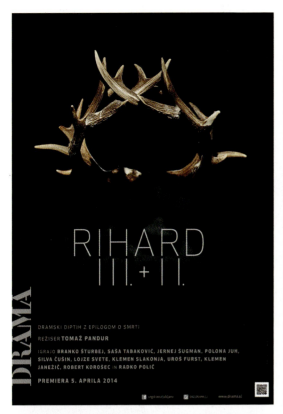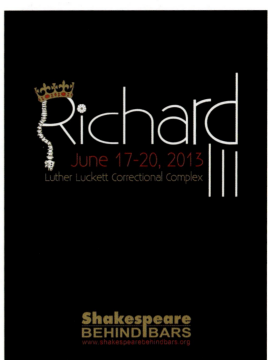

Slovene National Theatre, SI, 2014. d: Danijela Grgic, p: Aljosa Rebolj

Mecklenburgisches Staatstheater Schwerin, DE, 1972.
d: Karlheinz Effenberger
(Museum Folkwang, Deutsches Plakat Museum)

Shakespeare Behind Bars, Luther Luckett Correctional Complex, US, 2013. ad/d: Holly Stone

Teatr 77, PL, 1996. d: Tadeusz Piechura (Dydo Poster Collection)

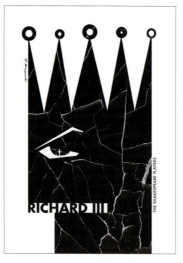

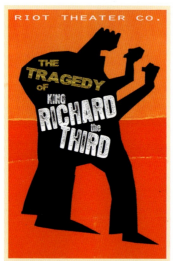

**Harrisburg Shakespeare Festival at Gamut Theatre Group**, Gamut Classic Theatre, US, 2009. **ad/d:** Rob Smith

**Theatre des gens de la place**, CA, 2014.
**ad:** Sebastien Roy (Egzakt), **d:** Philippe Lepage (Egzakt), **p:** Rozie Bouchard (Egzakt)

**Pavilion Theater**, US, 2002.
**d:** Lanny Sommese

**The Shakespeare Players**, DE, 2014.
**d:** Filip Kujawski

**Riot Theater Company**, US, 2000.
**ad/d:** Kaveh Haerian

**Teatro da Cornucopia**, PT, 1985. **ad:** Cristina Reis, Luis Miguel Cintra, **d/p:** Cristina Reis

**Baltimore Theatre Project**, US, 2006.
**ad/d:** David Plunkert

**The Globe Tokyo**, JP, 2006.
**ad:** Kiyoaki Ichikawa, **d:** Kaori Sato, **ill:** 100% Orange

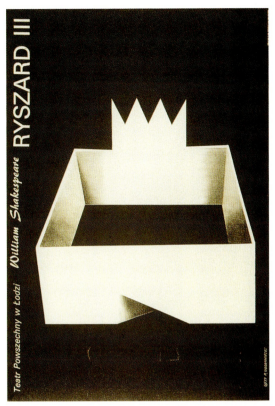

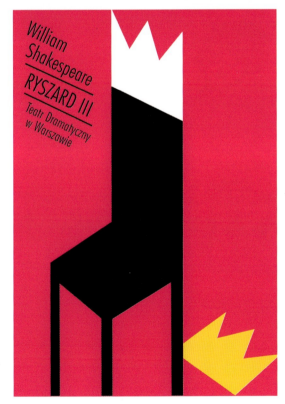
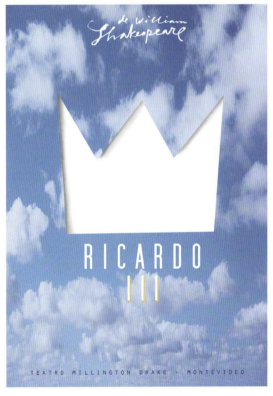

**Teatr Powszechny**, PL, 1971. **d:** Pawel Udorowiecki
(Dydo Poster Collection)

**Teatr Dramatyczny w Warszawie**, PL, 2005. **d:** Piotr Grabowski
(Dydo Poster Collection)

**Teatr Narodowy**, PL, 1969. **d:** Leszek Holdanowicz
(Dydo Poster Collection)

**Teatro Millington Drake**, UY, 1997. **ad/d:** Fidel Sclavo

The Histories I | 131

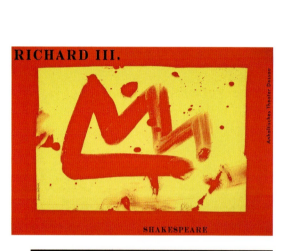

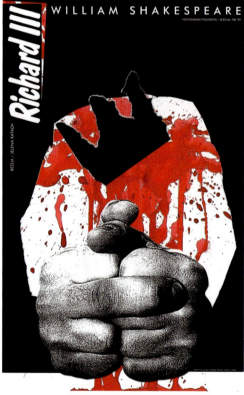
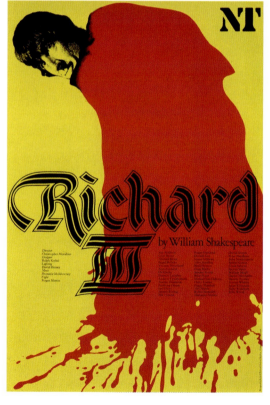

**Anhaltisches Theater**, DE, 2008. **d:** Erhard Gruttner (Museum Folkwang, Deutsches Plakat Museum)

**Novosadsko pozoriste**, RS, 1998. **ad/d:** Atila Kapitanj

**Teatr Ochoty**, PL, 1984. **d:** Andrzej Pagowski (Dydo Poster Collection)

**National Theatre, Olivier Theatre**, UK, 1979. **cd:** Richard Bird, Michael Mayhew, **ad:** Peter Hall

132  Presenting Shakespeare

New York Shakespeare Festival, The Public Theater, Delacorte Theater, US, 1990. ad/d/ill: Paul Davis

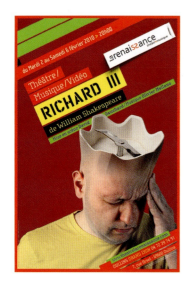

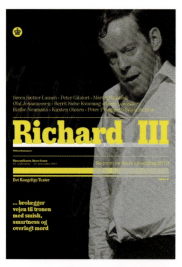
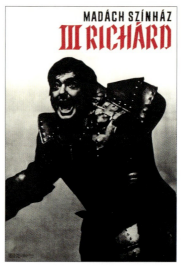
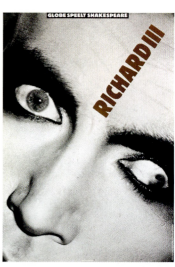

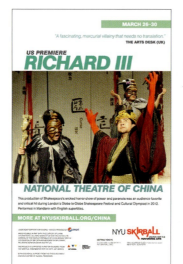
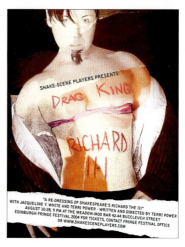

**Theatre de la Renaissance**, FR, 2010.
**ad/d/p:** Cedric Gatillon

**The Royal Danish Theatre**, DK, 2010.
**ad/d:** Soren Ajspur, **p:** Natascha Thiara

**Setagaya Public Theatre**, JP, 2007.
**ad/d:** Tatsuya Ariyama, **p:** Yasuhide Kuge

**Theatre 13**, FR, 2012. **ad/d/p:** Cedric Gatillon

**Madach Theatre**, HU, 1969. **d:** n/a

**National Theatre of China**, NYU Skirball Center, US, 2012. **d:** Kristina Deckert

**Royal Shakespeare Company, Roundhouse**, UK, 2012. **ad:** Claudio Baltar, Fabio Ferreira, **d:** Brigida Baltar, Ilana Braia, **p:** Emmanuelle Bernard

**Zuidelijk Toneel Globe**, NL, 1983.
**ad/d/p:** Anthon Beeke

**Shake-scene Players**, UK, 2004.
**ad/d:** Lynne R. Holmes

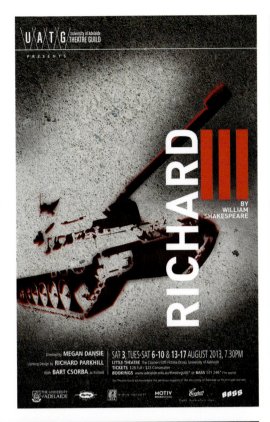
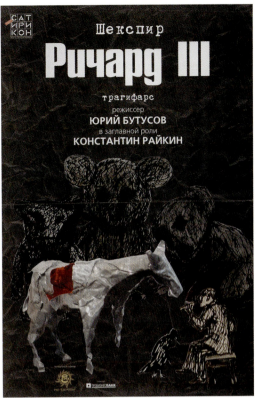
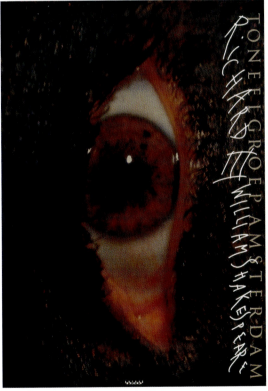

University of Adelaide Theatre Guild, AU, 2013. ad/d: Peter Hirte

Toneelgroep Amsterdam, NL, 1994. ad/d/p: Anthon Beeke

Satirikon Theatre, RU, 2004. d: A.R. Shishkin

Audimax, DE, 2008. ad/d/p: Ole Friedrich

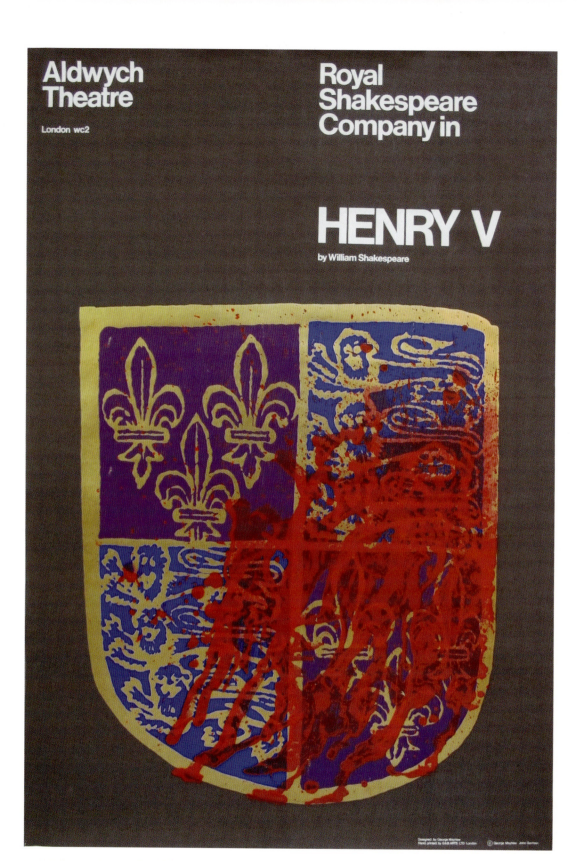

Royal Shakespeare Company, Aldwych Theatre, UK, 1966. d: George Mayhew

# THE HISTORIES PART II

### Henry IV (Part I)
King Henry IV, who unseated Richard II from his throne, now fights with rebels as well as his own estranged son, Prince Hal (the future Henry V), who, as war rages, wastes his time with women and drink.

### Henry IV (Part II)
Intrigue revolves around King Henry, who dies in the midst of war, leaving his kingdom and all its troubles to his oldest son, Prince Hal.

### Henry V
With Henry IV dead, the young Henry V must earn the respect of the common people. He laments his duties as king, yet under his command the English army wins a battle that forces the French king to surrender.

### Henry VI (Part I)
Henry V dies prematurely. His heir is yet to be crowned and is too young to rule the embattled kingdom. War breaks out between France and England. The duke of Gloucester remains in charge in England, and the duke of Exeter sets out to prepare young Henry for his coronation.

### Henry VIII
The most iconic of all English kings plans to divorce his wife, Katharine, so that he might produce a male heir. He announces his marriage with Anne Bullen. Katharine is demoted to "Princess Dowager." Anne gives birth to a girl, who is named Elizabeth.

### King John
King John must address French demands that he renounce his throne in favor of his nephew, Arthur, whom the French king, Philip, believes is the rightful heir to the throne. John is later poisoned by an angry monk.

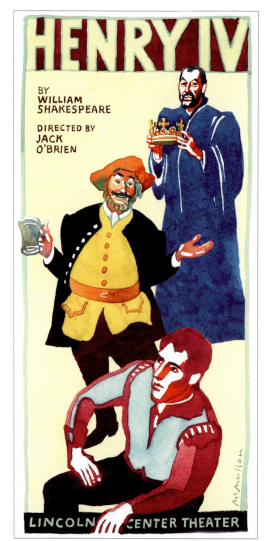

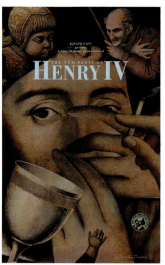
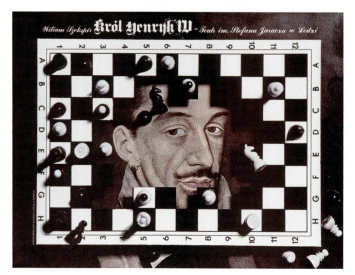
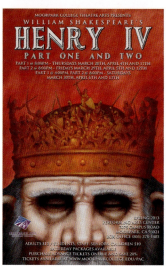

Lincoln Center Theater, US, 2003. ad: Jim Russek, d: James McMullan

Teatr im. Stefana Jaracza Olsztyn, PL, 1979. d: Marcin Mroszczak, p: Zbigniew Kapuscik (Dydo Poster Collection)

Royal Shakespeare Company, Barbican Theatre, UK, 1982. d: Ginni Moo-Young

New York Shakespeare Festival, The Public Theatre, US, 1991. ad/d/ill: Paul Davis

Moorpark College Performing Arts Center, US, 2013. ad: John Loprieno, d: Brian Koehler, p: Kurin Johansson

138  Presenting Shakespeare

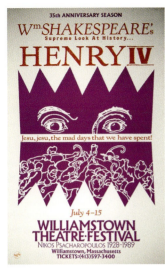
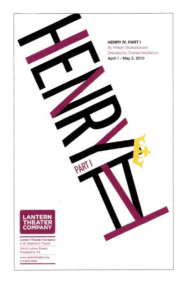

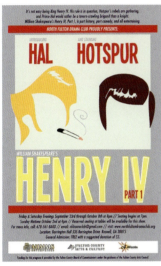
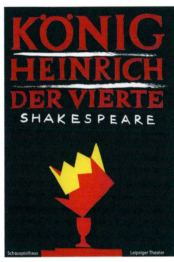

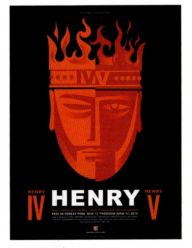

Williamstown Theatre Festival, US, n/a. d: n/a

North Fulton Drama Club, US, 2011.
ad/d: Erica Cruz

Royal Shakespeare Company,
Aldwych Theatre, UK, 1976. d: Ginni Gillam

Lantern Theater Company, US, 2010.
ad/d: Allan Espiritu, d: Christian Mortlock

Schauspielhaus Leipziger Theater, DE, 1986.
ad: Damm & Fiedler, d: Jutta Damm-Fiedler

Shakespeare Festival of St. Louis, US, 2014.
ad/d/ill: Rich Nelson

Harrisburg Shakespeare Festival at Gamut Theatre Group, Gamut Classic Theatre, US, 2005. ad/d: Rob Smith

Children's Shakespeare Theatre, US, 2005.
ad/d/p: David Green (Brightgreen Design)

Royal Shakespeare Company,
Launceston College, UK, 1980.
d: CS&S Design Partnership,
ill: Paul Broughton

The Histories II  139

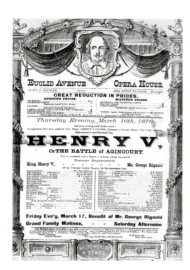

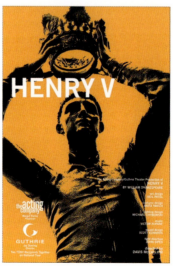

Euclid Avenue Opera House, US, 1876. d: n/a

Advice to the Players, US, 2009.
ad/d: Janina Lamb

North Fulton Drama Club, US, 2013.
ad/d: Erica Cruz

The Public Theater, Delacorte Theater, US, 1976. ad: Reinhold Schwenk, d/ill: Paul Davis

The Acting Company, US, 2008.
d/p: Kevin Sprague

Oxford Student's Troupe, Rustaveli Theatre,
GE, 2009. ad: Telma Holt

140  Presenting Shakespeare

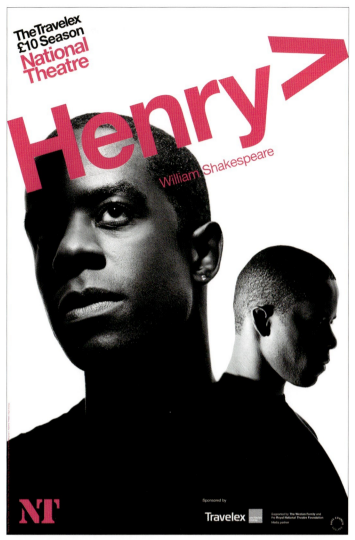

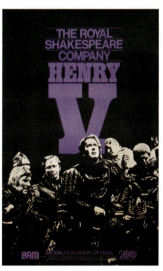

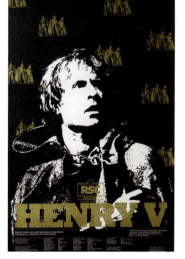

**National Theatre**, UK, 2003. **ad:** Nicholas Hytner, **cd:** Michael Mathew, **d:** Time Hatley, **p:** Hugo Glendinning

**Royal Shakespeare Company,**
**Brooklyn Academy of Music,** US, 1976. **d:** n/a
(Collection of Chisholm Larsson Gallery, NYC)

**Royal Shakespeare Company,**
**Royal Shakespeare Theatre,** UK, 1984.
**d:** Bob Crowley, **p:** Stephen MacMillan

**Prague Shakespeare Company**, CZ, 2013.
**d:** Martin Hula

**Royal Shakespeare Company,**
**Royal Shakespeare Theatre,** UK, 1994.
**d:** Amanda Bostock, **p:** William Webster

**Royal Shakespeare Company,**
**Aldwych Theatre,** UK, 1978. **d:** Ginni Gillam

The Histories II 141

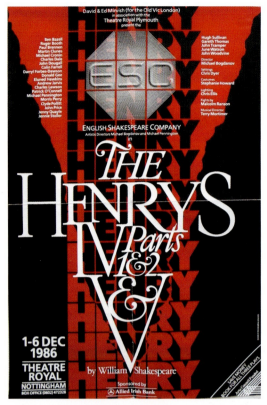
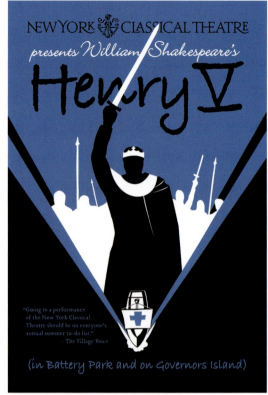

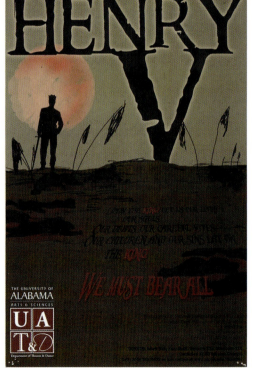

English Shakespeare Company, Theatre Royal Nottingham, UK, 1986. **d:** Richard Bird & Associates

Oxford University Drama Society, UK, 2009. **ad/d/p:** James Kennard

New York Classical Theatre, US, 2011. **ad:** Stephen Burdman, **ad/d/ill:** Todd Alan Johnson

University of Alabama, Department of Theatre and Dance, Marian Gallaway Theatre, US, 2009. **d:** n/a

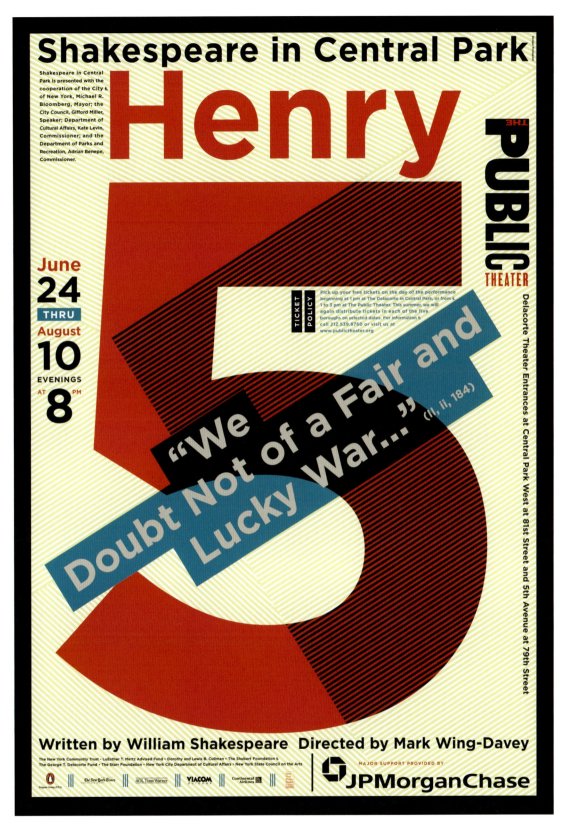

Shakespeare in Central Park, The Public Theater, US, 2003. ad/d: Paula Scher (Pentagram)

National Theatre in Belgrade, RS, 2011. d: Jovan Tarbuk

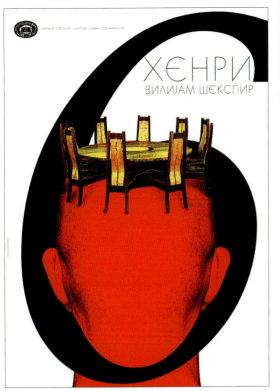
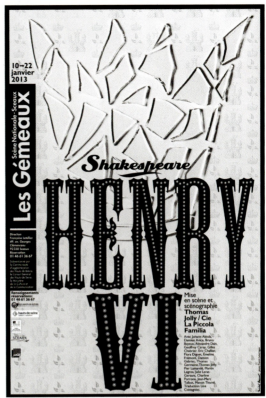
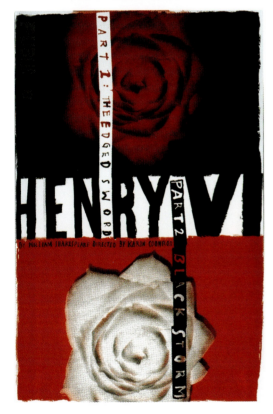
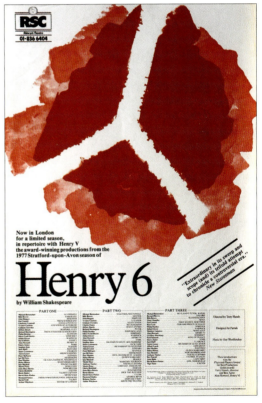

National Theatre in Belgrade, RS, 2012. d: Jovan Tarbuk

The Public Theater, US, 1996. ad/d: Paula Scher (Pentagram)

Les Gemeaux/Scene Nationale-Sceaux, FR, 2013. ad/d: Michel Bouvet, p: Francis Laharrague

Royal Shakespeare Company, Aldwych Theatre, UK, 1977. d: Allen-Beresford

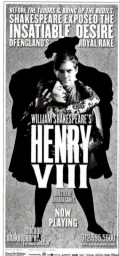

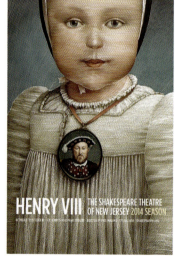

Chicago Shakespeare Theater, US, 2013.
ed: Criss Henderson, d: Allison Leake,
p: Bill Burlingham

Royal Shakespeare Company, Aldwych Theatre, UK, 1970. ad: George Mayhew, d: Royal Shakespeare Company

Royal Shakespeare Company, Swan Theatre, UK, 1996. d: Royal Shakespeare Company

Royal Shakespeare Company, Barbican Theatre, UK, 1984. d: The Partners, ill: Ralph Steadman

Shakespeare Theatre of New Jersey, US, 2014. ad/d/ill: Scott McKowen

National Theatre, MK, 2013.
ad: Blagoj Micevski, d: Sergej Svetozarev,
art: Borislav Traikovski

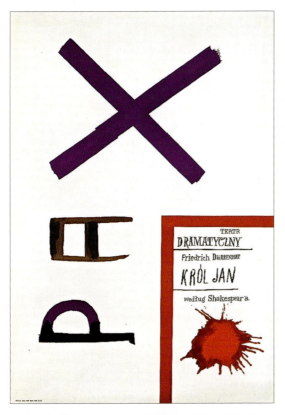

Teatr Dramatyczny, PL, 1970. d: Henryk Tomaszewski (Dydo Poster Collection)

Teatr Studio, PL, 1975. d: Andrzej Klimowski

Harrisburg Shakespeare Festival at Gamut Theatre Group, US, 2001. ad/d: Rob Smith

The Alley Theater, US, 2014. ad/d: Joey Arena

Theatre for a New Audience, US, 2013. ad: Julie Taymor, d: Milton Glaser, Sue Walsh, p: Josef Astor

# A MIDSUMMER NIGHT'S DREAM

*I'll follow you, I'll lead you about a round,*
*Through bog, through bush, through brake, through brier:*
*Sometime a horse I'll be, sometime a hound,*
*A hog, a headless bear, sometime a fire;*
*And neigh, and bark, and grunt, and roar, and burn,*
*Like horse, hound, hog, bear, fire, at every turn.*
—Puck

Puck gleefully transforming the boastfully arrogant Nick Bottom's head into that of an ass is the signature moment in Shakespeare's comedy *A Midsummer Night's Dream*. Puck is the quintessential trickster, and *Midsummer Night's Dream* is the essential—and most frequently performed—Shakespearean absurdity. Not surprisingly, the number of posters and placards announcing these countless performances, adaptations, parodies, and updates are large in volume. It is, however, curious there are not more posters featuring the wily Puck.

The plot, in which Puck plays a key role, centers on the marriage of Theseus (the Duke of Athens) and Hippolyta (Queen of the Amazons). There are three parallel plots that take Elizabethan aim at marriage, chastity, and, of course, death, and they are all neatly tied together by Puck's omnipresence.

One of the secondary plot lines involves Oberon, king of the fairies that populate the forest, and his estranged wife, Titania. The queen has defied the king by not giving up her "changeling" (servant) to her husband, and so she is being severely punished. Puck is called into service by Oberon to work his mischief, which includes anointing Titania's eyes with a love potion, causing her to fall in love with the misshapen Bottom, who does not yet realize he has metamorphosed into a donkey. Then, there is also the story of Helena, a lovesick girl who is the most romantic of the many characters, seeking to win loyalty and love wherever she might find it. There is also a play within the play, in which some characters take on a second role.

Love is a primary theme and deceit the main subtext. Many of the posters collected here illustrate these concepts in both overt and subtle ways. And since the scene is set in a moonlit fairyland forest outside of Athens, images of trees and vegetation recur. Winged fairies make frequent poster appearances in the guise of insect-size creatures. But the most commonly interpreted image, and the core of the comedy, is the hapless donkey in love.

Savoy Theatre, UK, 1914. d: Graham Robertson

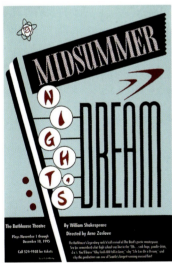

Narodno Pozoriste Sarajevo, BA, 1921. d: n/a

Royal Shakespeare Company, Aldwych Theatre, UK, 1977. d: Ginni Gillam

Bathhouse Theatre, US, 1995. ad: Art Chantry

Adams Memorial Theatre, US, 1962. d: n/a

Shakespeare on the Sound, US, 2009. ad/p: Noah Scalin

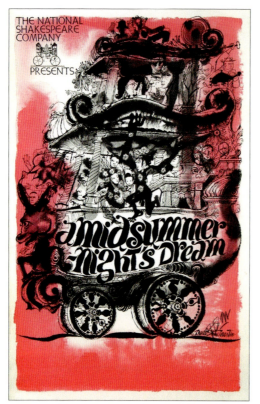
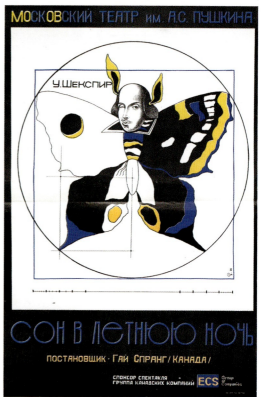

**The National Shakespeare Company**, US, 1970.
**d/ill:** David Stone Martin

**Moscow A.S. Pushkin Drama Theatre**, RU, 1990.
**d:** Fomin Valery Yakovlevich

**Tbilisi Theatre-Rustaveli Theatre**, GE, 1964. **d:** Mikhail Tumanishvili

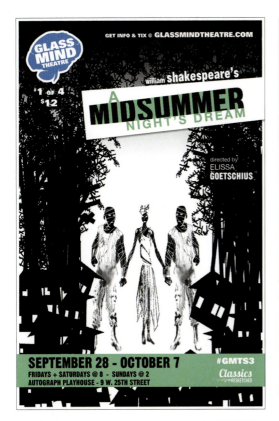

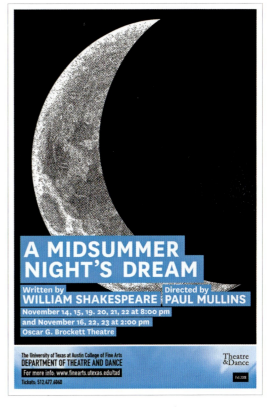

**Glass Mind Theatre**, US, 2012. **d:** Andrew Peters. **ill:** Aaron Marcovy

**Shakespeare's Globe**, UK, 2012. **ad:** Adrian Hastings (Premm Design)

**Harrisburg Shakespeare Festival at Gamut Theatre Group**, US, 2004. **ad/d:** Robinson Smith

**University of Texas Department of Theatre & Dance**, US, 2008. **ad/d:** Daniel Lievens

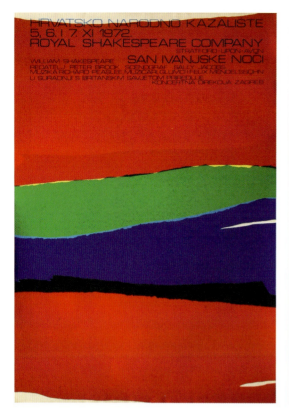
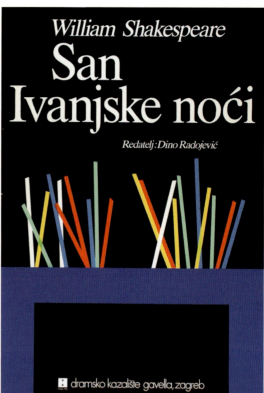

Croatian National Theatre Zagreb, HR, 1972. **d:** Vladimir Straza  Dramsko kazaliste Gavella, HR, 1984. **d:** Ivan Picelj

Narodno Pozoriste Sarajevo, BA, 1996. **d:** Art Institute Akademija likovnih umjetnosti, Aksamija '97

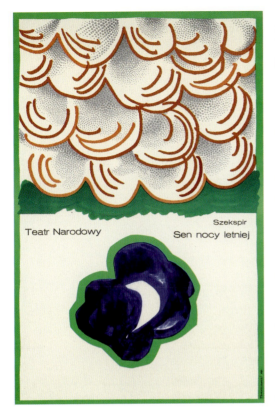

**Teatr Narodowy**, PL, 1968. d: Henryk Tomaszewski
(Dydo Poster Collection)

**Gogol Center**, RU, 2013. ad/d: Peter Bankov

**Teatr Dramatyczny**, PL, 1981. d: Eugeniusz Get Stankiewicz
(Dydo Poster Collection)

**Rustaveli Theatre**, GE, n/a. ad: Mikhail Tumanishvili

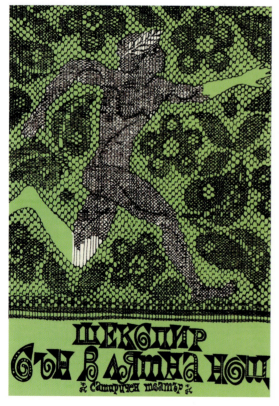
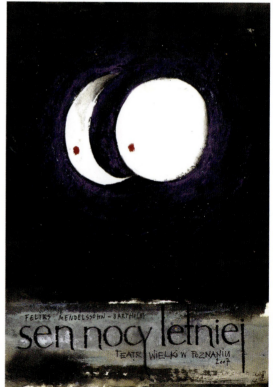

**Teatr Wspolczesny**, PL, 1982. **d:** Waldemar Swierzy
(Dydo Poster Collection)

**Satirical Theatre**, BG, n/a. **d:** Ludmil Chelarov

**Teatr im. Jana Kochanowskiego**, PL, 1982. **d:** Waldemar Swierzy
(Dydo Poster Collection)

**Teatr Wielki w Poznaniu**, PL, 2007. **ad:** Gray Veredon, **d:** Ryszard Kaja

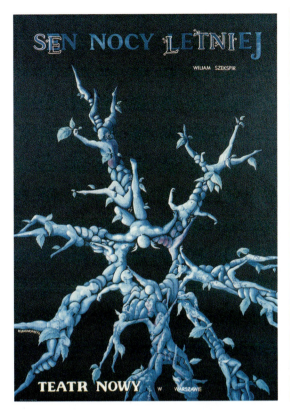
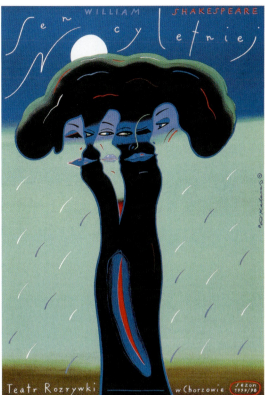

Teatr Nowy w Warszawie, PL, 1979. d: Marek Zadworny
(Dydo Poster Collection)

Teatr Poezji, PL, 1954. d: Jan Kurkiewicz (Dydo Poster Collection)

Teatr Rozrywki w Chorzowie, PL, 1997. d: Roman Kalarus
(Dydo Poster Collection)

Teatr Dzieci Zaglebia, PL, 1972. d: Tadeusz Grabowski
(Dydo Poster Collection)

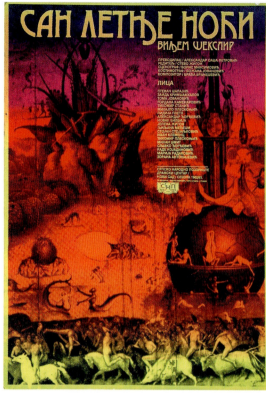

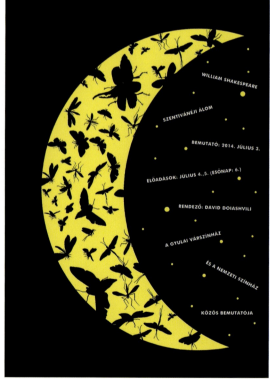

Royal Shakespeare Company, Nissei Theatre, JP, 1973. d: n/a

The Globe Tokyo, JP, 2007.
ad: Kiyoaki Ichikawa, d: Kaori Sato, ill: 100% Orange

Serbian National Theatre, RS, 1982. ad: Stevo Zigon, d: Radule Boskovic

Gyula Castle Theatre, The National Theatre, HU, 2011.
ad: David Doiashrili, d: Istrain Orosi

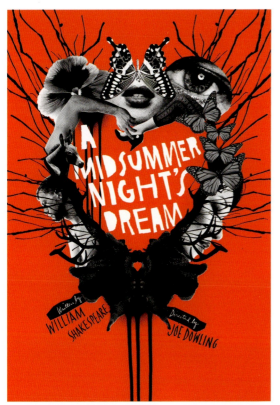

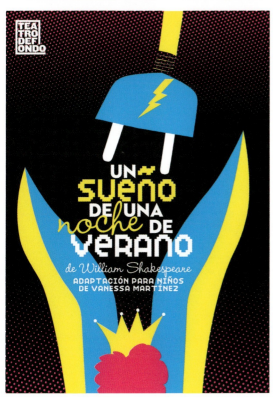

Guthrie Theater, US, 2008.
ad: Gail Anderson (SpotCo), d: Frank Gargiulo (SpotCo), p: Ian Allen

Teatro Defondo, ES, 2011. ad: Diego Areso Nieva

Centro Cultural Vila Flor, Teatro Oficina, PT, 2010.
ad/d: Atelier Martino & Jana

Jugendtheater Willisau, CH, 1997. ad/d: Niklaus Troxler

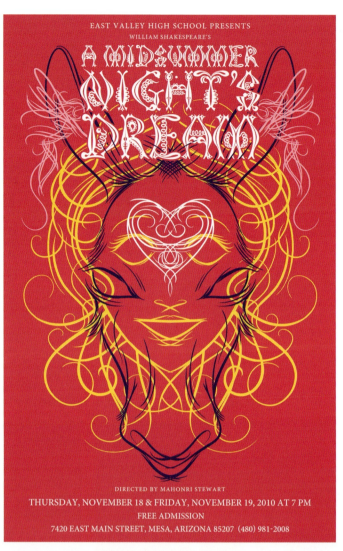
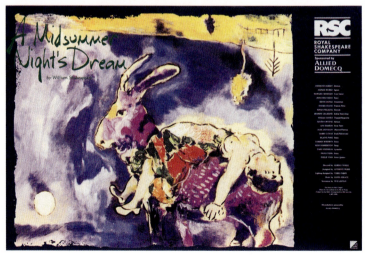

Teatro Persiani Recanati, IT, 2013.
ad/d: Salvatore Cuccu, Andrea Sopranzi

Asociacion Antiguos Alumnos Colegio de
Nuestra Senora del Pilar, ES, 2013.
ad: Diego Areso Nieva

Nottingham Playhouse, UK, n/a.
d: Merrygo Round

East Valley High School, US, 2010. d: David "Habbenink" Habben

Royal Shakespeare Company, Royal Shakespeare Theatre, UK, 1994.
d: Sue Rudd, art: Marc Chagall

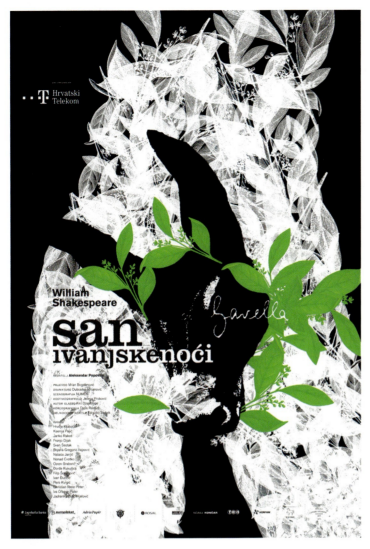
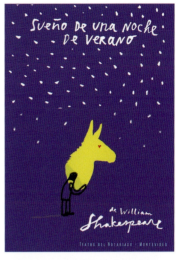
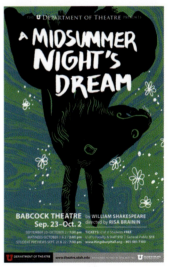
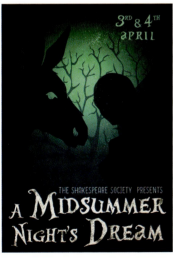

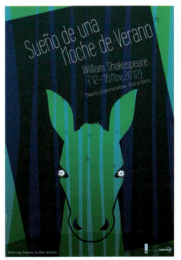

Gradsko dramsko kazaliste Gavella, HR, 2007. ad/d: Vanja Cuculic

The Shakespeare Society, St. Stephen's College, IN, 2014. d: Tanya Mathew

The Shakespeare Society, St. Stephen's College, IN, 2014. d: Tanya Mathew

Teatro Millington Drake, UY, 1994. ad/d: Fidel Sclavo

University of Utah Department of Theatre, US, 2011. ad/d: Whitney Shaw

Teatro Voz y Grito, BO, 2012. ad/d: Susana Machicao

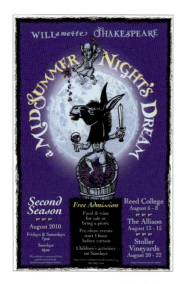
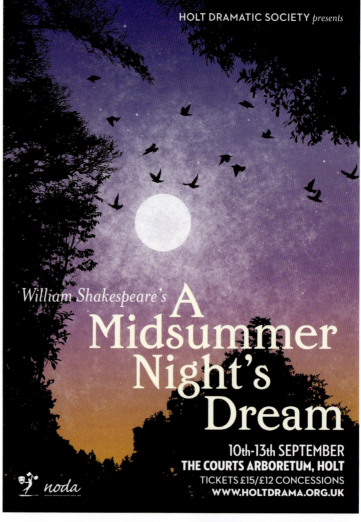

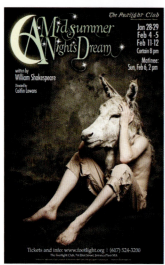

Willamette Shakespeare, US, 2010.
ad/d/ill: Dee Boyles

Tennessee Shakespeare Company, US, 2009.
d/p: Kevin Sprague

The Footlight Club, US, 2010.
ad: Sandi Mcdonald, d/p: Matt Mckee

Holt Dramatic Society, The Courts Arboretum, UK, 2014. d: Marc Bessant

Royal Shakespeare Company, Royal Shakespeare Theatre, Barbican Theatre, UK, 1989. p: Joe Cocks Studio

Shakespeare & Company, US, 2001.
d: Mary Garnish, p: Kevin Sprague

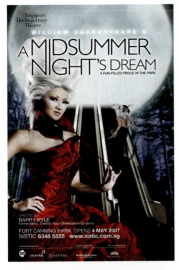
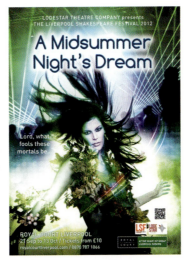

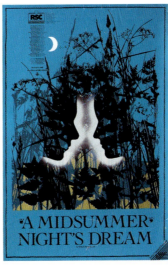
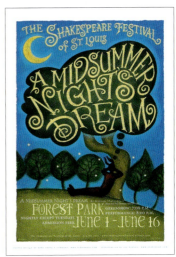

**Singapore the Repertory Theatre**, SG, 2007.
**d:** Zachary Goh

**Santa Monica High School Humanities Center Theatre**, US, 2010. **ad/d:** Josh Freeman, **p:** Jialiang Gao

**Factory Compagnia Transadriatica**, IT, 2014. **ad:** Tonio De Nitto, **d:** Francesco Maggiore (Big Sur), **p:** Alessandro Colazzo

**Royal Court Liverpool**, UK, 2012. **ad:** Damon Scott, Nomad Associates, **d:** Jason Brown

**The Bacchanals**, NZ, 2005. **ad:** William J. Earl, **d:** Earlyworm Digital, **p:** William J. Earl

**Royal Shakespeare Company**, Royal Shakespeare Theatre, Barbican Theatre, UK, 1986. **d:** The Drawing Room

**Children's Shakespeare Theatre**, US, 2014. **ad:** David Green (Brightgreen Design), **d:** David Green, **p:** Chris Carroll

**Trinidad Theatre Workshop**, TT, 2013. **ad/d/p:** Patrick Rasoanaivo, **ad:** Timmia Hearn Feldman

**Shakespeare Festival of St. Louis**, US, 2002. **ad/d:** Rich Nelson, **ill:** Joe Keylon

A Midsummer Night's Dream   163

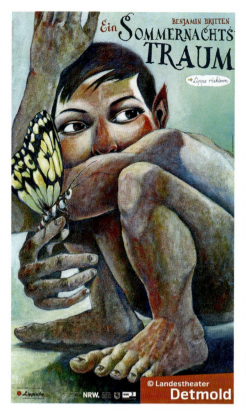
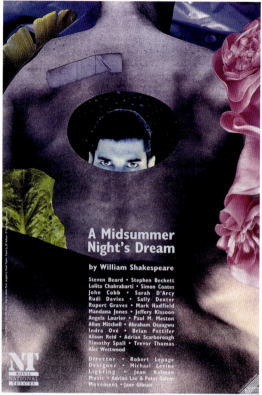

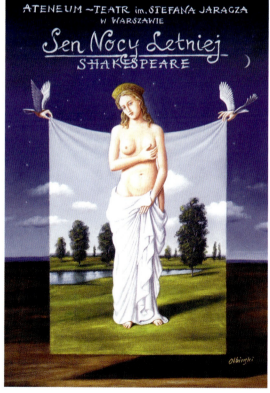

**Landestheater Detmold**, DE, 2007. **d:** Michael Hahn
(Museum Folkwang, Deutsches Plakat Museum)

**People's Light & Theatre**, US, 2004. **ad/d:** Rafal Olbinski

**National Theatre, Olivier Theatre**, UK, 1992. **cd:** Michael Mayhew,
**ad:** Richard Eyre, **d:** Michael Levine, **p:** Andrew Pavitt

**Ateneum Theater**, PL, 2011. **ad/d:** Rafal Olbinski

Junges Theater Sempach, CH, 2014. ad/d: Erich Brechbuhl

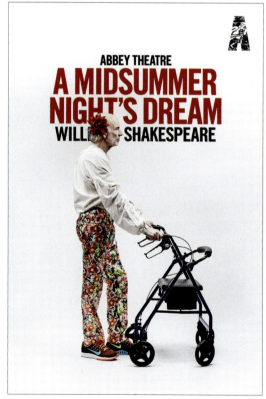

Royal Shakespeare Company, Royal Shakespeare Theatre, UK, 1970. art: Sally Jacobs

Bosko Buha Theatre, RS, 2015. ad: Miodrag Mandic, d: Iva Cukic,
p: Vladimir Jablanov, Iva Cukic

Abbey Theatre, IE, 2015. ad: Jason Delahunty, Zero-G,
d: Jason Delahunty, p: Sarah Doyle

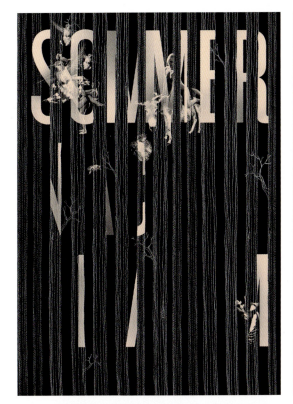

**Od-Theater**, CH, 2009. **d:** Jiri Oplatek, Simon Stotz (Claudiabasel)

**Royal Shakespeare Company, Royal Shakespeare Theatre**, UK, 2011.
**ad/d:** Andy Williams, **ill:** Emmanuel Polanco

**Teatr Dramatyczny w Elblagu**, PL, 1988. **d:** Jerzy Krechowicz
(Dydo Poster Collection)

A Midsummer Night's Dream

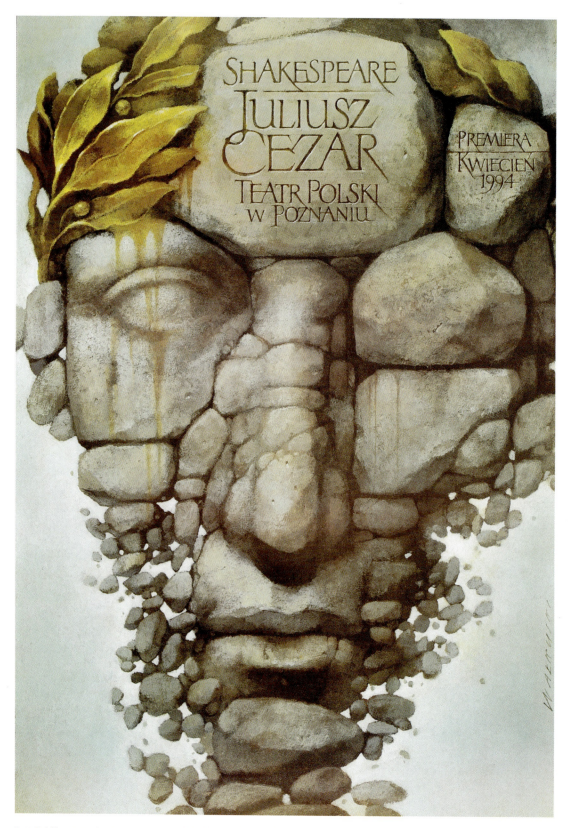

Teatr Polski w Poznaniu, PL, 1994. d: Wieslaw Walkuski (Dydo Poster Collection)

# JULIUS CAESAR

> Let us be sacrificers, but not butchers, Caius.
> We all stand up against the spirit of Caesar;
> And in the spirit of men there is no blood:
> O, that we then could come by Caesar's spirit,
> And not dismember Caesar! But, alas,
> Caesar must bleed for it! And, gentle friends,
> Let's kill him boldly, but not wrathfully;
> Let's carve him as a dish fit for the gods,
> Not hew him as a carcass fit for hounds:
> And let our hearts, as subtle masters do,
> Stir up their servants to an act of rage,
> And after seem to chide 'em. This shall make
> Our purpose necessary and not envious:
> Which so appearing to the common eyes,
> We shall be call'd purgers, not murderers.
> And for Mark Antony, think not of him;
> For he can do no more than Caesar's arm
> When Caesar's head is off.
>
> —Brutus

Distinctive characters in Julius Caesar run amuck, including monarchs, conspirators, idealists, artists, and a soothsayer, caught up in a vortex of loyalty and perfidy, power and abuse, truth and lies on a sociopolitical stage. The play's namesake appears in only five scenes, while Caesar's best friend, the guilt-ridden assassin Marcus Brutus, has more startling scenes and lines. Likewise, Mark Antony plays a key role (and later gets his own spotlight with Cleopatra). The drama leads to assassination, suicide, and heroic deaths by the sword. With so many compelling characters and scenes, designers have had many options for how to illustrate the play.

Julius Caesar is one of many Shakespearean tragedies that seamlessly translate into contemporary political scenarios, allowing poster designers license to reject cliché historical imagery for modern styles and methods.

Connections to present times notwithstanding, 44 BC Rome is the historical setting for Julius Caesar, which was influenced by accounts in Plutarch's Lives (1517). The Roman Empire, which spanned broadly from Britain to North Africa and from Persia to Spain, was undermined by the schism between ranking citizens and plebian masses. Fears that Caesar was planning to change the republic into a monarchy resulted in his murder, which led to civil war. The play follows the tragic outcome.

Caesar's visage is commonly used on posters in abstract and realistic ways, but the play inspires other imagery, too. A turn-of-the-century chromolithographic poster shows a realistic depiction of Brutus startled by "great Caesar's ghost" (page 170), while more contemporary versions emphasize the laurel-leaf wreath (the sign of victory) as a symbol of Caesar's station and his downfall. Another trope is the approximation of a dagger's violent slash through type and image, suggesting the weapon with which Caesar was murdered.

Following Caesar's death, his assassin, Marcus Brutus, explains to the public the reason for this necessary act of regicide. But the rhetorical brilliance of Julius Caesar's ally, Mark Antony ("Friends, Romans, countrymen, lend me your ears…"—the quintessence of PR spin), quickly turns the masses against the conspirators and provides designers with more illustrative fodder for their posters.

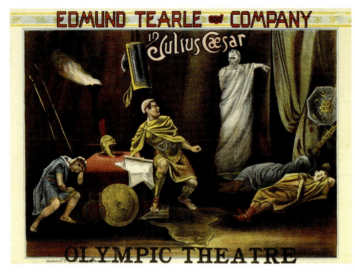

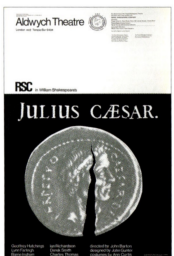

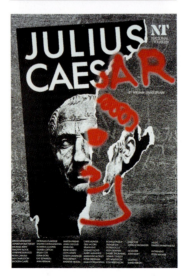
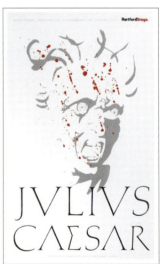

Edmund Tearle and Company, Olympic Theatre, UK, 1892. d: Jordison & Co. Ltd

Hrvatsko narodno kazaliste Zagreb, HR, 1970.
d: Grbic

Orlando Shakespeare Theater, US, 2014.
ad: Jim Helsinger, d: Landon St. Gordon

Royal Shakespeare Company,
Aldwych Theatre, UK, 1968.
ad: George Mayhew,
d: Royal Shakespeare Company

National Theatre, Olivier Theatre, UK, 1977.
cd: Richard Bird, Michael Mayhew,
ad: Peter Hall

Narodno Pozoriste Sarajevo, BA, 1976. d: n/a

Royal Shakespeare Company,
Royal Shakespeare Theatre, UK, 1979.
d: Jeff Jones, Chris Frampton, p: n/a

Hartford Stage, US, 1991.
ad/d/ill: Christopher Passehl,
ad: William Wondriska, art: n/a

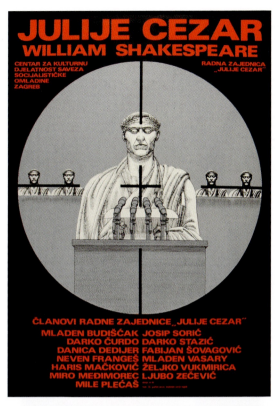
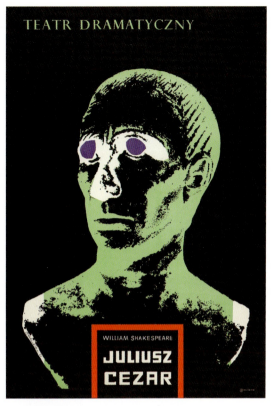
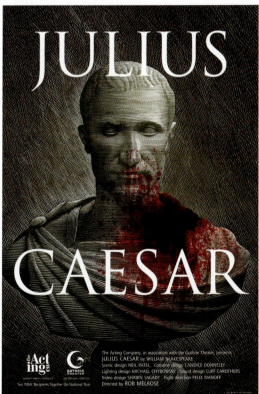
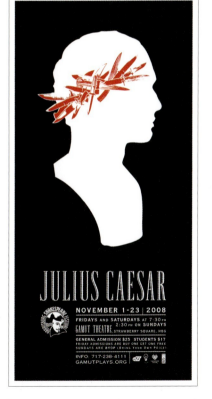

Centar za kulturnu djelatnost Saveza socijalisticke omladine Zagreb, HR, 1979. ad/d/ill: Mirko Ilic

The Acting Company, US, 2011. ad: Christina Poddubiuk, d/ill: Scott McKowen

Teatr Dramatyczny, PL, 1971. d: Henryk Tomaszewski (Dydo Poster Collection)

Harrisburg Shakespeare Festival at Gamut Theatre Group, Gamut Classic Theatre, US, 2008. ad/d: Rob Smith

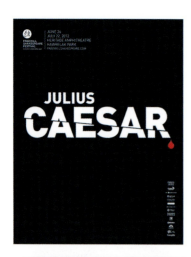
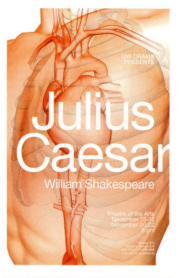
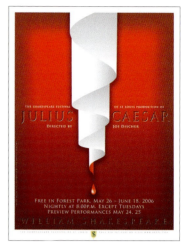

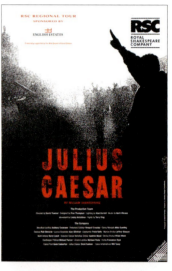

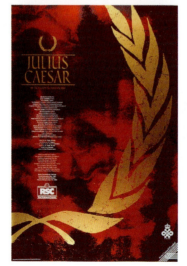

**Free Will Players, Freewill Shakespeare Festival**, CA, 2012. **ad/d:** Brad Blasko

**Tennessee Shakespeare Company**, US, 2010. **ad/p:** Kevin Sprague, **d:** Dan McCleary, Susannah Millonzi

**Royal Shakespeare Company, Royal Shakespeare Theatre**, UK, 1983. **d:** Lloyd Northover, **art:** Juan Genoves

**Theatre of the Arts, University of Waterloo**, CA, 2008. **d:** Yen Chu, **d:** n/a

**Bckseet Productions**, US, 2013. **ad/d/p:** Kyle Cassidy

**Royal Shakespeare Company, Royal Shakespeare Theatre**, UK, 1987. **ad/d:** John David Lloyd, Jim Northover

**Shakespeare Festival of St. Louis**, US, 2006. **ad/d/ill:** Rich Nelson

**Royal Shakespeare Company, The Other Place**, UK, 1993. **d:** January Design Consultants, **p:** David Turnley

**Children's Shakespeare Theatre**, US, 2010. **ad/d:** David Green (Brightgreen Design), **p:** Chris Carroll

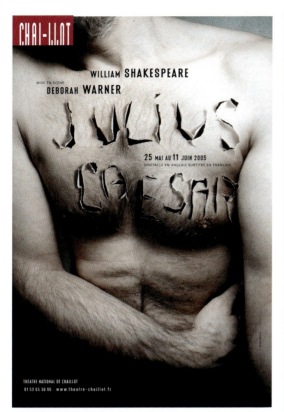
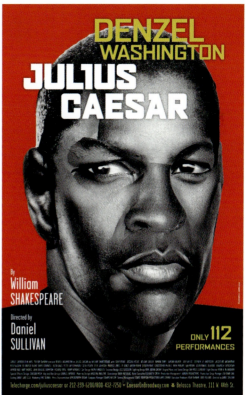
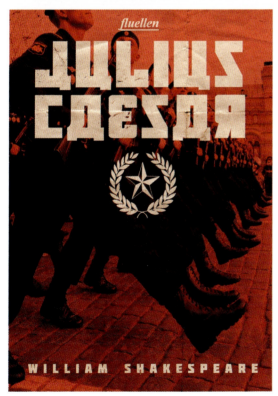

Theatre National de Chaillot, FR, 2005. d/p: Michal Batory

Fluellen Theatre Company, UK, 2014. ad/d: Camille Gajewski

Belasco Theater, US, 2005. ad: Gail Anderson (SpotCo), ill: Eddie Guy

Royal Shakespeare Company, Royal Shakespeare Theatre, UK, 1991.
d: Ginny Crow, art: Andrea Mantegna

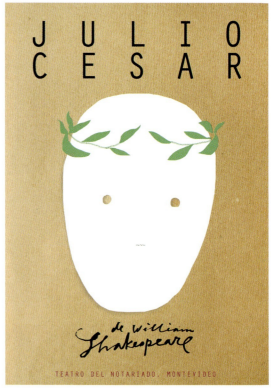
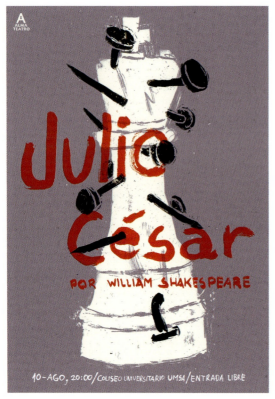
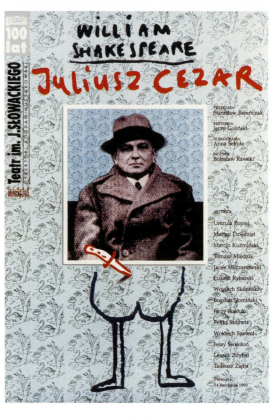

Owl Spot, JP, 2013. ad: Kiyoaki Ichikawa, d: Kaori Sato, ill: 100% Orange

Teatro Alma, BO, 2013. ad/d: Bruno Rivera

Teatro del Notariado, UY, 1994. ad/d: Fidel Sclavo

Teatr im. Juliusza Slowackiego, PL, 1983. d: Marek Pawlowski
(Dydo Poster Collection)

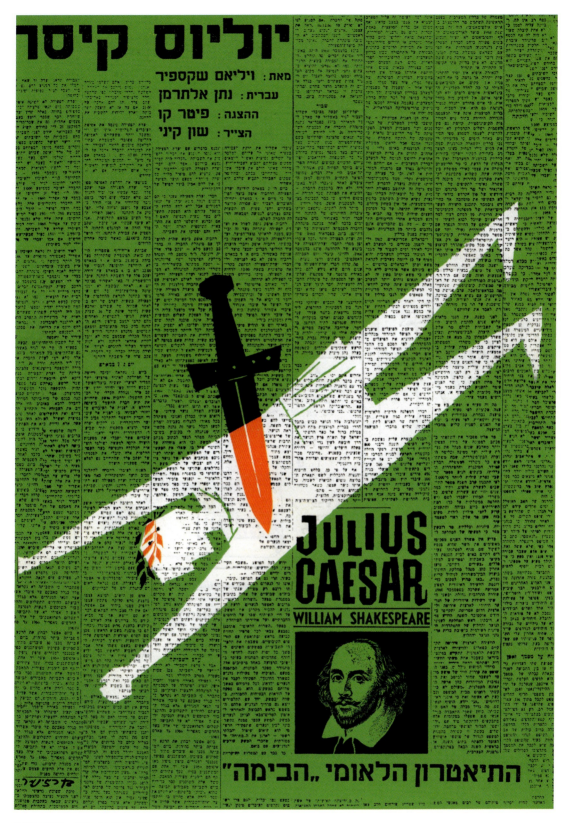

Habima National Theatre, IL, 1961. d: Dan Reisinger

Teatr Ludowy, PL, 1998. **ad:** Krzysztof Dydo, **d:** Wieslaw Grzegorczyk (Dydo Poster Collection)

# THE COMEDIES

### The Merry Wives of Windsor

Mistress Page and Mistress Ford are married to two prosperous men of Windsor. They attest that wives can be merry and faithful to their husbands. Mr. Page understands but Mr. Ford does not. The wives deceive a sexual predator named Falstaff while curing Mr. Ford of his jealousy.

### Love's Labor's Lost

The King of Navarre and his three companions put a moratorium on the company of women for three years. But they become infatuated with the Princess of Aquitaine and her ladies in waiting. Unable to thwart their own desires, they succumb (although with the death of the princess's father, the weddings are delayed for a year).

### Two Gentlemen of Verona

Valentine and Proteus from Verona are best friends. Valentine ventures out into the world; Proteus stays home, in love with Julia—they promise to wed. Valentine has fallen in love with the Duke's daughter, Silvia. But, as it happens, so has Proteus, who vows to do anything he can to win her away from Valentine.

### All's Well That Ends Well

Well-meaning, likeable characters seed this comedy about the long-suffering Helena's attempts to domesticate her husband, the wayward Bertram. The ending is about romance, but it is a cynical comedy, whereby manipulation trumps love.

### Pericles

In the kingdom of Antioch, King Antiochus and his daughter are engaging in incest. Unknowing suitors have been prevented from marrying her because Antiochus demands that they answer a riddle correctly or die. Pericles, Prince of Tyre, correctly answers the challenge and reveals the incestuous relationship.

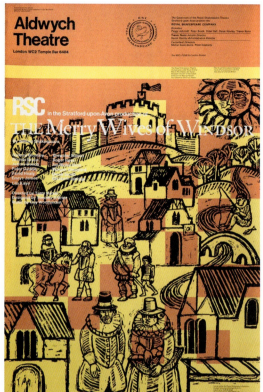
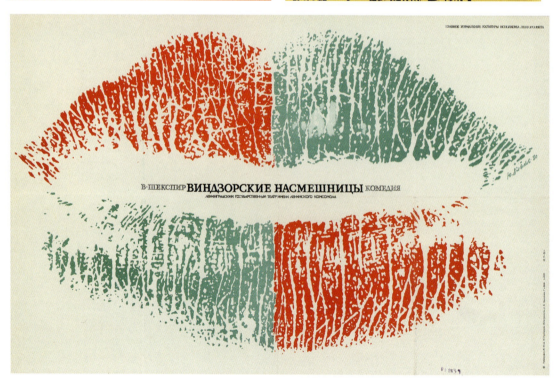

Narodno pozoriste Subotica, RS, 1953. d: n/a

Royal Shakespeare Company, Aldwych Theatre, UK, 1968.
ad: George Mayhew, d: Royal Shakespeare Company, ill: Ruth Bribram

Lenin Komsomol Leningrad State Theater, RU, 1980. ad/d: Gunter Rambow, ill: Henri de Tou

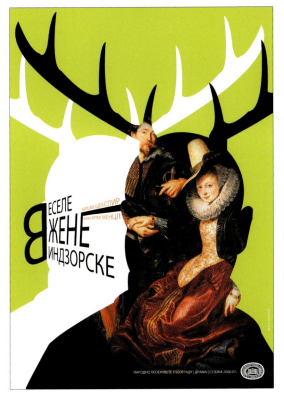
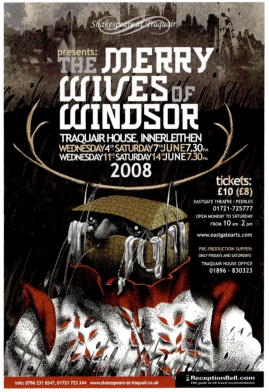

Teatro Millington Drake, UY, 1996. ad/d: Fidel Sclavo

National Theatre in Belgrade, RS, 2006. d: Jovan Tarbuk

Teatr Szkolny, PL, 2007. ad/d: Andrzej Pagowski
(Dydo Poster Collection)

Shakespeare at Traquair Theatre, UK, 2008. d: Michal Stachowiak

The Comedies 179

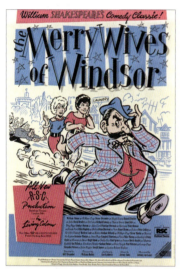

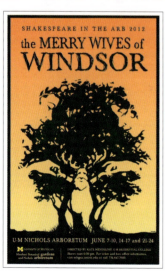

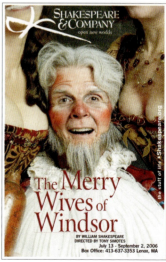

**Teatr Powszechny**, PL, 2000.
**d**: Grzegorz Marszalek
(Dydo Poster Collection)

**Royal Shakespeare Company,
Barbican Theatre**, UK, 1986. **d**: n/a

**University of Michigan Matthaei Botanical
Gardens and Nichols Arboretum**,
US, 2013. **ad/d**: David Zinn

**Royal Shakespeare Company, Royal Shakespeare Theatre**, UK, 1996. **d**: Chris Moody, **ill**: Paul Cox

**Shakespeare Festival of St. Louis**, US, 2009.
**ad/d/ill**: Rich Nelson

**Shakespeare & Company**, US, 2006.
**d**: Amanda Bettis **p**: Kevin Sprague

180 Presenting Shakespeare

# HELP ME

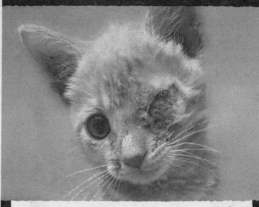

Please give **£18** today to help ill, injured, and abandoned animals enjoy the second chance at life they deserve. **Your gift will help pay for urgently needed medicines, operations, warmth, and specialist food.**

To donate £18 please complete the coupon below, call **0300 303 9876** or visit **www.woodgreen.org.uk/urgent**

---

**Here's my donation towards more second chances:**

£18 ☐ or £ ☐ (please choose your own amount)

Name _____

Address _____

_____ Postcode _____

Please send cheques/postal orders/CAF charity vouchers payable to **'Wood Green, The Animals Charity'** with this coupon to: Freepost RTLR-XJZG-BERC, Wood Green, The Animals Charity, London Road, Godmanchester, Huntingdon PE29 2NH.

We'd love to send you updates on how your donations make a difference. We'd also like to send you news, event details and tips to care for pets – and fundraising messages with details of how you can continue to help homeless pets in need.

You may contact me by telephone. ☐

Tel No: _____

We promise not to share personal details of our supporters. You can change the way you hear from us by visiting our online permission portal https://woodgreen.yourpreferencecentre.com

Wood Green, The Animals Charity, is the Registered Trademark of Wood Green Animal Shelters. Registered Charity No. 298348.

PRSAO1812TT32

Theatre Behind the Gate, CZ, 1970. d: Pavel Brom, Milan Kopriva, p: Joseph Koudelka

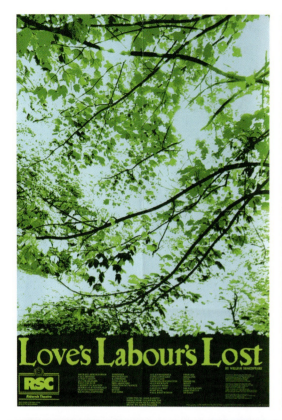
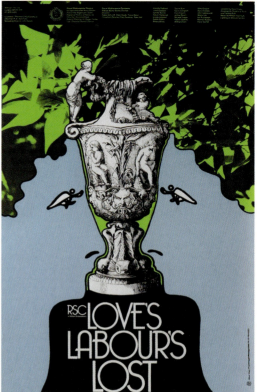

Royal Shakespeare Company, Aldwych Theatre, UK, 1979.
d: Ginni Moo-Young Taymor, p: Ian Moo-Young

Royal Shakespeare Company, Aldwych Theatre, UK, 1975. d: Blue Egg

Royal Shakespeare Company, Royal Shakespeare Theatre, UK, 1990. d: Ginny Crow, p: Ivan Kyncl

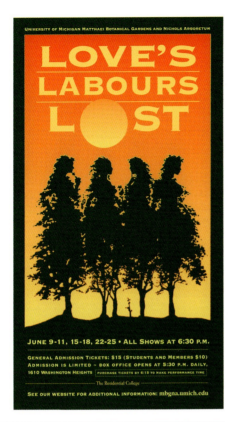
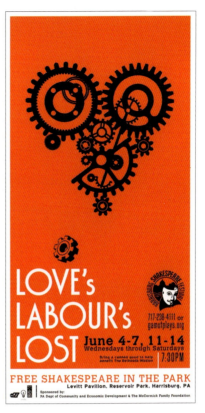

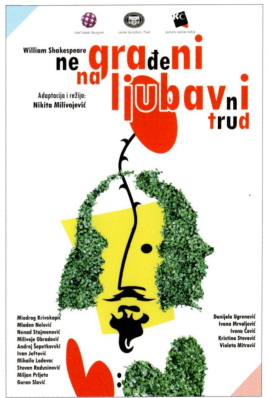

University of Michigan Matthaei Botanical Gardens and Nichols Arboretum, US, 2006. ad/d: David Zinn

The Philadelphia Shakespeare Theatre, US, 2014. d: n/a

Harrisburg Shakespeare Festival at Gamut Theatre Group, US, 2008. ad/d: Robinson Smith

Centar za Kulturu Tivat, Bitef teatar Beograd, ME, 2007. ad: Milena Radojevic, d: Neven Stanicic

Royal Theatre Podgorica, ME, 2002. ad: Milan Karadzic, d: Zora Mojsilovic Popovic, p: Goran Saban

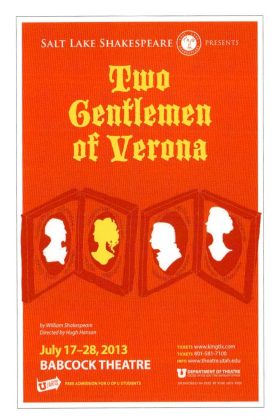
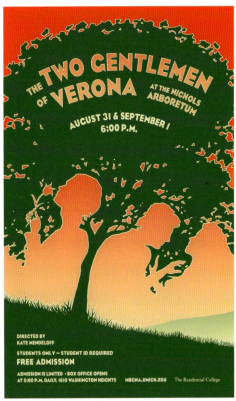
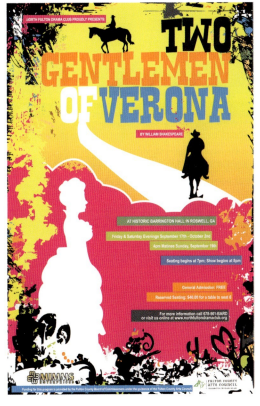

**University of Utah Department of Theatre**, US, 2013.
ad/d: Whitney Shaw

**North Fulton Drama Club**, US, 2010. **ad/d:** Erica Cruz

**University of Michigan Matthaei Botanical Gardens and Nichols Arboretum**, US, 2008. **ad/d:** David Zinn

**Teatr Jednego Znaku**, PL, 2005. **d:** Marian Nowinski
(Dydo Poster Collection)

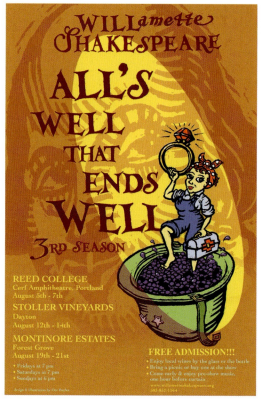

Harrisburg Shakespeare Company at Gamut Theatre Group, US, 2011.
ad/d: Rob Smith

Royal Shakespeare Company, Royal Shakespeare Theatre, UK, 1981
ad/d: Ginni Moo-Young

Triad Stage, US, 2014. ad: Bluezoom, d: Kyle Webster

Williamette Shakespeare, US, 2011. d/ill: Dee Boyles

Presenting Shakespeare

# All's Well That Ends Well

William Shakespeare's

**12 OCT – 2 NOV**
ST NICOLAS' CHURCH,
BURY STREET, GUILDFORD,
GU2 4AW
BOX OFFICE: 01483 304384
GUILDFORD-SHAKESPEARE-COMPANY.CO.UK

**6 – 30 NOV**
JERMYN STREET THEATRE,
16B JERMYN STREET,
LONDON, SW1Y 6ST
BOX OFFICE: 020 7287 2875
JERMYNSTREETTHEATRE.CO.UK

JERMYN STREET THEATRE

e English accents, and some would be
pressed by how posh they are, but they are
ot aristocratic in the least. (If you doubt me,
o on YouTube and listen to Bertrand Russell
Deborah Devonshire). I remember the his-
torian Elizabeth Longford (a doctor's daughter
who was a countess) asking me, of a snobbish
acquaintance of ours, "Do you think he
believes an aristocrat is a rich person who lives
in a castle?" The success of *Downton* depends
on the majority of viewers sharing the simpli-
fied view of our snobbish friend.

The explanation is easily found. Most senti-
mental *Downton* fans of today, if transported
back to the time when aristocrats still did exer-
cise political power and social clout, would
find resentment surfacing in their bosoms very
quickly. The exclusivity of the aristocratic
world was stronger on the Continent than it
was in Britain – where, since the Reformation,
the newly rich could purchase landed estates
and titles for themselves and pretend to be of
noble birth. Even in Britain, though, in Victo-
rian or Edwardian times, the class barriers
were tangible and difficult to surmount even
for the most determined of counter-jumpers.

In the *Downton* fantasy, however, counter-
jumping is as easy as falling off a horse. Julian
Fellowes knows how to pander to his audiences, and he plays down the one element which
made the aristocratic system work – namely its
exclusivity. In the new film, for example, the
hero is really Tom Branson (played by Allen
Leech), Lord Grantham's lovable Irish son-in-
law, who started life as the chauffeur. Now
Branson is a widower, it's inevitable that he
would fall in love with the lady's maid of the
Dowager Lady Grantham's arch-enemy –
Lady Bagshaw (Imelda Staunton). Complicated shenanigans ensue, but the message
becomes clear. With a bit of luck, anyone
uld find themselves the master and mistress of

Downton. In the comforting Fellowes world,
the hard edges of class no longer quite exist.
The titles and the beautiful houses are in a sort
of limbo, with none of the painful facts of class
remaining.

Michael Engler, whose success as a director
began with *Sex and the City*, knows, even
better than Fellowes, how to flatter and cajole
audiences with such sweeteners. American
viewers may love the fact that the hero is a
perky Irish Republican who compounds his
lovability by bravely preventing an assassination attempt on King George V.

You may feel that Fellowes has come a long way
since his first essay in this genre of snob-pic –
*Gosford Park*, directed by that ironist Robert
Altman. In *Gosford*, partly because Stephen
Fry was allowed to camp things up so outra-
geously as the detective in a classic country
house murder-mystery, there was no attempt
to make things authentic. Servants, for example, walked in through the front door of the
stately home as if they were friends of the
family; the whole drama made Agatha Christie
seem like gritty social realism.

In the new film collaboration, this time with
Engler, Fellowes goes out of his way to flatter
the prejudices of class-ignorant cinema audiences. When Lord Grantham asks his American wife (Elizabeth McGovern) whether it is
very "common" to be so much looking for-
ward to entertaining the King, she replies,
"Not if you are an American" – before snog-
ging him. In addition to the plebeian Irishman
being the hero, there is a whole gay subplot in
which the butler, Barrow, dances the tango
with a man he met in a bar. The police raid
which follows is regarded as an outrage to
human dignity.

Yet in other aspects, the new *Downton* does
aim, on one level, for authenticity. The story

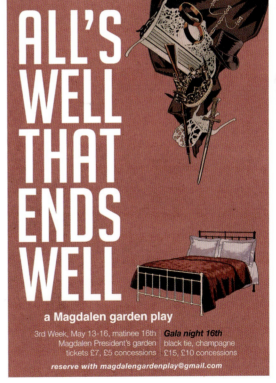

Royal Shakespeare Company, Swan Theatre at the Pit, UK, 1992.
ad/d: Amanda Bostoch, p: Bob Carlos Clarke

Royal Shakespeare Company, Royal Shakespeare Theatre, UK, 2013.
ad/d: Royal Shakespeare Company, p: Nik Keevil (Arcangel Images)

Royal Shakespeare Company, Royal Shakespeare Theatre, Barbican Theatre, UK, 1989. ad/d: The Drawing Room

Magdalen Players, Magdalen College, UK, 2009. ad/d: James Kennard

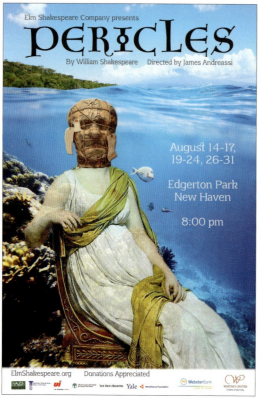

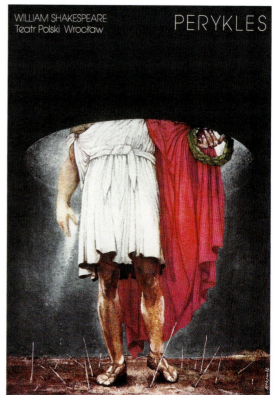

The Croatian National Theatre, HR, 1986. ad/d: New Collectivism

Elm Shakespeare Company, US, 2014. ad/d: Sue Surina Rollins,
p: Shutterstock, art: Jacques-Louis David, Genpei Akasegawa

Teatr Polski we Wrocławiu, PL, 1982. d: Jan Jaromir Aleksiun
(Dydo Poster Collection)

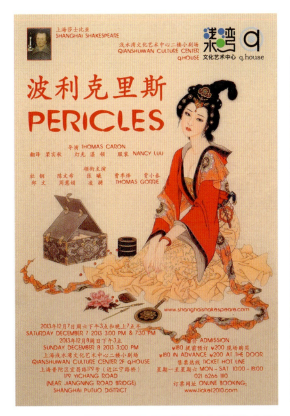
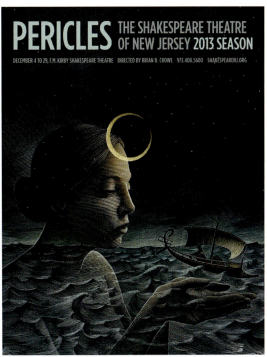
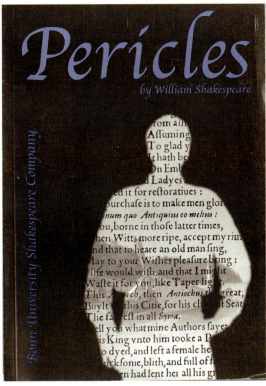
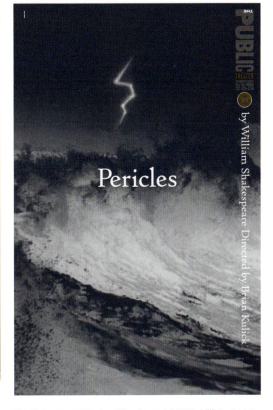

Shanghai Shakespeare, CN, 2013. ad/d: Thomas Caron

Bonn University Shakespeare Company, DE, 1995.
d: Jan Hendrik Junker

The Shakespeare Theatre of New Jersey, US, 2013. d/ill: Scott McKowen

The Public Theater, US, 1998. ad/d: Paula Scher (Pentagram)

Theater Haus, DE, 1994. ad/p: Frieder Grindler

# OTHELLO

*Lie with her! lie on her! We say lie on her, when they belie her. Lie with her! that's fulsome. —Handkerchief—confessions—handkerchief!—To confess, and be hanged for his labour;—first, to be hanged, and then to confess.—I tremble at it. Nature would not invest herself in such shadowing passion without some instruction. It is not words that shake me thus. Pish! Noses, ears, and lips. —Is't possible—Confess—handkerchief!—O devil!*

—**Othello**

The names Othello and Desdemona may just be as well known as Romeo and Juliet. Yet only a small number of the posters for Shakespeare's *Othello* zero in directly on the beautiful wife of the Moorish general. This is not to say that references to the female protagonist don't exist, but in poster art she is usually suggested and only rarely overtly shown. Othello is the lead character, and he is the star in the majority of posters. Still, Desdemona makes cameo appearances in some of the early chromolithographic posters, such as the one for Thos. W. Keene's performance, where she lies on a bed (page 192), and she has become increasingly more visible in contemporary examples as well.

*Othello* is set in Venice. Desdemona, the daughter of Venetian senator Brabanzio, has eloped with Othello, the black Venetian general. Their wedding triggers intrigues that are sparked by Iago, Othello's ensign, who hates Othello for passing him over for promotion. Iago plots to defame his commander before the eyes and ears of the Duke of Venice. But the plot fails, and Othello leaves Venice for Cyprus to command the Venetian army against an invading Turkish fleet. He is accompanied by Desdemona; Cassio, his trusted lieutenant; Iago; and Iago's wife, Emilia. While in Cyprus, Iago produces false evidence—a handkerchief—that convinces Othello of Cassio's betrayal, an affair with Desdemona. The tormented Othello smothers poor Desdemona in bed and asks Iago to kill the framed Cassio. Of course, he eventually realizes that his suspicions and his murder of Desdemona were fomented by Iago's lies, so Othello kills himself with a dagger.

Many Othello posters represent him as a proud and strong Moor. But equally striking are some white Othellos. The classic portrait, however, is of John McCullough as Othello (page 192), about which was written in *Sixty Years of the Theater* by John Ranken Towse: "His Othello was an imposing and martial figure, with authority in voice and mien and all the external indications of the 'frank and noble nature' with which Iago credited him."

Theater: n/a, US, 1878. d: Forbes Co.

Theater: n/a, US, 1884. d: W.J. Morgan & Co. Lith.

Lakhuti Tadjik State Academic Drama Theater, RU, 1941. d: Aleksander Andreadi

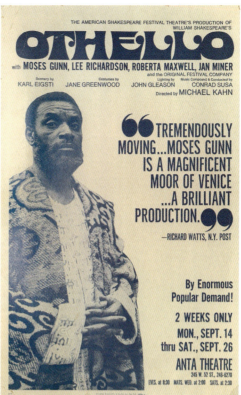

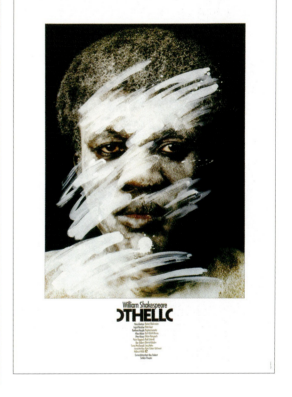

Adams Memorial Theatre, US, 1961. d: n/a

Anta Theatre, US, n/a. d: n/a

Marjanishvili Theatre, GE, n/a. d: n/a

Schiller Theater, DE, 1981. d: Holger Matthies
(Museum Folkwang, Deutsches Plakat Museum)

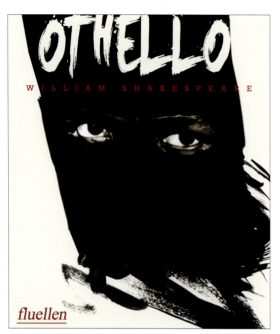

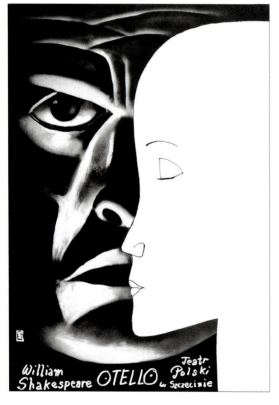

Fluellen Theatre Company, UK, 2012. ad/d: Camille Gajewski

Teatr Polski w Szczecinie, PL, 2000. d: Lezek Zebrowski

Hessisches Staats Theater Wiesbaden, DE, 1999. ad/d: Gunter Rambow

The Philadelphia Shakespeare Theatre, US, 2013. d: n/a

Schauspiel Frankfurt, DE, 1978. ad/d/p: Gunter Rambow, Studio Rambow, Lienemeyer, van de Sand

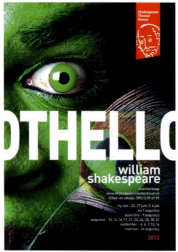
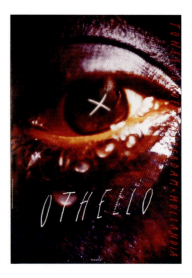

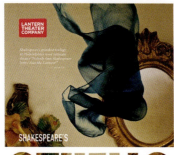

Badisches Saatstheatre Karlsruhe, DE, 2007.
ad/d: Gunter Rambow.

Setagaya Public Theatre, JP, 2013.
ad: Kazuya Kondo

Lantern Theater Company, US, 2008.
ad/d: Allan Espiritu, d/p: Mike Sung Park

Shakespeare Theater Diever, NL, 2013.
ad: Jack Nieborg, d: Paulien Schutten,
p: Koen Timmerman

The Public Theater, US, 2009.
d: Paula Scher (Pentagram)

Narodni teatar iz Bitolja, MK, 2014. ad: Blagoj Micevski, d/p: Sergej Svetozarev

Toneel groep Amsterdam, NL, 1989.
ad/d: Anthon Beeke

Kaspar Theatre, CZ, 2013.
ad: Marek Pistora (Studio Najbrt),
p: Johana Posova

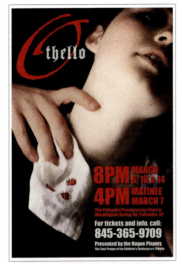
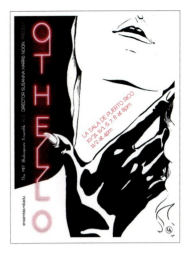

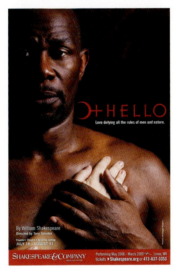

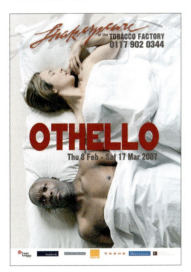

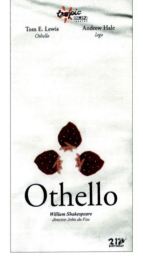

Stephen Joseph Theatre in the Round, UK, 1990. ad/d: Patrick Argent

Singapore Repertory Theatre, SG, 2013. d: Ching Kai

The Tobacco Factory, UK, 2007. d: Alpha Charlie Design, p: Graham Burke

Children's Shakespeare Theatre, US, 2009 ad/d: David Green (Brightgreen Design) p: Chris Carroll

Shakespeare & Company, US, 2008. d/p: Kevin Sprague

M.C. 93 Bobigny, FR, 1986. d: n/a

Massachusetts Institute of Technology Shakespeare Ensemble, US, 2014. d: Alison Malouf

Romateatern, SE, 2012. ad/d: Johan Brunzell, p: Niclas Brunzell

Tropic Sun Theatre, PT, 2007. d: Rui Guerra, art: Previdencia Rossa

**Royal Shakespeare Company,
Royal Shakespeare Theatre**, UK, 1985.
**ad/d:** John David Lloyd, Jim Northover
(Lloyd Northover)

**The Mobtown Players**, US, 2012.
**ad/d:** Shannon Light Hadley

**University of Tehran**, IR, 1975.
**ad/d/p:** Ebrahim Haghighi
(Alliance Graphique Internationale)

**Joburg Theatre**, ZA, 2013. **ad/d:** Ryan Honeyball, **p:** Lies Meirlaen

**Croatian National Theatre Split**, HR, 1979.
**d:** Gorki Zuvela

**Royal Shakespeare Company,
Royal Shakespeare Theatre**, UK, 1999.
**d:** Andy Williams, **p:** Harry Borden, Mark Hall

Les Gemeaux/Scene Nationale-Sceaux, FR, 2001. **ad/d:** Michel Bouvet, **p:** Francis Laharrague

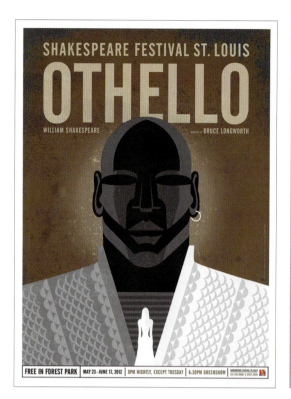

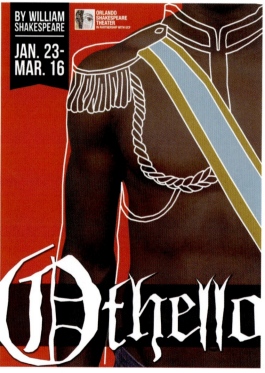

Shakespeare Festival of St. Louis, US, 2012. ad/d/ill: Rich Nelson

Orlando Shakespeare Theater, US, 2013. ad: Jim Helsinger, d: Betsy Dye

This New Theater, US, 2008. ad/d: Kristopher Pollard

The Moor's Bar Theatre, UK, 2014. d: Sah Starr

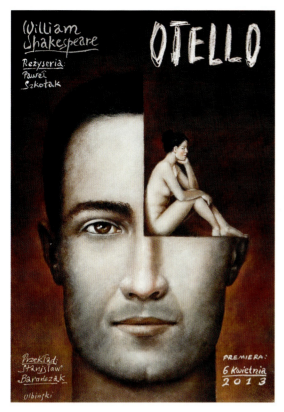
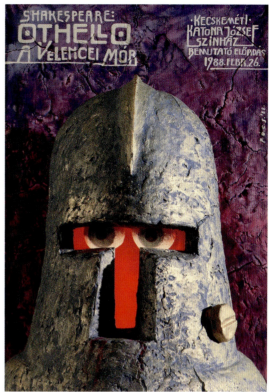

Poznan Theater, PL, 2013. ad/d: Rafal Olbinski

Shakespeare at Traquair Theatre, UK, 2009. d: Michal Stachowiak

Jozsef Katona Theatre, AL, 1988. ad/d: Peter Pocos, p: Peter Walter

The Public Theater, Delacorte Theater, US, 1991. ad/d/ill: Paul Davis

Pavilion Theater, US, 2002. ad/d: Lanny Sommese

Teatr Jednego Znaku, PL, 1995. d: Marian Nowinski (Dydo Poster Collection)

Hrvatsko narodno kazaliste Split, HR, 1983. **d:** Boris Bucan

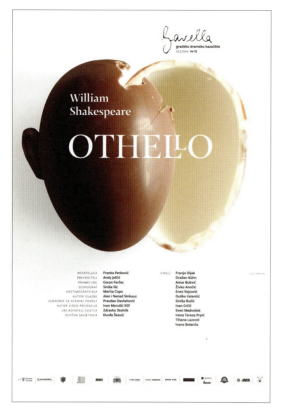
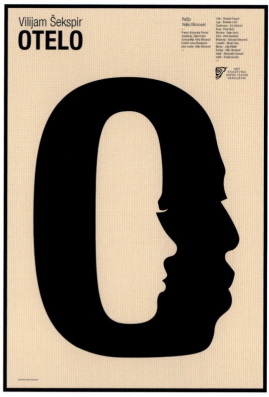
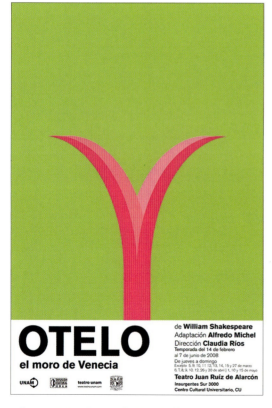

Gradsko dramsko kazaliste Gavella, HR, 2015. ad/d: Vanja Cuculic

Teatro U.N.A.M. I Teatro Juan Ruiz de Alarcon (Centro Cultural Universitario, C.U.), MX, 2008. ad/d: Sergi Rucabado Rebes

Knjazevsko-srpski Teatar, RS, 2012. ad/d/ill: Ivan Misic

Teatr Stajnia Pegaza, PL, 2012. d: Leszek Zebrowski

204 Presenting Shakespeare

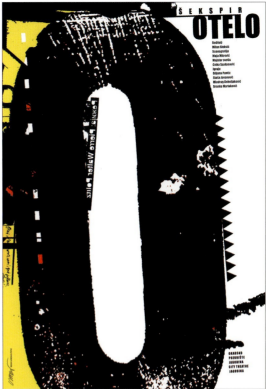
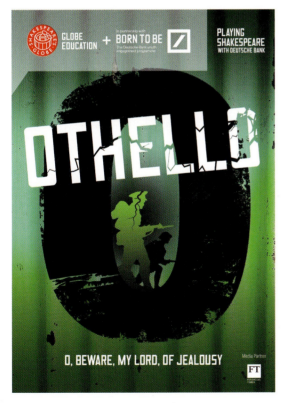
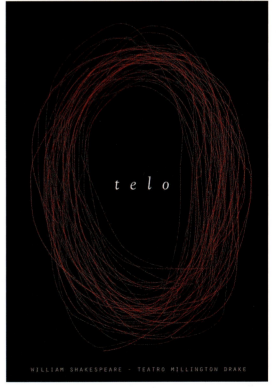

Yugoslav Drama Theatre, RS, 2012. ad/d: Slavimir Stojanovic

Shakespeare's Globe, UK, 2015. ad: Adrian Hastings (Premm Design), d: Sophie Adams (Premm Design)

Jagodina City Theatre, RS, 2013. ad/d: Slobodan Stetic

Teatro Millington Drake, UY, 1991. ad/d: Fidel Sclavo

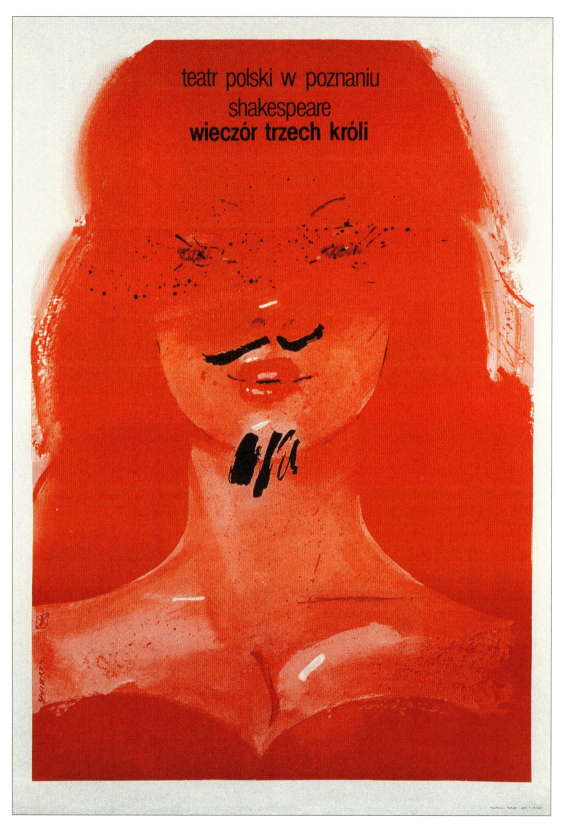

**Teatr Polski w Poznaniu**, PL, 1980. **d**: Waldemar Swierzy (Dydo Poster Collection)

# TWELFTH NIGHT

*I left no ring with her: what means this lady?*
*Fortune forbid my outside have not charm'd her!*
*She made good view of me; indeed, so much,*
*That sure methought her eyes had lost her tongue,*
*For she did speak in starts distractedly.*
*She loves me, sure; the cunning of her passion*
*Invites me in this churlish messenger.*
*None of my lord's ring! why, he sent her none.*
*I am the man: if it be so, as 'tis,*
*Poor lady, she were better love a dream.*
*Disguise, I see, thou art a wickedness,*
*Wherein the pregnant enemy does much.*
*How easy is it for the proper-false*
*In women's waxen hearts to set their forms!*
*Alas, our frailty is the cause, not we!*

—*Viola*

Yet another comedy about separated twins, *Twelfth Night* is the play that gives us "If music be the food of love, play on." *Twelfth Night* focuses on Viola, a young woman of aristocratic birth, and her brother, Sebastian. She has been shipwrecked and believes her brother is dead. To survive she disguises herself as a young man named Cesario and becomes a favorite of Orsino, who makes Cesario his page. Viola begins to fall in love with Orsino, which is complicated by the fact that Orsino thinks that she is a man. And there's more: Orsino sends Cesario to deliver his love messages to the disinterested Olivia, and she falls for the handsome young Cesario, believing her to be a man. So, Viola loves Orsino, Orsino loves Olivia, and Olivia loves Cesario—and they are all miserable. Which doubtless made Shakespeare very happy.

Sebastian, as it happens, is actually alive and well and believes his sister, Viola, is dead. He arrives in Illyria with his friend Antonio, who has cared for Sebastian since the shipwreck and has strong feelings for him. He follows Sebastian to Orsino's home, although he and Orsino are old enemies. Intrigue among the various lovers and their families ensues until the end, when all is somehow unraveled and revealed.

Much poster imagery involves the cross-dressing Viola, with visuals that echo Marcel Duchamp's *L.H.O.O.Q.*, his mustachioed riff on the Mona Lisa. Another frequent graphic theme builds on the threesome concept. The shipwreck is introduced in a few posters, too, as are *Twelfth Night*'s clowns, who indicate the comedic side of this tremendously likable play.

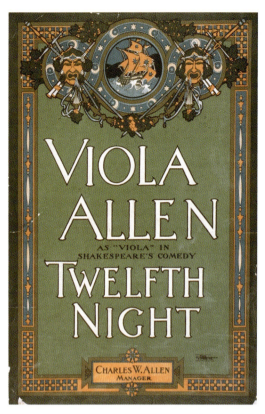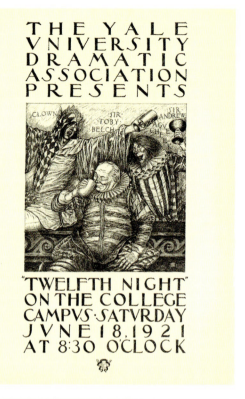

Theater: n/a, US, 1903. d: Strobridge & Co. Lith.

The Yale University Dramatic Association, US, 1921. d: n/a

State Comedy Theater, RU, 1938. d: Nikolai Akimov

Central Children's Theatre Moscow, RU, 1983. d: Zmoyro E.P.

Theater: n/a, HU, 1964. art: Janos Istvanfy

Teatr Polski w Poznaniu, PL, 1965. d: Zbigniew Kaja

Bulgarian Army Theatre, BG, n/a. d: Asen Stareishinski

Theater: n/a, HU, 1966. art: Istvan K. Bocz

Twelfth Night **209**

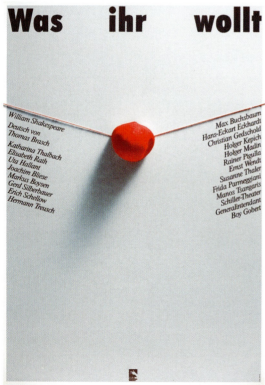

Teatr im. Juliusza Slowackiego, PL, 1996. d: Wladyslaw Pluta
(Dydo Poster Collection)

Schiller Schlosspark Werkstatt, DE, 1984. d: Holger Matthies
(Museum Folkwang, Deutsches Plakat Museum)

Shakespeare Festival of St. Louis, US, 2013. ad/d/ill: Rich Nelson

Teatr im. Jana Kochanowskiego, PL, 1980. d: Maciej Urbaniec
(Dydo Poster Collection)

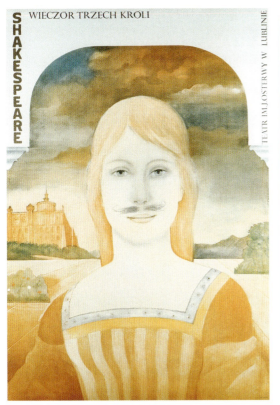
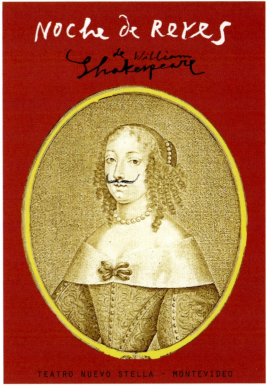

Teatr im. Juliusza Osterwy, PL, 1973. d: Maciej Urbaniec (Dydo Poster Collection)

University of Illinois at Chicago, US, 2013. ad/d/p: Matthew Gaynor

Teatro Nuevo Stella, UY, 1998. ad/d: Fidel Sclavo

Shakespeare at Traquair Theatre, UK, 2012. d: Michal Stachowiak

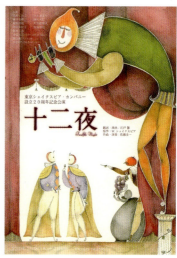

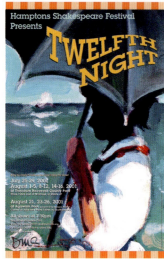

Royal Shakespeare Company, Royal Shakespeare Theatre, UK, 1987.
ad/d: John David Lloyd, Jim Northover,
d: Ruth Newsome (Lloyd Northover)

The Philadelphia Shakespeare Theatre, US, 2012. d: n/a

Hamptons Shakespeare Festival, US, 2001.
ad/d: Dennis Ascienzo,
art: Dinah Maxwell Smith

Theater Company Subaru, Sanbyakunin Gekijo, JP, 1997. ad/d: Takeshi Kitamura, ill: Yuuki Kitazawa

Maxim Gorki Theater, DE, 1991. d: Voker Pfuller (Museum Folkwang, Deutsches Plakat Museum)

Teatr Wspolczesny we Wroclawiu, PL, 1981. d: Jan Jaromir Aleksiun (Dydo Poster Collection)

Tokyo Shakespeare Company, Iwato Theatre, JP, 2010. ad: Kaoru Edo, d: Masami Tajiri, ill: Tomoko Kawaichi

212  Presenting Shakespeare

Lincoln Center Theater, US, 1998. ad: Jim Russek, d: James McMullan

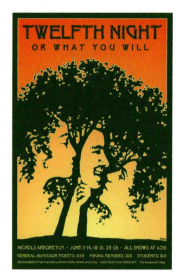

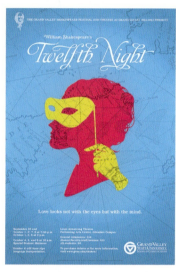

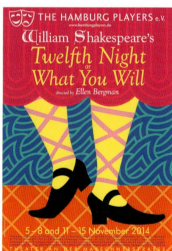

University of Michigan Matthaei Botanical Gardens and Nichols Arboretum, US, 2009.
ad/d: David Zinn

Repertory Theater of Lincoln Center, Vivian Beaumont Theater, US, 1972.
wd: Karen Beckhardt

Our Lady's High School, UK, 1980.
ad/d/ill: John Angus

Shakespearian Youth Theatre, US, 2008.
ad/d: Steven Verdoorn

Saratoga Shakespeare Company, US, 2000. ad/d: Nicholas Parslow

San Jose Youth Shakespeare, Historic Hoover Theatre, US, 2012. d: Karen Macauley

Kingsmen Shakespeare Festival, California Lutheran University, US, 2014.
ad/d: Cary Hanson

Grand Valley State University, Louis Armstrong Theatre, US, 2011.
ad: Nancy Crittenden

The Hamburg Players, DE, 2014.
ad/d: Alexander Ruehl

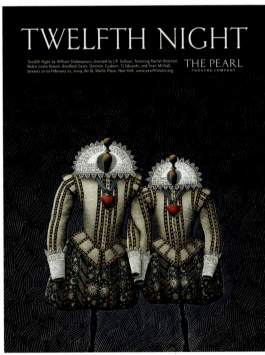

Royal Shakespeare Company, Royal Shakespeare Theatre, UK, 1983.
d: Jeff Jones, Chris Frampton

The Pearl Theatre Company, US, 2009. ad/d/ill: Scott McKowen

Royal Shakespeare Company, Royal Shakespeare Theatre, UK, 1979.
d: Allen-Beresford

The Acting Company, US, 1995. ad/d/ill: Scott McKowen

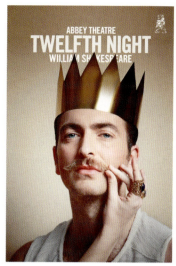
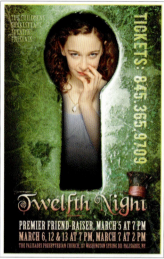
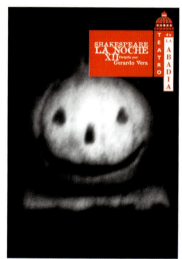
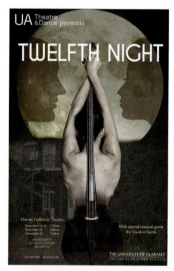

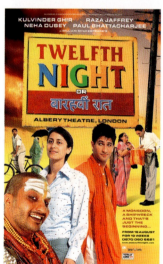

**Abbey Theatre**, IE, 2014. **ad:** Jason Delahunty, Stephen Ledwidge, Zero-G, **d:** Simon Roche, **p:** Sarah Doyle

**Children's Shakespeare Theatre**, US, 2010.
**ad/d:** David Green (Brightgreen Design),
**p:** Chris Carroll

**Romateatern**, SE, 2011. **ad/d:** Johan Brunzell,
**p:** Niclas Brunzell

**Teatro de La Abadia**, ES, 1996.
**d:** Oyer Corazon

**Royal Shakespeare Company**,
The Courtyard Theatre, UK, 2009.
**ad/d:** Andy Williams, **d:** Jillian Edelstein

**University of Alabama Theatre and Dance**,
Marian Gallaway Theatre, US, n/a.
**d:** Meghan Lalonde

**Background Productions**, Albery Theatre, UK,
2004. **ad/d:** Shaun Webb (Shaun Webb Design),
**p:** Hugo Glendinning

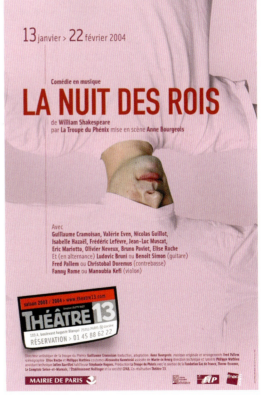

**Cheek by Jowl Theatre Co.**, UK, 2006. **ad:** Ian Vickers, **d:** Ranald Graham, **p:** Patrick Baldwin

**Pilgrim Theater Company, American Repertory Theater**, US, 2007. **ad:** Chaz Mariyane-Davies, **d:** Isaiah King, **p:** Alvin Booth

**The Soho Group**, UK, 1997. **ad/d:** Luke Dixon, **p:** Sarah Ainslie

**Theatre 13**, FR, 2004. **ad/d/p:** Cedric Gatillon

Teatr Rekwizytornia, PL, 2006. **d**: Tomasz Boguslawski (Dydo Poster Collection)

# THE TRAGEDIES

### Titus Andronicus
The bloodiest and most graphically violent of the Bard's plays, this is the fictional story of Titus, a general of Roman legions who is consumed by the spirit of revenge. Tamora, Queen of the Goths, takes on the spirit incarnation of revenge, which serves her tragically by the end.

### Coriolanus
Rome has transitioned from monarchy to republic, and the patrician Coriolanus emerges heroic in battle. He should be a leader in this new system but has contempt for the lower classes and popular rule. He is born to command, yet exists in a republican state that he cannot abide. Not surprisingly, things end badly for Coriolanus.

### Timon of Athens
With money as the play's central character, the question of "What does it truly buy?" is pervasive. Timon is a highly respected citizen of Athens, with a generosity that fatefully exceeds all common sense. He gives his fortunes to parasitic "friends" interested in squandering his wealth, which he loses in a tragic manner at the hands of the greedy for whom he was benefactor.

### Antony and Cleopatra
In the most famous suicide ever staged, Cleopatra kills herself by allowing an asp to bite her after Antony dies at her feet. Cleopatra imagines meeting Antony in the afterlife. Her serving maids, Iras and Charmian, also kill themselves. Antony's former ally Octavius discovers their bodies and realizes that their deaths leave him free to become the Roman Emperor.

### Troilus and Cressida
Two plots involve the ill-fated love of the eponymous Troilus and Cressida and the war between the Greek leader, King Agamemnon, and the Trojan, Priam. Agamemnon attempts to get the legendary Achilles to return to battle against the great Trojan warrior Hector. Cressida is eventually traded to the Greeks, to Troilus's sorrow, and Hector is slaughtered by Achilles on the battlefield.

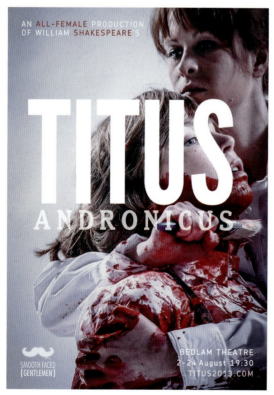

Theaterhaus Jena, DE, 2013. ad/d/p: David Eckes, Paul Steinmann

Smooth Faced Gentlemen, UK, 2013. ad: Yaz Al-Shaater, d: Brother Brother, p: Haz Al-Shaater

Royal Shakespeare Company, Swan Theatre, UK, 2013. d: Royal Shakespeare Company, p: Kahn & Selesnick

Theatre National de Chaillot, FR, 2003. d/p: Michal Batory

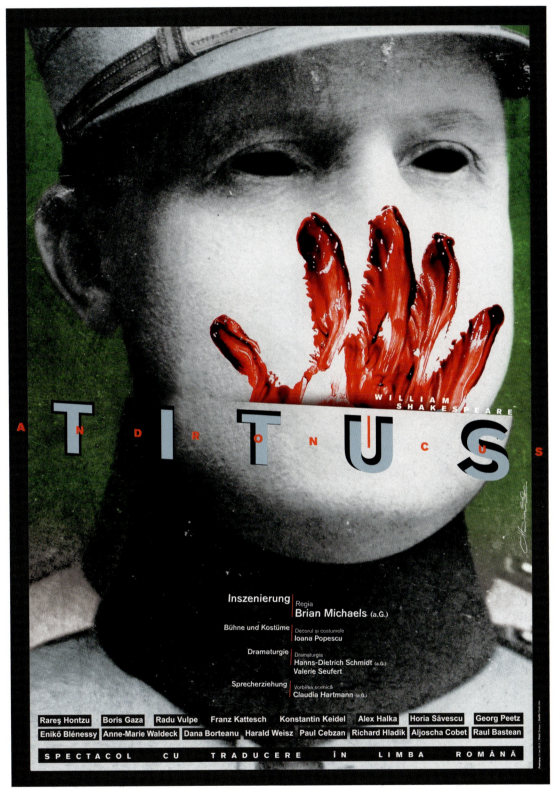

Deutsches Staatstheater Temeswar, RO, 2013. ad/d: Ovidiu Hrin, p: Richard Aumann

Harrisburg Shakespeare Festival, Gamut Theatre Group at Gamut Classic Theatre, US, 2007. **ad/d:** Robinson Smith

Knjazevsko-srpski teatar Kragujevac, RS, 2011. **ad/d/p:** Ivan Misic

Teatr im. Stefana Jaracza, PL, 1897. **d:** Stasys Eidrigevicius (Dydo Poster Collection)

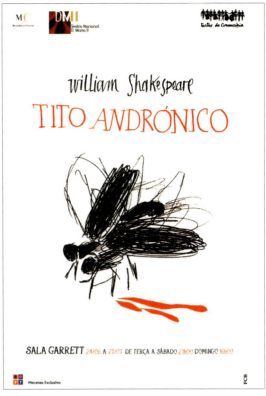
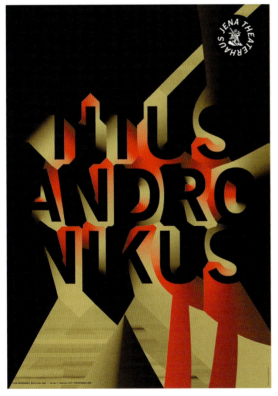

Teatro Zifio, CL, 2013. ad/d: Diego Becas Villegas

Theaterhaus Jena, DE, 2013. ad/d: David Eckes, Paul Steinmann

Teatro da Cornucopia, Teatro Nacional D. Maria II, PT, 2003.
ad/d: Cristina Reis, ad: Luis Miguel Cintra

Royal Shakespeare Company, Swan Theatre, UK, 2013.
d: Annette Bowery

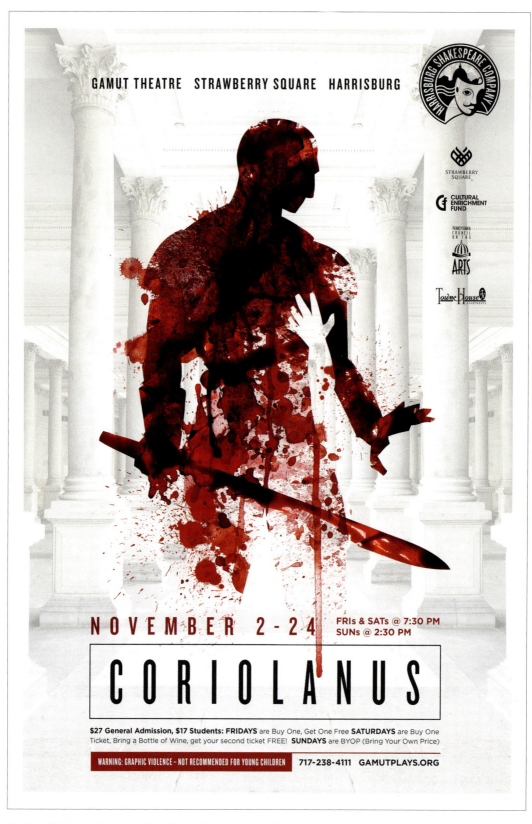

Harrisburg Shakespeare Company at Gamut Theatre Group, Gamut Classic Theatre, US, 2013. ad/d: Rob Smith

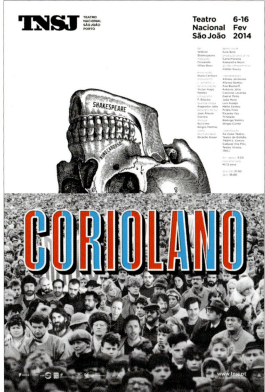

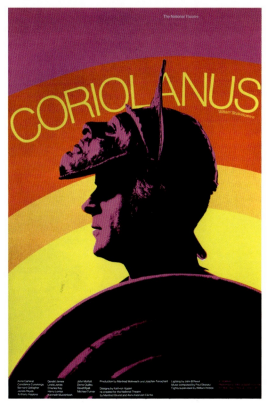

Gabriel Sundukyan National Academic Theatre, AM, 1978. d: K. Shch.

National Theatre, UK, 1984. cd: Richard Bird, ad: Peter Hall, d: John Bury, p: John Haynes

Ao Cabo Teatro, Teatro Nacional Sao Joao, PT, 2014. ad/d/art: Joao Faria (Drop), art: Victor Hugo Pontes

National Theatre, UK, 1971. d: n/a

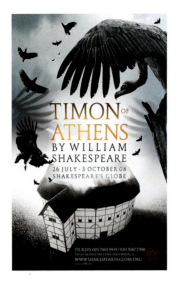
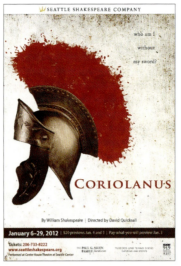

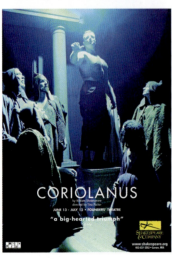

Shakespeare's Globe, UK, 2008.
ad: Shawn Webb, d: Shawn Webb Design

Teatr Powszechny, PL, 1966.
d: Andrzej Bilewicz, p: Edward Hartwig
(Dydo Poster Collection)

Shakespeare & Company, US, 2001.
d: Mary Garnish, p: Kevin Sprague

Seattle Shakespeare Company, US, 2012.
ad: Jeff Fickes, d: Thea Roe

Royal Shakespeare Company,
Barbican Theatre, UK, 1995.
ad/d: Amanda Bostock, p: Mark Dovet

Shakespeare & Company, US, 2000.
d/p: Kevin Sprague

Royal Shakespeare Company, Aldwych
Theatre, UK, 1978. d: Allen-Beresford

Royal Shakespeare Company,
Royal Shakespeare Theatre, UK, 1989.
ad/d: Ginny Crow, p: Ivan Kyncl

Royal Shakespeare Company, Swan Theatre,
UK, 1994. ad/d: Sue Rudd, p: Richard Levy

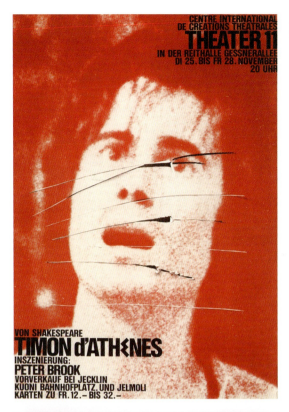

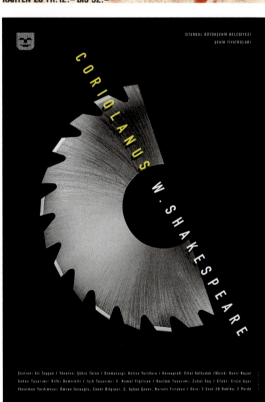

**Theater 11**, CH, 1975. **d:** Paul Bruhwiler

**Istanbul Municipal Theatre**, TR, 2009. **ad/d:** Ardan Erguven

**Teatr Polski Bydgoszcz**, PL, 2007. **d:** Joanna Gorska, Jerzy Skakun (Dydo Poster Collection)

**Teatr Klasyczny**, PL, 1963. **d:** Henryk Chylinski (Dydo Poster Collection)

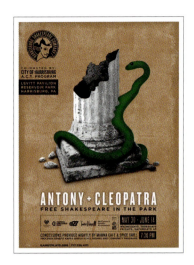

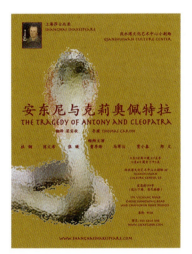

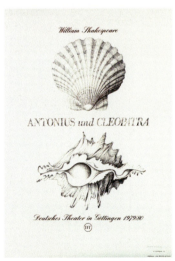

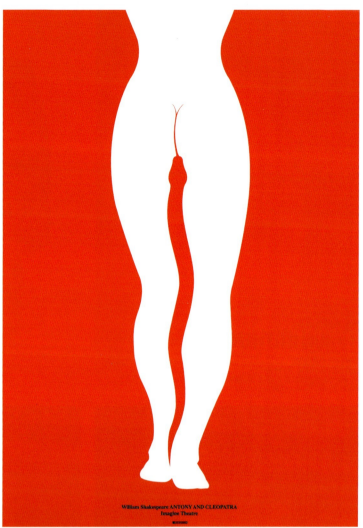

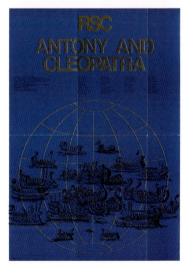

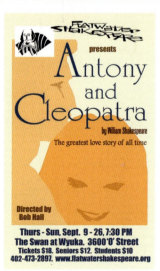

Harrisburg Shakespeare Company at Gamut Theatre Group, US, 2014. ad/d: Rob Smith

Shanghai Shakespeare, CN, 2012.
ad/d: Thomas Caron, p: Nancy Luu

Deutsches Theater in Gottingen, DE, 1979.
d: Mariusz Chwedczuk
(Dydo Poster Collection)

Imagine Theatre, DE, 2013. d: Lex Drewinski

Royal Shakespeare Company,
Royal Shakespeare Theatre, Aldwych Theatre,
UK, 1972. d: n/a

Flatwater Shakespeare Company, US, 2010.
d: Bob Hall

228  Presenting Shakespeare

Royal Shakespeare Company, Royal Shakespeare Theatre, UK, 1978. ad: Chris Frampton, d: Jeff Jones

Zuidelijk Toneel Globe, NL, 1980. **ad/d/p:** Anthon Beeke

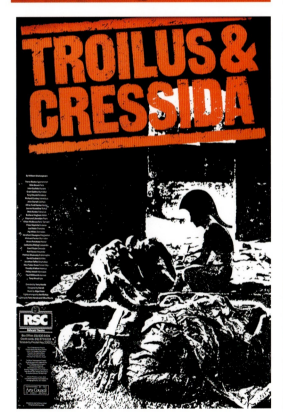
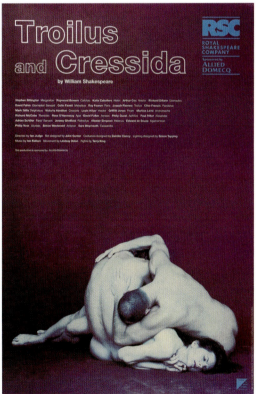

Deutsches Schauspielhaus in Hamburg, DE, 1966. **d:** Holger Matthies (Museum Folkwang, Deutsches Plakat Museum)

Bonn University Shakespeare Company, Brotfabrik Theater, DE, 2008. **d:** n/a

Royal Shakespeare Company, Aldwych Theatre, UK, 1981. **d:** Lloyd Northover

Royal Shakespeare Company, UK, 1996. **d:** Chris Moody, **p:** Clare Park

The Tragedies  231

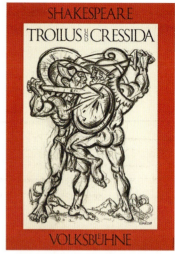

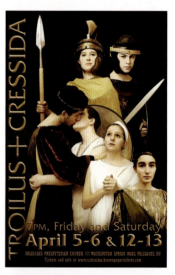
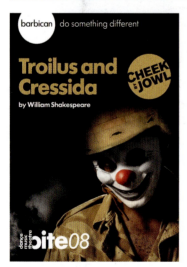

Munchner Kammerspiele, DE, 1985. d: Volker Pfuller (Museum Folkwang, Deutsches Plakat Museum)

Teatr im. Jana Kochanowskiego w Opolu, PL, 1972. d: Boleslav Polnar (Dydo Poster Collection)

Cheek by Jowl Theatre Co., Barbican Centre, UK, 2008. ad: Ian Vickers, d: Ranald Graham, p: Patrick Baldwin

Harrisburg Shakespeare Company at Gamut Theatre Group, US, 2015. ad/d: Robinson Smith

Volksbuehne, DE, 1969. d: Ronald Paris (Museum Folkwang, Deutsches Plakat Museum)

Children's Shakespeare Theatre, US, 2010. ad/d: David Green (Brightgreen Design), p: Chris Carroll

Royal Shakespeare Company, Royal Shakespeare Theatre, UK, 1976. d: Ginni Gillam

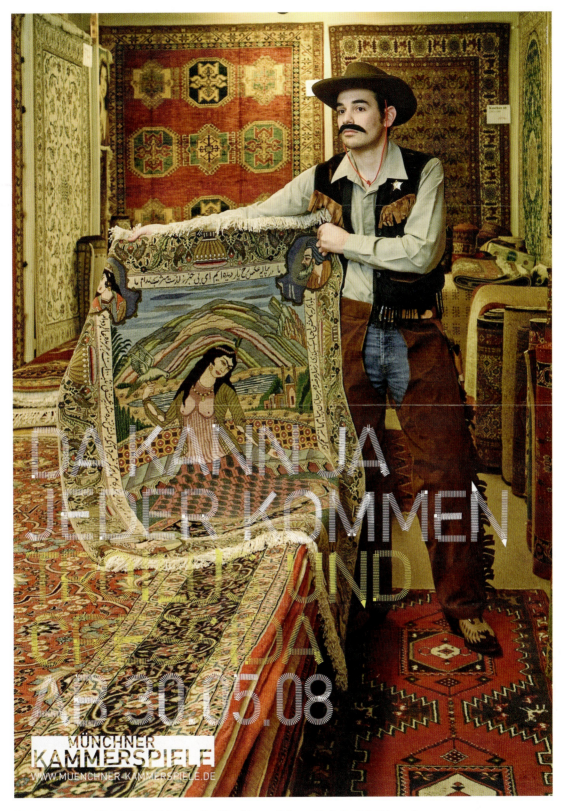

Munchner Kammerspiele, DE, 2008. d: Velvet Creative Office (Museum Folkwang, Deutsches Plakat Museum)

University of Memphis Department of Theatre and Dance, US, 2010. ad/d: Gary Golightly

# THE COMEDY OF ERRORS

*There's none but witches do inhabit here;*
*And therefore 'tis high time that I were hence.*
*She that doth call me husband, even my soul*
*Doth for a wife abhor. But her fair sister,*
*Possess'd with such a gentle sovereign grace,*
*Of such enchanting presence and discourse,*
*Hath almost made me traitor to myself:*
*But, lest myself be guilty to self-wrong,*
*I'll stop mine ears against the mermaid's song.*
—Antiphoulus of Syracuse

What a gift to poster artists is *The Comedy of Errors*, one of Shakespeare's earliest and shortest plays, about the disruptive antics of two sets of identical twins who have no idea that they have become entwined in each others' lives.

The play is introduced with a scene that sets up the slapstick to follow. Egeon, a merchant from Syracuse, is sentenced to death for entering Ephesus. However, he tells a story about the birth of his twin sons and their twin slaves, from whom he was separated after a tempest at sea sank his ship. Egeon lashed himself to a mast with one son and one slave. His wife, Emilia, and his other son and his slave were separately rescued and never seen again. Years later, his grown son, Antiphoulus of Syracuse, and slave, Dromio of Syracuse, had left for Ephesus to find their kin and had not returned. Egeon had set out after them and was arrested.

The action begins with Egeon's search for funds to pay a fine so he will not be executed. The rest is the famous comedy of errors, as the identical duos are mistaken for one another by everyone, including Antiphoulus of Ephesus's wife, who embraces Antiphoulus of Syracuse while barring her real husband from his own house. With two sets of identical twins, the hilariously tragic consequences are exponentially outrageous.

Consequently, the primary graphic conceit has been the representation of the twins as mirror images. These visual means have varied from realism to cartoons, photographs to drawings, but the fundamental concept has been fairly constant throughout the decades. Many posters have attempted to express the play's central use of slapstick humor typographically, with varying degrees of success. And since *The Comedy of Errors* can be set in so many different eras, styles and period details have always been in flux.

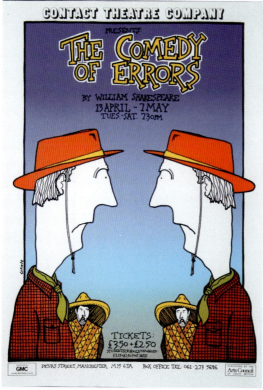

**Theater:** n/a, US, 1879. **d:** Forbes Co. Boston

**Contact Theatre Company,** UK, 1983. **ad/d/p:** John Angus

**Theater:** n/a, n/a, 1879. **ill:** Muller R, Metropolitan Litho. Studio

**Shakespeare at Traquair, Traquair House,** UK, 2014.
**d:** Michal Stachowiak

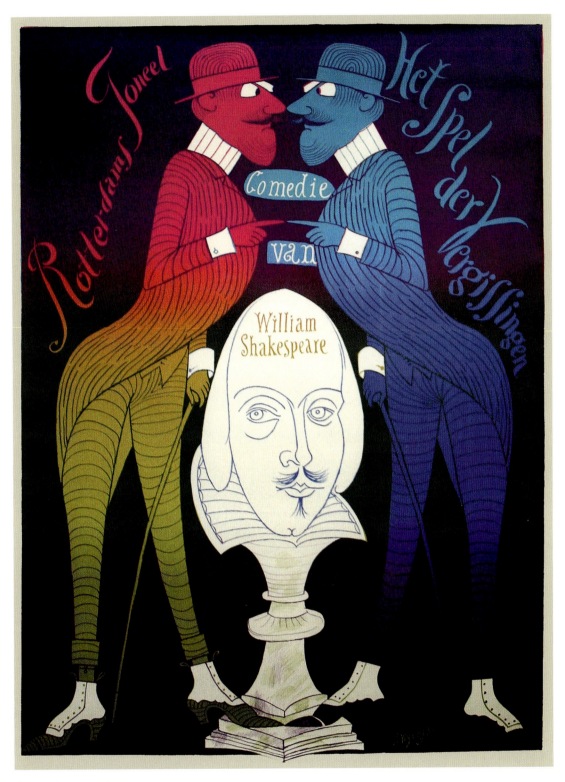

Rotterdam Toneel, NL, 1959. d: N. Wijnberg

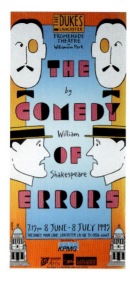
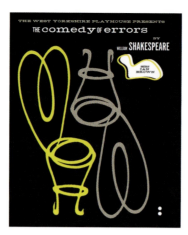
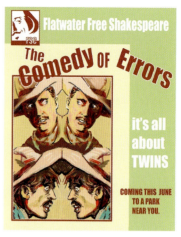

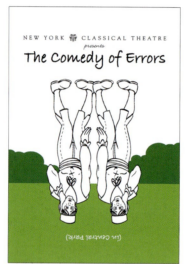
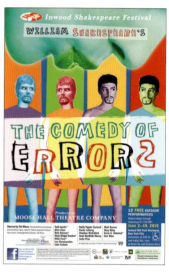
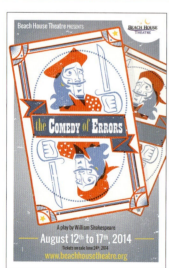

**The Dukes Playhouse**, UK, 1995.
ad/d/p: John Angus

**Types**, Tokyo Ryogoku Theater X, JP, 2011.
ad/d: Ayako Nagai

**Beach House Theatre**, CA, 2014.
d: Benjamin Thompson Stone

**West Yorkshire Playhouse**, UK, 1994.
ad/d: Laurie Rosenwald

**New York Classical Theatre**, US, 2005.
ad/d/ill: Todd Alan Johnson,
d: Stephen Burdman

**Teatr Wybrzeże**, PL, 2013. d: Maciej Hubner
(Dydo Poster Collection)

**Flatwater Shakespeare Co.**, US, 2014.
d: Bob Hall

**Moose Hall Theatre Co.**, Inwood Shakespeare Festival, US, 2010. d: Lee Kaplan

**San Jose Youth Shakespeare**, Historic Hoover Theatre, US, 2011. d: Karen Macauley

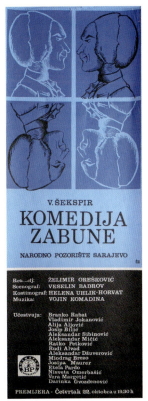
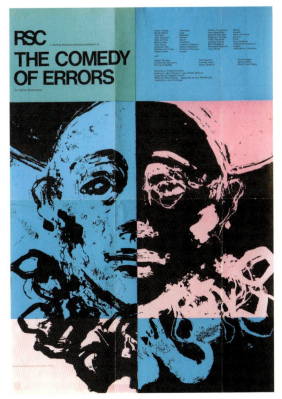

Clock Tower Theatre Company, The Gate Arts Centre, UK, 2015.
ad/d: Jonathan Dunn

Royal Shakespeare Company, Royal Shakespeare Theatre, UK, 1972.
d: Anthony Powell

Narodno pozoriste Sarajevo, BA, 1970. d: n/a

Royal Shakespeare Company, Royal Shakespeare Theatre, UK, 1983.
d: Mike Flowers, ill: X3

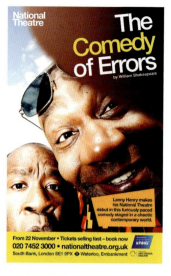

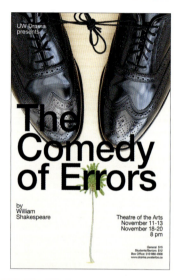

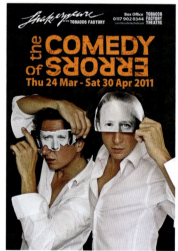

Shakespeare by the Bow, Theatre Calgary, CA, 2014. ad: Christina Poddubiuk, d: Scott McKowen, p: David Cooper

University of Waterloo, Department of Drama and Speech Communication, Theatre of the Arts, CA, 2010. d: Yen Chu

Shakespeare at the Tobacco Factory, UK, 2011 ad: Alan Coveney, d: Alpha Charlie Design

National Theatre, Olivier Theatre, UK, 2011. cd: Charlotte Wilkinson, ad: Nicholas Mytner, p: Phil Fisk

Shakespeare & Company, US, 2004. d: Mary Garnish

Royal Shakespeare Company, Royal Shakespeare Theatre, UK, 1990. d: Ginny Crow, p: Clive Barda

Setagaya Public Theatre, JP, 2002. ad/d: Tatsuya Ariyama, p: Yasuhide Kuge

Guildburys Theatre Company, UK, 2009. ad: Rob Sheppard, d/p: Phillip Griffith

Shakespeare & Company, US, 2011. d: Mary Garnish

Habima National Theatre, IL, 1962. ad/d: Dan Reisinger

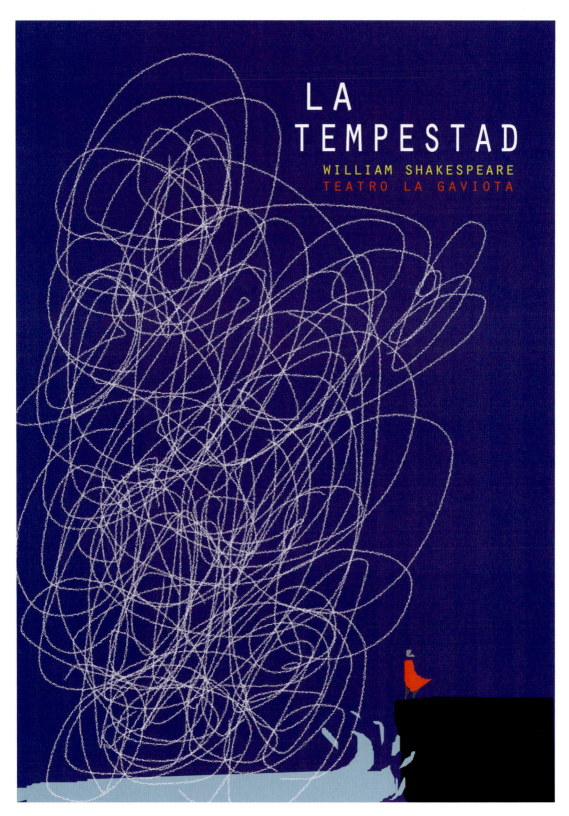

Teatro La Gaviota, UY, 1993. ad/d/ill: Fidel Sclavo

# THE TEMPEST

*Then, as my gift and thine own acquisition
Worthily purchased take my daughter: but
If thou dost break her virgin-knot before
All sanctimonious ceremonies may
With full and holy rite be minister'd,
No sweet aspersion shall the heavens let fall
To make this contract grow: but barren hate,
Sour-eyed disdain and discord shall bestrew
The union of your bed with weeds so loathly
That you shall hate it both: therefore take heed,
As Hymen's lamps shall light you.*
—**Prospero**

*The Tempest* might be seen as a seafaring romance, with some requisite intrigues and unusual fantastical conceits strung through three intersecting plots. It takes place on a fictional deserted island somewhere, perhaps, in the New World, where Prospero and his daughter Miranda have been abandoned by Prospero's jealous brother Antonio, who has usurped his station as Duke of Milan. Prospero, whom critics have argued represents Shakespeare at the end of his dramatic career, has become a sorcerer during their twelve years on the island, and is out to exact revenge on his brother and his ally, Alonso, the King of Naples, who deposed him. Enlisting his reluctant servant-spirit, Ariel, Prospero commands her to stir up a tempest at sea that wrecks the ship carrying, among others, brother Antonio and King Alonso, along with Alonso's brother Sebastian and son Ferdinand. The latter is in love with Miranda and ultimately, after many scenes, receives Prospero's blessing, as long as he does not break her virgin-knot before "All sanctimonious ceremonies" are final. After the requisite Shakespearean character twists and turns, Prospero decides to suppress his magical powers and allows the audience to set him free with its applause—an unusually happy ending.

Designing a poster for a play with three plot lines results in some curious juxtapositions of images and interpretations. The most common images relate to grounded boats and a raging sea. Some show ships, realistic or symbolic, atop or clashing with waves—look for the one with the paper boat sailing over the pages of a book (page 250). Others spotlight Prospero as a kind of Neptune. Depictions of Prospero and Miranda are realistic and abstracted. But perhaps the most clever conceptual image is that of a life preserver in the shape of a heart (page 245), a reference to the love between Miranda and Ferdinand.

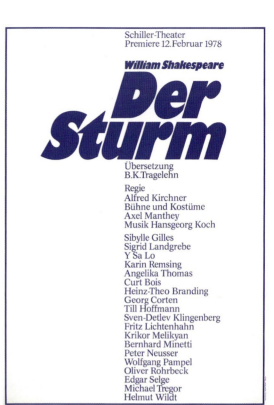

**Theatre Royal**, UK, 1823. **d:** n/a

**Vermont Shakespeare Company**, US, 2012. **ad/d:** Cristian Fleming, **d:** Gustavo Cordova

**Schiller Theater**, DE, 1978. **d:** Volker Noth (Atelier Noth+Hauer) (Museum Folkwang, Deutsches Plakat Museum)

**Knjazevsko-srpski teatar Kragujevac**, RS, 2013. **ad/d/p:** Ivan Misic

**ROYAL EXCHANGE THEATRE**

Box Office 0161 833 9833
royalexchange.co.uk

**15 - 18 August**

A Royal Exchange Theatre Young Company production

# The Tempest

at Abraham Moss

Directed by **NICKIE MILES-WILDIN**

A Royal Exchange Theatre Young Company Production

# The Tempest
## At Abraham Moss

By **WILLIAM SHAKESPEARE**
Directed by **NICKIE MILES-WILDIN**

*"This island's mine...which thou take from me!"*

School's out for summer. The school should be empty. A desolate prison. No more rules.

But wait, what's that on the CCTV? A person, a spirit, a mystical creation? Something strange is happening at Abraham Moss School just as exam results are released. Rules are broken, souls are bared and can you ever really forgive?

Following the successes of WE WERE TOLD THERE WAS DANCING and MIXTAPE, the Royal Exchange Theatre's award-winning Young Company present a unique twist on a familiar text, performed in promenade at Abraham Moss School, Crumpsall.

### Tickets £13 / £11 concessions

Do you live in Crumpsall or Cheetham Hill? £5 tickets available for anyone with an M8 postcode. Subject to availability. Book via Box Office or online.

**Box Office 0161 833 9833**
royalexchange.co.uk

**Wednesday 15 Aug** 7.30pm
**Thursday 16 Aug** 1pm, 3.15pm, 6pm & 8pm
**Friday 17 Aug** 3.15pm, 6pm & 8pm
**Saturday 18 Aug** 1pm, 3.15pm, 6pm & 8pm

With thanks to Andrew Lloyd Webber Foundation, The Garfield Weston Foundation, John Thaw Foundation, and to our anonymous donors for their generous support.

# Get Involved

There are loads of ways to get involved with the Royal Exchange Theatre for everyone aged 5+

### THE CHILDREN'S COMPANY

Aged 5 – 13? Our brand new children's company starts in September, with weekend and holiday opportunities for children to play and make theatre across the year.

**royalexchange.co.uk/childrenscompany**

### THE YOUNG COMPANY

If you are aged 14-25 and interested in any aspect of making theatre you can join our award-winning Young Company.

This is a year-long training programme in performance, technical theatre, writing, digital production, directing and producing.

For more information, visit
**royalexchange.co.uk/youngcompany**

### ELDERS MONTHLY

New Elders Monthly sessions from September - a day of opportunities every month for all older people to drop in, get involved, try something new, meet friends, and be creative!

Monday 10 Sep, 22 Oct, 12 Nov, 17 Dec, 21 Jan, 18 Feb. Anytime between 11-6pm at the Royal Exchange Theatre.

**royalexchange.co.uk/elderscompany**

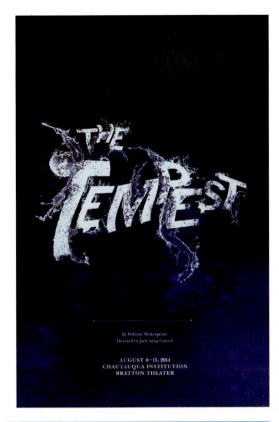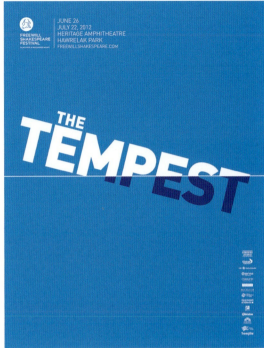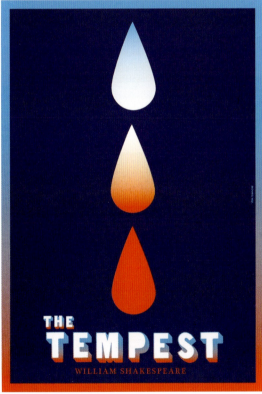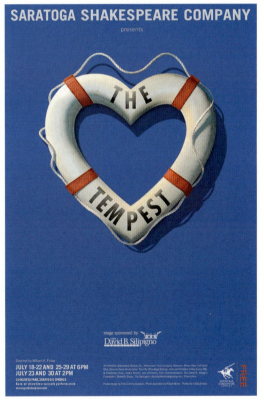

Chautauqua Theater Company, Bratton Theater, US, 2014.
d: Jordan Reading, p: Lukas Gojda, Deposit Photos

Association Tadaaa, FR, 2008. ad/d: Yann Legendre

Free Will Players, Free Will Shakespeare Festival, CA, 2012.
ad/d: Brad Blasko

Saratoga Shakespeare Company, US, 2006. ad/d: Tom Rothermel,
p: Robert Moore

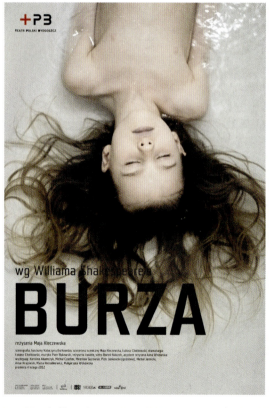

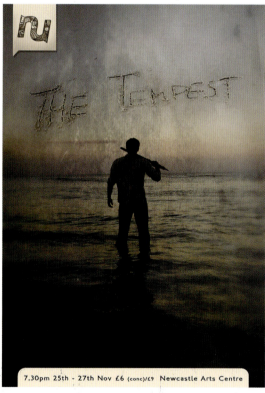

Pozoriste mladih Sarajevo, BA, 1982. ad/d: Cedomir Kostovic, p: Kemal Hadzic

Teatr Polski Bydgoszcz, PL, 2012. d: Joanna Gorska, Jerzy Skakun
(Dydo Poster Collection)

Newcastle University Theatre Society, 2014, UK. ad: Luke W. Robson,
d/p: Anna Kennedy, Anna Simmons, Chloe Marquand

Royal Shakespeare Company, Royal Shakespeare Theatre, UK, 1988. d: David Fielding (The Drawing Room), p: Richard Winslade

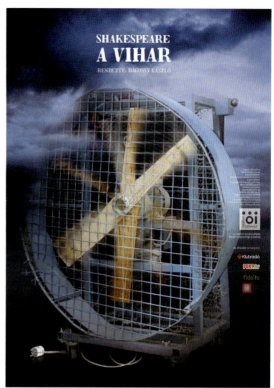
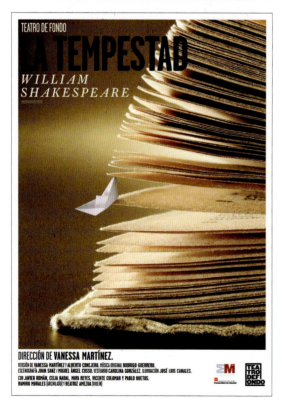

Royal Shakespeare Company, Royal Shakespeare Theatre, UK, 1993. d: Steve Xern, Avril Broadley

Teatro Defondo, ES, 2009. ad: Diego Areso Nieva, p: Zsuzsanna Kilian

Orkeny Istvan Szinhaz, HU, 2015. d: Levente Bagossy

Gyula Castle Theatre, HU, 2012. ad/d: Szergej Maszlobojscsikov

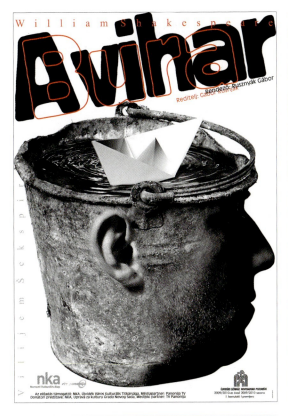

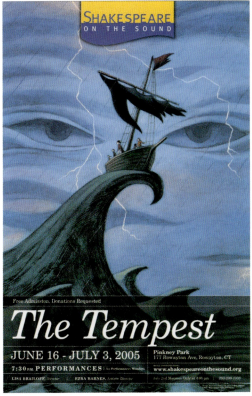

Novosadsko pozoriste, RS, 2010. ad/d: Atila Kapitanj

Shakespeare on the Sound, US, 2005. ad: Ezra Barnes, d: Nat Connacher

Ulysses Theatre, HR, 2010. ad/d: Eduard Cehovin, p: Damjan Kocijancic

The Shakespeare Theatre of New Jersey, US, 2014. ad/d/ill: Scott McKowen

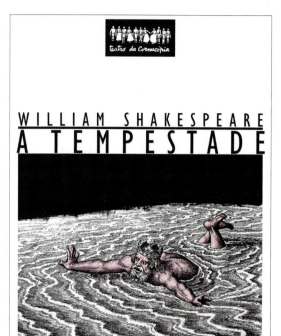

Teatro da Cornucopia, Teatro do Bairro Alto, PT, 2009.
ad/d: Cristina Reis

Royal Shakespeare Company, Barbican Theatre, UK, 1983.
d: Lloyd Northover, ill: Alan Adler

Royal Shakespeare Company, Royal Shakespeare Theatre, UK, 1978.
d: Jeff Jones, Chris Frampton

Riot Theater Company, US, 1999. ad/d: Kaveh Haerian

Galeria Forum, PL, 1988. **ad:** Krzystof Dydo, **d:** Mieczyslaw Gorowski (Dydo Poster Collection)

Teatr im. Jana Kochanowskiego, PL, 1977. **d:** Jan Sawka (Dydo Poster Collection)

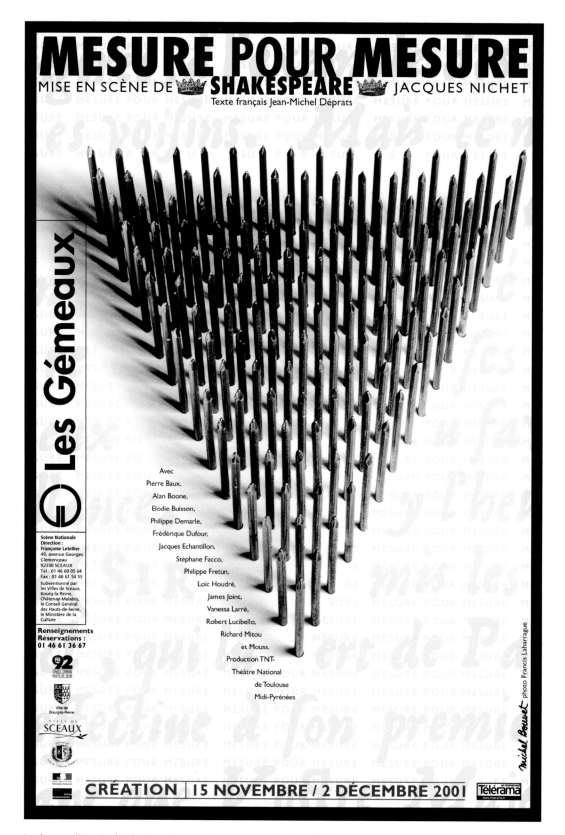

Les Gemeaux/Scene Nationale-Sceaux, FR, 2001. **ad/d:** Michel Bouvet, **p:** Francis Laharrague

# THE TRAGICOMEDIES

### Measure for Measure
Vienna is awash with sin, believes the moralistic judge Angelo, who vows to strictly expunge it. Claudio is arrested for the premarital pregnancy of his fiancée, Juliet, and sentenced to have his head severed as an example to all potentially offending Viennese citizens. With the help of Claudio's sister Isabella (who has been propositioned by Angelo) and the duke of Vienna, Claudio is eventually pardoned.

### The Merchant of Venice
Shylock, the seemingly villainous moneylender—the quintessential negative Semitic caricature and poster boy for this play—acts out *The Merchant of Venice*'s most dramatic scenes, especially his famous speech that begins "Hath Not a Jew eyes?"

### Cymbeline
Imogen, daughter of the British king Cymbeline, rebelliously marries the lowborn Posthumus instead of Cloten, the son of Cymbeline's villainous new queen. Posthumus goes into exile in Italy, where he meets Iachimo, who schemes to seduce Posthumus's beloved Imogen. After considerable drama and confusion, Imogen and Posthumus are at last reunited and the wicked queen dies.

### Two Noble Kinsmen
Based on Geoffrey Chaucer's *Knight's Tale*, this play depicts the capture of cousins and lifelong kinsmen Palamon and Arcite while fighting for Thebes against Athens. During their captivity they become enamored with Emilia, who is the sister of Hippolyta, wife of Theseus. Their friendship is harshly put to the test as the two vie for her attentions.

### The Winter's Tale
Following three acts of tragedy, two acts of comedy reign. The play is divided by sixteen years, the first part set during a most oppressive winter, when mistaken jealousy hangs over Leontes, King of Sicilia. In the play's second half spring intervenes, and joy is restored when a statue of the king's wife comes alive.

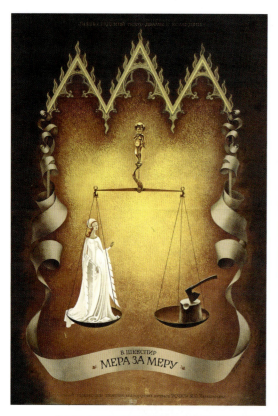
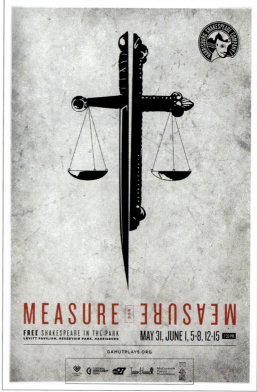

Leningrad Drama Theatre, RU, 1981. d: Komut G.P.

Illinois State University School of Theatre, Westhoff Theatre, US, 2010. ad: Julie Johnson, d/p: Nick Griffin

Harrisburg Shakespeare Company at Gamut Theatre Group, US, 2013. ad/d: Robinson Smith

Teatro La Candela, UY, 1987. d: Fidel Sclavo

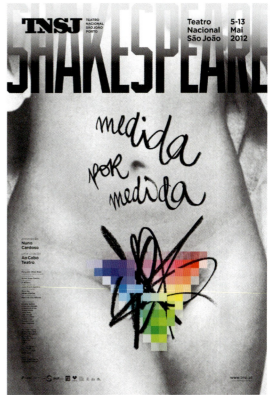
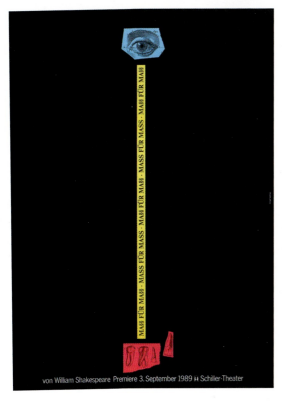
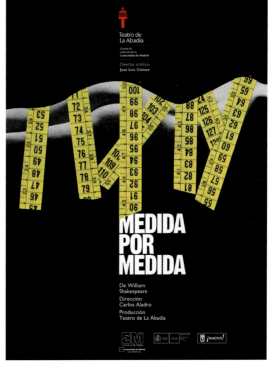

National Theatre, UK, 2004. ad: Nicholas Hytner, cd: Michael Mayhew, d: Tom Pye, p: Josef Astor

Schiller Theater, DE, 1989. d: Holger Matthies
(Museum Folkwang, Deutsches Plakat Museum)

Ao Cabo Teatro, Teatro Nacional Sao Joao, PT, 2012. ad/d: Joao Faria

Teatro de La Abadia, ES, 2008. ad/d: Manuel Estrada

The Tragicomedies 255

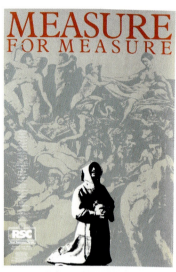

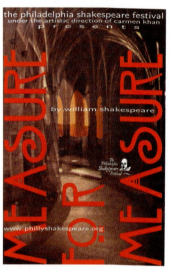
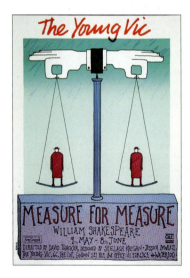
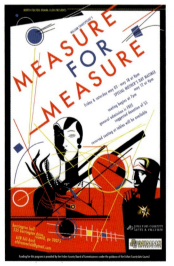

Royal Shakespeare Company,
Royal Shakespeare Theatre, UK, 1983.
d: The Partners, ill: Ian Pollock

Bonn University Shakespeare Company,
Brotfabrik Theater, DE, 2013.
d: Sebastian Klement, art: Eugen Schramm

The Young Vic, UK, 1985. ad/d: John Angus

Stratford Festival, CA, 1992.
ad: Christina Poddubiuk, d/ill: Scott McKowen

Royal Shakespeare Company,
Royal Shakespeare Theatre, UK, 1987.
d: Ginny Crow, p: Olive Barda

North Fulton Drama Club, Barrington Hall,
US, 2013. ad/d: Erica Cruz

Royal Shakespeare Company,
Royal Shakespeare Theatre, UK, 1978.
d: Lloyd Northover

The Philadelphia Shakespeare Theatre, US,
2001. d: n/a

Kinokuniya Southern Theatre, JP, 2005.
d: Kaori Sato, ill: 100% Orange

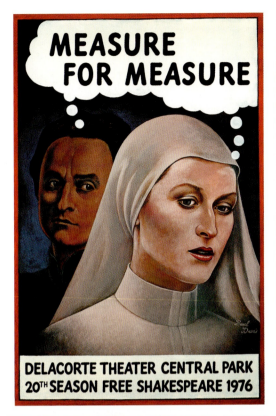

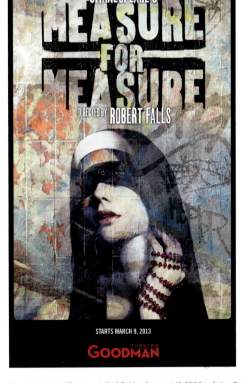

The Public Theater, Delacorte Theater, US, 1976. d/ill: Paul Davis, Reinhold Schwenk

Royal Shakespeare Company, Swan Theatre, UK, 2011. ad/d: Andy Williams, ill: Emmanuel Polanco

Lincoln Center Theater, Mitzi E. Newhouse, US, 1989. ad: Jim Russek, d: James McMullan

Goodman Theatre, US, 2013. ad/d: Kelly Rickert

The Tragicomedies 257

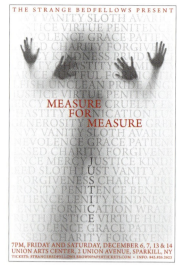
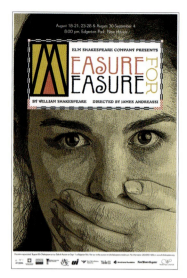

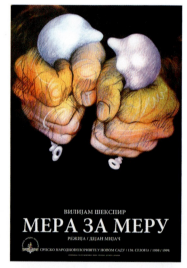

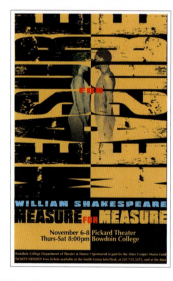

Chicago Shakespeare Theater, US, 2005.
ed: Criss Henderson, d: Paul Abel,
p: Peter Bosy

Royal Shakespeare Company,
Royal Shakespeare Theatre, UK, 1994.
d: Duncan Macaskill

Bowdoin College Department of Theater
and Dance, US, 2008. ad: Davis Robinson,
d: Judy Gailen

The Strange Bedfellows, US, 2013.
ad: Brightgreen Design, d: David Green
(Brightgreen Design), p: Thinkstock

Srpsko Narodno pozoriste, RS, 1998.
ad: Dejan Mijac, d: Radule Boskovic

Yokohama Yamate Theater and Tokyo Ginza Miyuki Theater, JP, 2006. ad/d: Yoko Abe,
p: Takayuki Ayanogi

Elm Shakespeare Company, Edgerton Park,
US, 2011. ad/d: Sue Surina Rollins,
p: Dreamstime

Szigligeti Theater Szolnok, HU, 1988.
ad/d: Peter Pocs, p: Peter Walter

Recinto de Rio Piedras, Teatro Universidad de Puerto Rico, PR, 1964. d: Lorenzo Homar

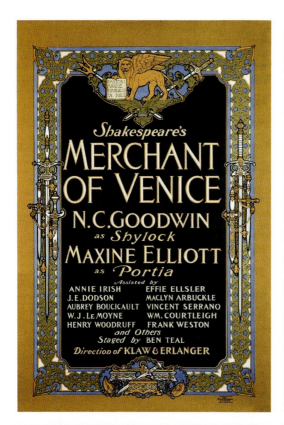

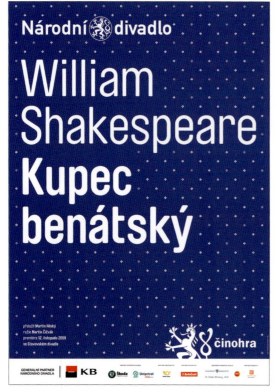

Theatre n/a, US, 1901. d: Strobridge & Co.

Narodni divadlo v Praze, CZ, 2009.
ad: Mikulas Machacek (Studio Najbrt)

Bakelit Multi Art Center, HU, 2013. ad: Csaba Paroczay,
d: Balazs Solyom

Theater Oberhausen, DE, 2007. d: Benning Gluth & Partner
(Museum Folkwang, Deutsches Plakat Museum)

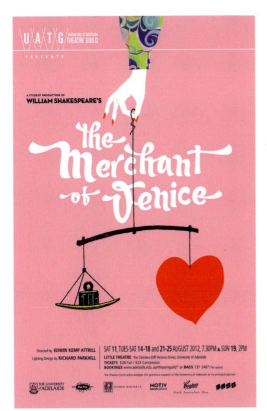
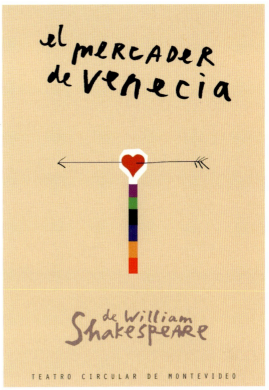
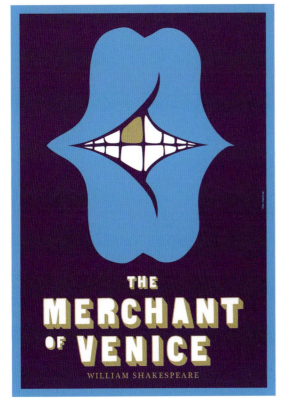
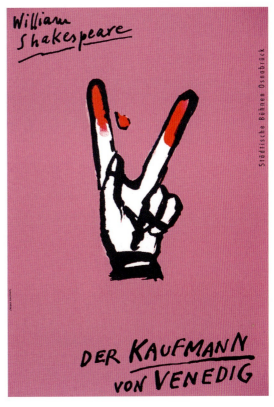

University of Adelaide Theatre Guild, AU, 2011. ad/d: Peter Day

Association Tadaaa, US, 2008. ad/d: Yann Legendre

Teatro Circular de Montevideo, UY, 1989. ad/d: Fidel Sclavo

Stadtische Buhnen Osnabruck, DE, 1992. d: Erhard Gruttner
(Museum Folkwang, Deutsches Plakat Museum)

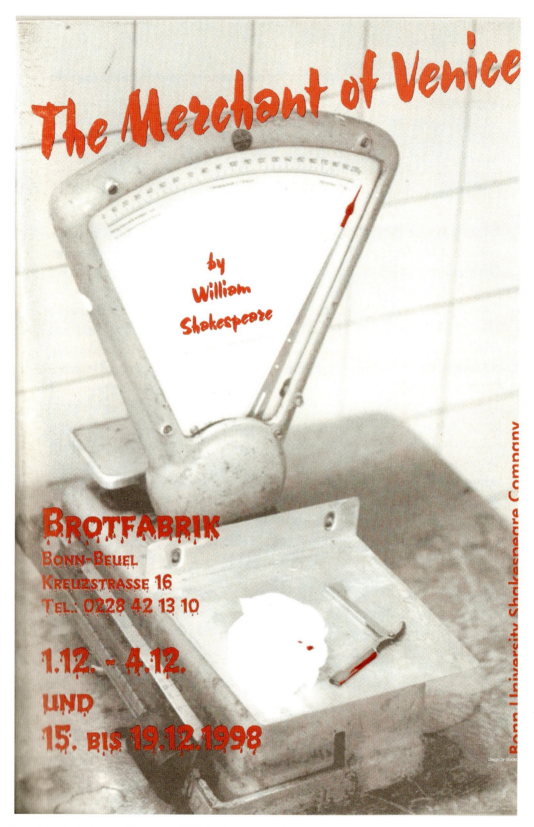

Bonn University Shakespeare Company, Brotfabrik Theater, DE, 1998. d: Thorsten Lohndorf

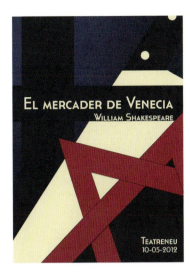
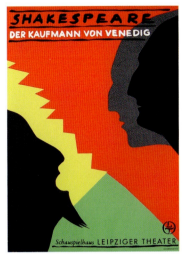

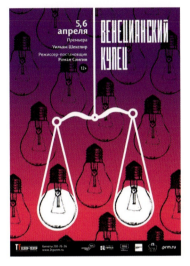

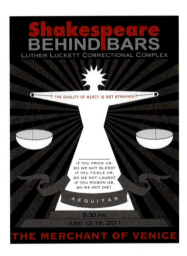

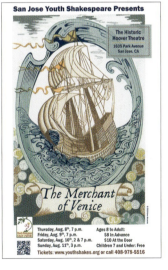

Teatreneu, ES, 2012.
ad/d: Enrique Hernandis

Perm Academic Theatre, RU, 2013.
d: Petya Stabrovskiy

Shimokitazawa Geki Syo Gekijyo, JP, 2014. ad: Kaoru Edo, d: Masami Tajiri, ill: Tomoko Kawaichi

Schauspielhaus Leipziger Theater, DE, 2008.
ad/d: Jutta Damm-Fiedler

Globe Theatre, Habima National Theatre of Israel, IL, 2012. d: David Bauminger

Players by the Sea, US, 2011.
ad/d: Jorge Brunet-Garcia,
d: Aerien Mull, Kedgar Volta

Shakespeare Behind Bars, Luther Luckett Correctional Complex, US, 2011.
ad/d: Holly Stone

San Jose Youth Shakespeare, Historic Hoover Theatre, US, 2013. d: Karen Macauley

The Tragicomedies 263

 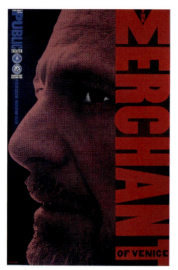 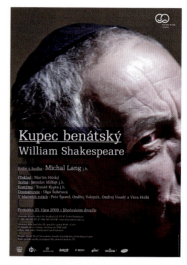

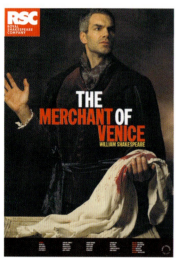  

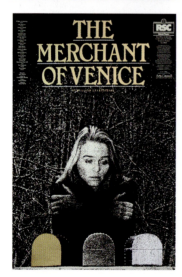  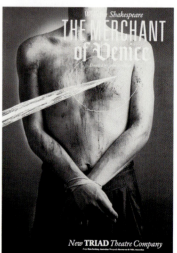

Compagnie nonante-trois, Theatre de L'oriental Vevey, CH, 2007. ad/d/p: Benjamin Knobil

Royal Shakespeare Company, The Courtyard Theatre, UK, 2008. ad/d: Andy Williams, d: Tamie Bridl, p: Jillian Edelstein

Royal Shakespeare Company, Aldwych Theatre, UK, 1981. ad/d: John David Lloyd, Jim Northover, d: Lloyd Northover, p: Donald Cooper

The Public Theater, US, 1995. ad/d: Paula Scher (Pentagram)

Deutsches Theater, DE, 2005. d: Sophia Paeslack (Museum Folkwang, Deutsches Plakat Museum)

Royal Shakespeare Company, Barbican Theatre, UK, 1988. d: Lloyd Northover, Kirby-Sessions

Jihoceske divadlo, CZ, 2009. ad: Michal Lang, d: Robert V. Novak, p: Ivan Pinkava

Saratoga Shakespeare Company, US, 2000. ad/d: Nicholas Parslow

New Triad Theatre Company, NL, 1985. ad/d: Hans Bockting, p: Reinier Gerritsen

Royal Shakespeare Company, Royal Shakespeare Theatre, UK, 1993. ill: Ralph Steadman

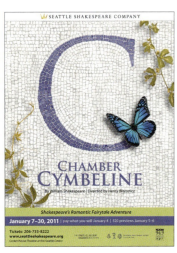

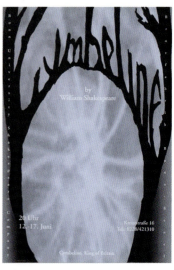
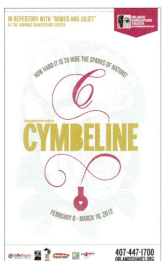

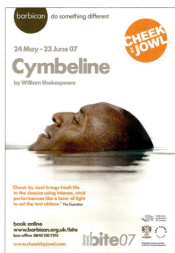

Owl Spot, JP, 2008. ad: Kiyoaki Ichikawa, d: Kaori Sato, ill: 100% Orange

Seattle Shakespeare Company, US, 2011. ad: Jeff Fickes, d: Thea Roe

Orlando Shakespeare Theater, US, 2012. ad: Jim Helsinger, d: Betsy Dye

I Pit Mejiro, JP, 2011. ad: Kaoru Edo, d: Masami Tajiri, ill: Tomoko Kawaichi

Barrow Street Theatre, US, 2011. ad/d: Frank "Fraver" Verlizzo

Royal Shakespeare Company, Stratford-Upon-Avon, UK, 1979. d: Jeff Jones

Teatro del Notariado, UY, 1998. ad/d: Fidel Sclavo

Bonn University Shakespeare Company, DE, 2001. art: Imke Pannen, Eva Dinnessen

Cheek by Jowl Theatre Co., Barbican Centre, UK, 2007. ad/d: Ian Vickers, Ranald Graham, p: Patrick Baldwin

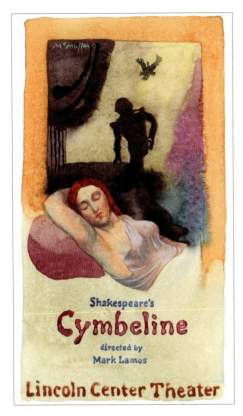
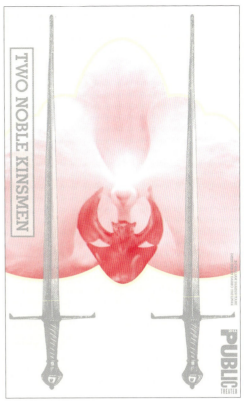
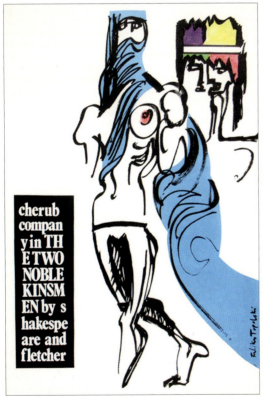

**Lincoln Center Theater**, US, 2007. **ad:** Jim Russek, **d:** James McMullan

**The Cherub Company London**, Young Vic Theatre, UK, 1979.
**d:** Feliks Topolski

**The Public Theater**, US, 2003. **ad/d:** Paula Scher (Pentagram)

**Harrisburg Shakespeare Festival, Gamut Theatre Group**, US, 2009.
**ad/d:** Robinson Smith

The Tragicomedies

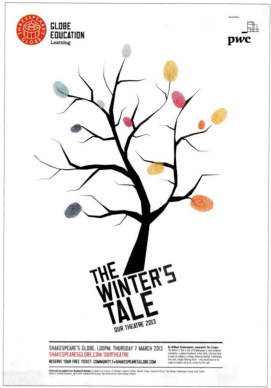
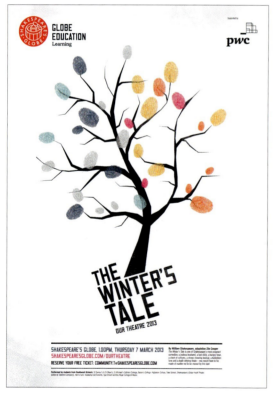
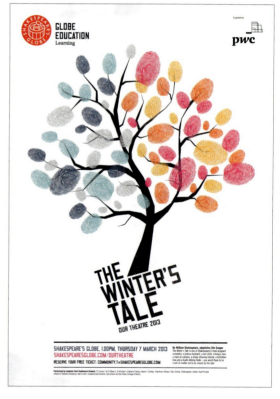

Shakespeare's Globe, UK, 2013. ad/d: Embrace

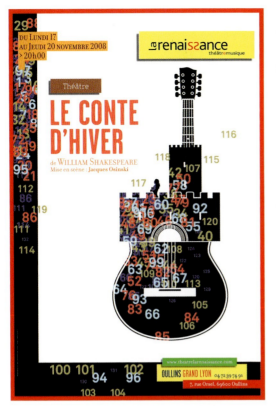

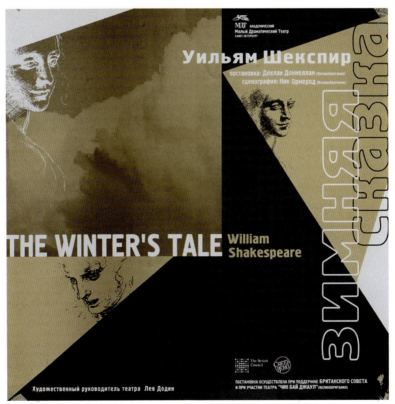

Theatre de La Renaissance, FR, 2008. ad/d/p: Cedric Gatillon

Stadttheater Ingolstadt, DE, 2012. ad/d: Sascha Lobe, d: Ina Bauer

Leningrad Maly Drama Theatre, RU, 1997. d: A. Andreychuk

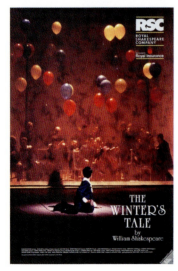

Qianshuiwan Culture Center, CN, 2013.
ad/d/p: Thomas Caron

Shakespeare & Company, US, 2000.
d/p: Kevin Sprague

Royal Shakespeare Company,
Royal Shakespeare Theatre, UK, 1992.
d: Ginny Crow, p: Donald Cooper

University of Rochester International Theatre
Program, Todd Theatre, US, 2011.
ad/d/p: Nigel Maister

Royal Shakespeare Company, UK, 1986. d: n/a

Vermont Shakespeare Company, US, 2013.
ad: Cristian Fleming, d: Cristian Fleming,
Wendy Qi

Kingsmen Shakespeare Festival, US, 2010.
ad/d: Michael Adams

California Shakespeare Theater, US, 2013.
ad: Jonathan Moscone, d: Callie Cullum,
p: Jeff Singer

Royal Shakespeare Company,
Barbican Theatre, UK, 1981.
d: The Drawing Room

**Sakura Hall of Shibuya Cultural Center Owada**, JP, 2011. **ad:** Kiyoaki Ichikawa, **d:** Kaori Sato, **ill:** 100% Orange

**Teatro da Cornucopia, Teatro da Trindade**, PT, 1994. **ad/d:** Cristina Reis

**Teatr Wspolczesny w Warszawie**, PL, 1994. **d:** Wieslaw Rosocha (Dydo Poster Collection)

**The Dukes Playhouse**, UK, 1985. **ad/d/p:** John Angus

**Schauspiel Bonn**, DE, 1995. **d:** Zygmunt Januszewski (Dydo Poster Collection)

**University of Michigan Matthaei Botanical Gardens and Nichols Arboretum**, US, 2011. **ad/d:** David Zinn

The Tragicomedies

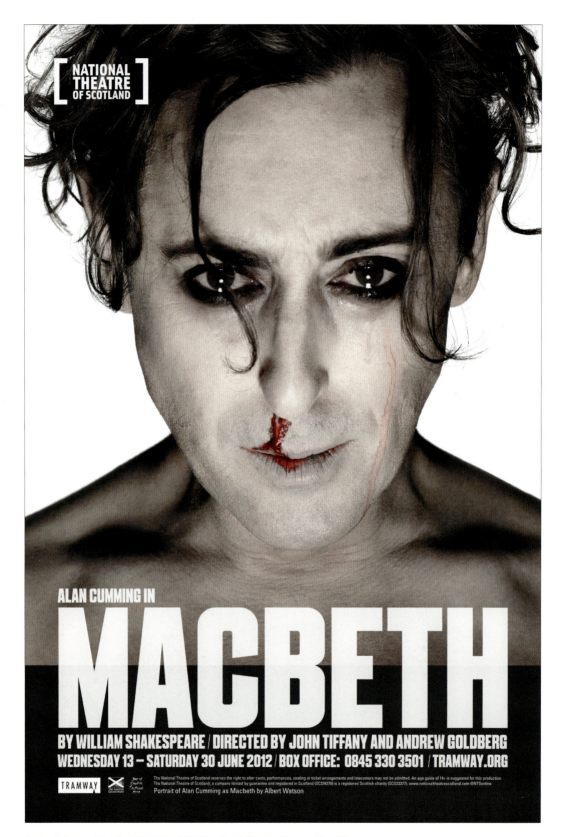

National Theatre of Scotland, UK, 2012. ad: Neil Maguire, d: After the News, p: Albert Watson

# MACBETH

*Who can be wise, amazed, temperate and furious,*
*Loyal and neutral, in a moment? No man:*
*The expedition my violent love*
*Outrun the pauser, reason. Here lay Duncan,*
*His silver skin laced with his golden blood;*
*And his gash'd stabs look'd like a breach in nature*
*For ruin's wasteful entrance: there, the murderers,*
*Steep'd in the colours of their trade, their daggers*
*Unmannerly breech'd with gore: who could refrain,*
*That had a heart to love, and in that heart*
*Courage to make's love known?*

—Macbeth

There is more red ink used in the printing of posters promoting performances of *Macbeth* than in the inkwells for any other of Shakespeare's tragedies. Red, or shall we say blood, is everywhere in this play—it soaks deep into Macbeth's hands and drips profusely from his dagger's blade.

It is Lady Macbeth who encourages—indeed demands—that her husband follow the serious prophecies of three witches who have foretold Macbeth's accession as King of Scotland after the murder of the current King Duncan. Consumed by his own irredeemable ambition, with his wife egging him on, Macbeth murders King Duncan and assumes the throne for himself. Shakespeare—being Shakespeare—makes certain that Macbeth is genuinely guilt-ridden for what he's done. Yet rather than curtail his evil, Macbeth keeps the blood flowing from his murderous hand. He is compelled to commit ever-more-heinous acts of carnage to protect himself from his enemies, among them Duncan's rebel sons. His bloodbath and the resulting civil war waged against him swiftly consume Macbeth and Lady Macbeth in madness. Even Lady Macbeth feels the guilt. Yet guilt doesn't stop the crimes.

In addition to the surfeit of red, shining dagger blades appear frequently in this poster art. When these daggers are also bloodstained and used to represent the points of a crown they take on a macabre quality, suggesting malice or pain—the inescapability of violence. The best *Macbeth* posters suggest how trapped he is in his horror. Although Macbeth's conscience is increasingly haunted, he refuses to stop his savagery until the very end, when he is slain at the hands of Duncan's vengeful elder son, Malcolm (who should have a poster all his own).

Drury Lane Theatre, UK, 1865. d: Thomas Way

Boston Theatre, US, 1868. d: n/a

Theater: n/a, US, 1884. d/art: W.K. Morgan & Co. Lith.

Euclid Avenue Opera House, US, 1876. d: n/a

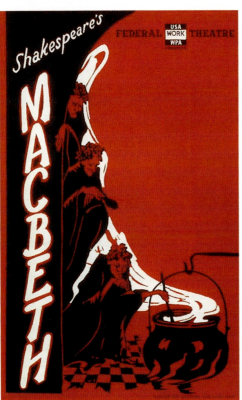
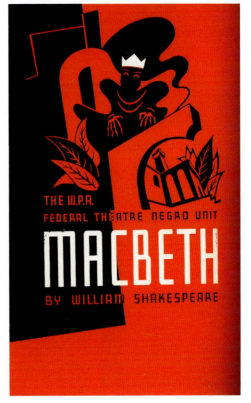

His Majesty's Theatre, UK, 1911. d/art: Edmund Dulac

Copley Theatre, US, n/a. d: n/a

USA Work W.P.A., Federal Theatre, US, 1935. d: n/a

The W.P.A. Federal Theatre Negro Unit, US, 1938. art: Anthony Velonis

 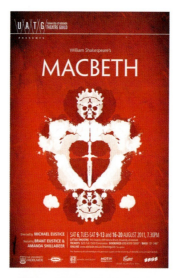 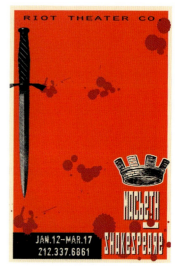
 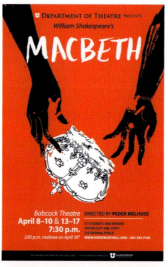 
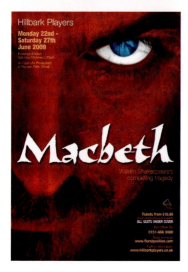 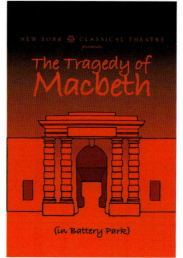 

**Orlando-UCF Shakespeare Festival**, US, 1999.
d: Paul Mastriani

**University Players**, DE, 2005.
ad/d: Ole Friedrich

**Hillbark Players**, UK, 2009.
ad/d: Nick Sample, p: Dundanim

**University of Adelaide Theatre Guild**, AU, 2011.
ad/d: Peter Day

**University of Utah Department of Theatre**, US, 2011. ad/d: Whitney Shaw

**New York Classical Theatre**, US, 2008. ad: Todd Alan Johnson, Stephen Burdman, d/ill: Todd Alan Johnson

**Riot Theater Company**, US, 2001.
ad/d: Kaveh Haerian

**Setagaya Public Theatre**, JP, 2009.
ad: Kiyoaki Ichikawa, d: Kaori Sato,
ill: 100% Orange

**Florence English Speaking Theatrical Artists**, IT, 2010. ad/d/p: David Ballerini,
d: Miles DeCoster

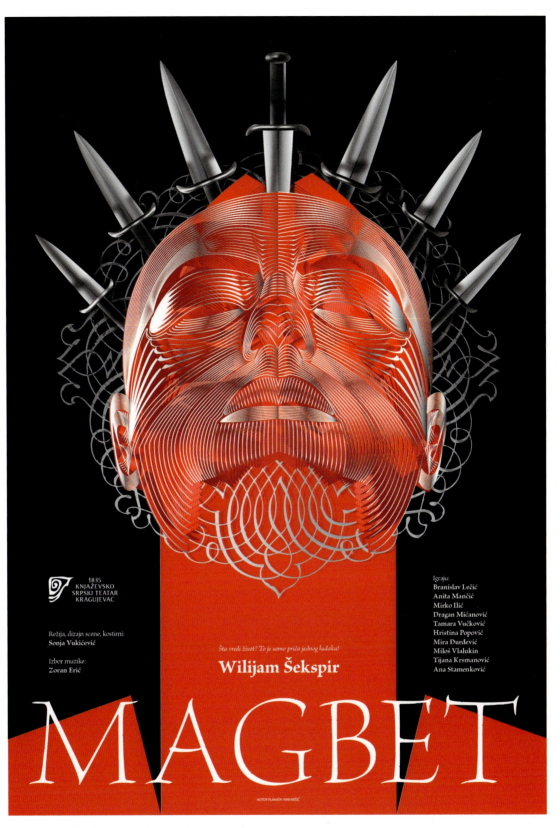

Knjazevsko-srpski teatar Kragujevac, RS, 2010. ad/d/p: Ivan Misic

Les Gemeaux/Scene Nationale-Sceaux, FR, 2010. **ad/d:** Michel Bouvet, **p:** Francis Laharrague

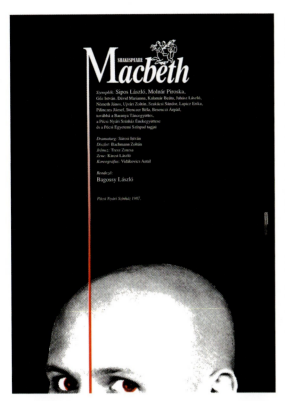
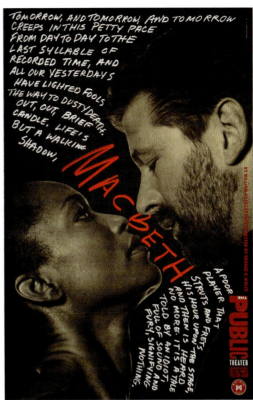
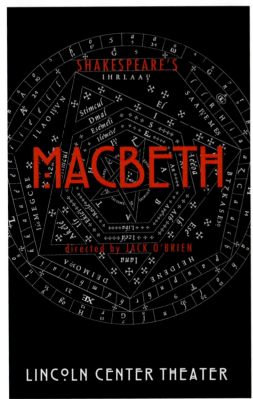
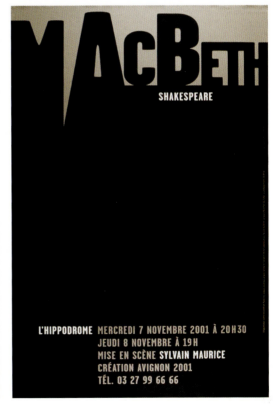

Pecsi Nyari Szinhaz, HU, 1997. d: Levente Bagossy

Lincoln Center Theater, US, 2014. ad: Lincoln Center Theater

The Public Theatre, US, 1998. ad/d: Paula Scher (Pentagram)

L'Hippodrome, Scene Nationale de Douai, FR, 2001.
ad/d: Catherine Zask

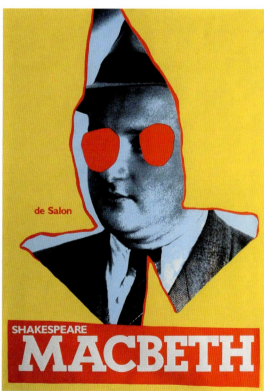

**Theatre der Altmark**, DE, 1992. **d:** Erhard Gruttner (Museum Folkwang, Deutsches Plakat Museum)

**Theatergroep de Salon**, NL, 1986. **ad/d:** Marc Warning

**Setagaya Public Theatre**, JP, 2013. **ad/d:** Kazuya Kondo, **p:** Jun Ishikawa

**Classical Theatre Project, Shakespeare Toronto, Bathurst Street Theatre**, CA, 2011. **ad:** Iam Coulter, **d:** Christopher Rouleau

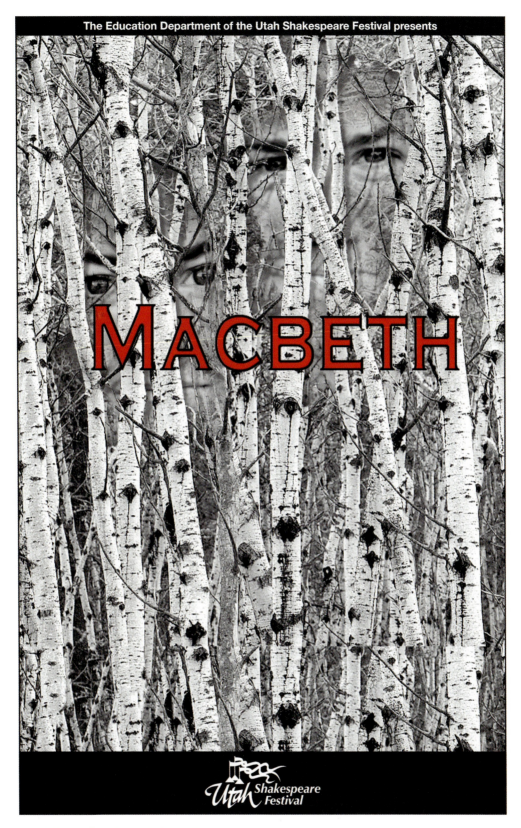
Utah Shakespeare Festival, US, 2015. ad: Philip Hermansen

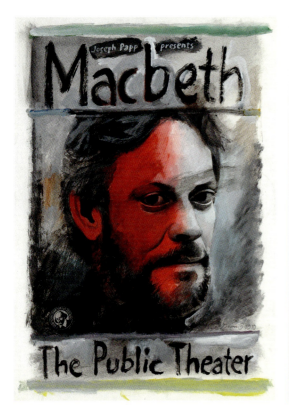

New York Shakespeare Festival, The Public Theater, US, 1989. ad/d/ill: Paul Davis

Teater Arena, BE, 1979. d: n/a

Capitol Shakespeare, US, 2014. d/ill: Bree Reetz

K.S. Stanislavsky Yerevan Russian Drama Theater, RU, 1978. d: K. Shch

Royal Shakespeare Company, Royal Shakespeare Theatre, Barbican Theatre, UK, 1982. d: CS&S Design Partnership, ill: Ralph Steadman

Stadtische Buhnen Munster, DE, 1980. d: Franciszek Starowieyski (Dydo Poster Collection)

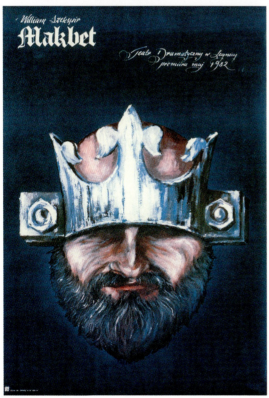

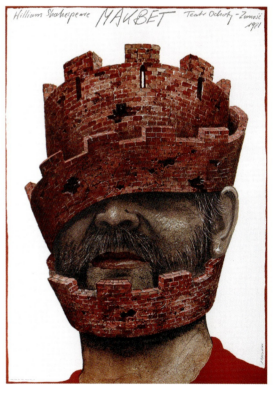

**Teatr Ludowy**, PL, 1998. **ad:** Krzysztof Dydo, **d:** Wiesław Grzegorczyk (Dydo Poster Collection)

**Teatr Dramatyczny w Legnicy**, PL, 1982. **d:** R. Kabanow
(Dydo Poster Collection)

**Teatr Ochoty w Warszawie**, PL, 1981. **ad/d:** Andrzej Pągowski
(Dydo Poster Collection)

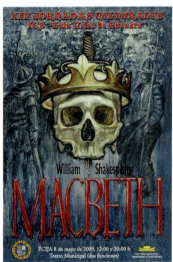
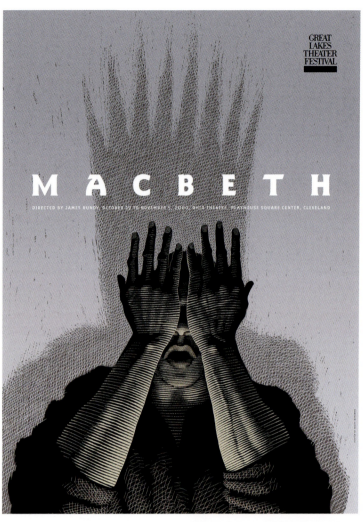
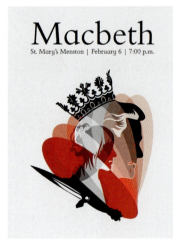
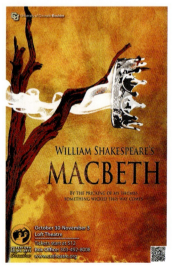

Shakespeare Festival of St. Louis, US, 2003.
ad/d/ill: Rich Nelson

Shakespeare at Traquair Theatre, UK, 2010.
d: Michal Stachowiak

Teatro Municipal de Ecija, ES, 2009.
ad: Providencia Molina Pintar,
d: Rafael Amadeo Rojas Alvarez,
p: Javier Pastor Lopez

Great Lakes Theater Festival, US, 2000. ad: Christina Poddubiuk, d/ill: Scott McKowen

St. Mary's Menston Catholic School, UK 2014.
ad/d/p: Jonathan Biggs

University of Colorado Boulder Theatre & Dance Dept., US, 2013. ad/d: Daniel Leonard

286 Presenting Shakespeare

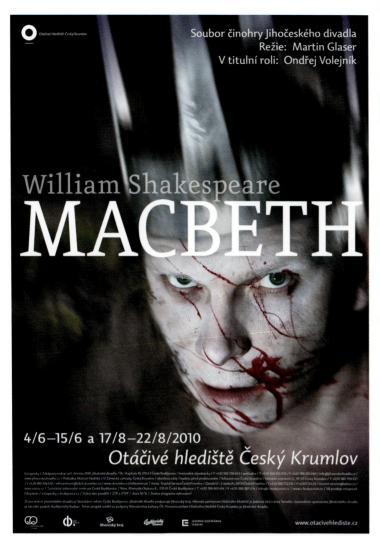

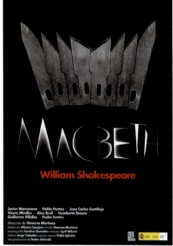
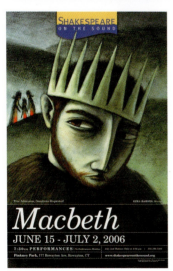
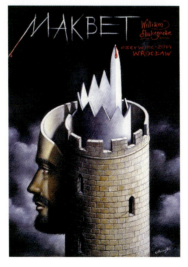

Jihoceske Divadlo, Otacive hlediste Cesky Krumlov, CZ, 2010. ad: Martin Glaser, d: Robert V. Novak, p: Ivan Pinkava

Shakespeare on the Sound, US, 2006.
ad: Ezra Barnes, d: Nat Connacher

Wroclaw Opera & Theater, PL, 2014.
ad/d: Rafal Olbinski

Saratoga Shakespeare Company, US, 2014.
ad/d: Frank Edwards/Tonner Holford,
p: Mark McCarthy, Taylor James

Teatre Defondo, ES, 2010.
ad: Diego Areso Nieva

New Triad Theatre Company, NL, 1989.
ad/d/p: Hans Bockting

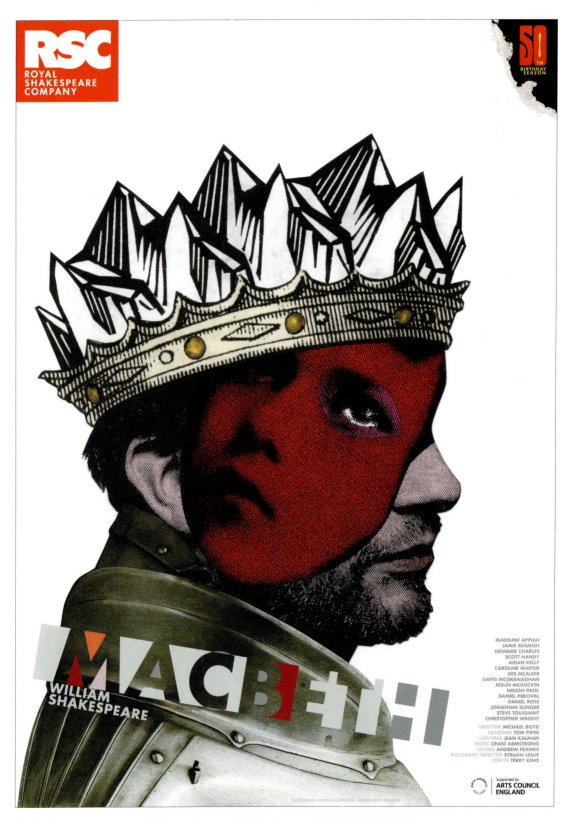

Royal Shakespeare Company, Royal Shakespeare Theatre, UK, 2011. ad/d: Andy Williams, ill: Andrzej Klimowski

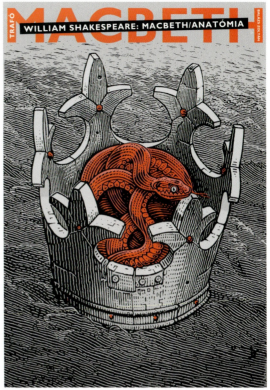

**University of San Francisco and College Players, Gill Theatre Campion Hall**, US, 1997. **d/ill**: Jack DeGovia

**Maladype, Trafo Theatre**, HU, 2013. **d**: Istvan Orosz

**Volksbuhne**, DE, 1959. **d**: Roman Weyl (Museum Folkwang, Deutsches Plakat Museum)

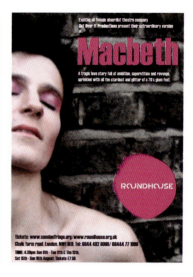

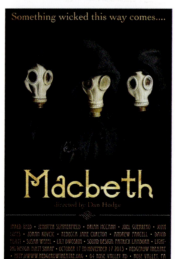
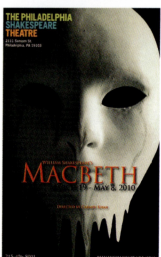

**Stark Naked Theatre Company**, US, 2013.
ad: Kim Tobin-Lehl, d: Chip Schneider,
d/p: Gabrielle Nissen

**Shake-scene Players**, Edinburgh Fringe Festival 2005, UK, 2005.
ad/d: Lynne R. Holmes (LRH Creatives, LLC)

**Nikola Vaptzarov Drama Theatre**, BG, 2012.
ad: Grigor Antonov, d/p: Venelin Shurelov

**The Liverpool Shakespeare Festival, Lodestar Theatre Company**, Royal Court Liverpool, UK, 2012. ad: Damon Scott, Nomad Associates, d: Jason Brown

**Children's Shakespeare Theatre**, US, 2010.
ad/d: David Green (Brightgreen Design),
p: Chris Carroll

**Hedgerow Theatre**, US, 2013.
ad/d/p: Kyle Cassidy

**Camden Fringe, The Roundhouse**, UK, 2009.
ad/p: Paula Benson, d: Velenzia Spearpoint

**Shakespeare & Company**, US, 2002.
d: Mary Garnish, p: Kevin Sprague

**The Philadelphia Shakespeare Theatre**, US, 2010. d: n/a

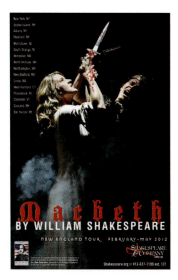
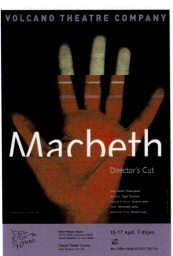
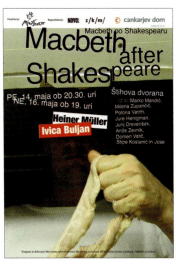

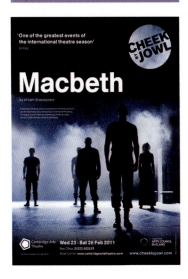

Setagaya Public Theatre, JP, 2004.
ad: Kiyoaki Ichikawa, d: Kaori Sato,
ill: 100% Orange

Volcano Theatre Company, UK, 1999.
ad/d/ill: Scott Doran

Cheek by Jowl Theatre Co., UK, 2011.
ad/d: Ranald Graham, p: Johan Persson

Milwaukee Shakespeare Festival, US, 2007.
ad: Linsey Sierger, Third Sector Creative

Mini Teater, SI, 2009. ad: Robert Waltl,
d: Maja Gspan, p: Marko Mandic Archive

Theatre Nanterre-Amandiers, FR, 2013.
ad/d: Pascal Bejean, Nicolas Ledoux,
p: Image Bank

Shakespeare & Company, US, 2012.
d: Mary Garnish, p: Kevin Sprague

Bandt Gutbrodt die Verschwender E.V., DE,
1998. ad/d: Ole Friedrich

Prague Shakespeare Company, Divadlo
Kolowrat, CZ, 2013. d: Martin Hula,
p: Ashe Kazanjian

Macbeth  291

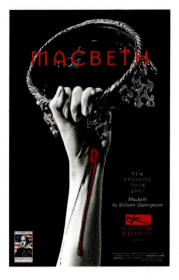
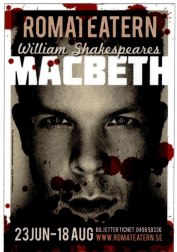
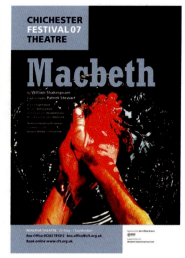

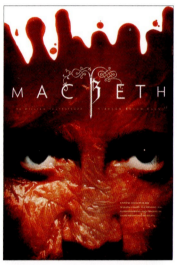

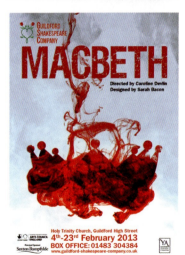
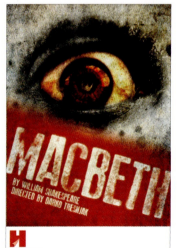
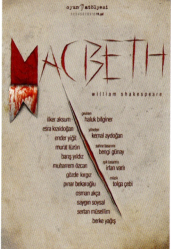

Shakespeare & Company, US, 2007.
d/p: Kevin Sprague

The Rondo Theatre, UK, 2011.
ad/d: Daniel Shearn

Guildford Shakespeare Company, UK, 2013.
d: Little Yellow Duck

Romateatern, SE, 2010. ad/d: Johan Brunzell,
p: Niclas Brunzell

Grupo Delirio Cia de Teatro, BR, 2006.
ad/d: Marcos Minini, p: Marcos Minini, Stock

Hartford Stage, US, 2013.
ad/d: Taylor Goodell Benedum

Chichester Festival Theatre, UK, 2007.
ad: Shaun Webb, d: Shaun Webb Design,
p: Shaun Webb

Theater Aeternam, CH, 2008.
ad/d: Erich Brechbuhl

Theater: n/a, TR, 2010. ad: Haluk Bilginer,
d: Oyun Atolyesi

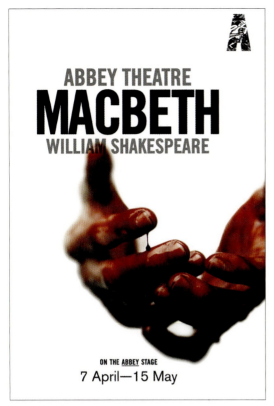

Abbey Theatre, The National Theatre of Ireland, IE, 2010.
ad/d: Ciaran OGaora, p: Ryan Jay

Theatre 13, FR, 2013. ad/d/p: Cedric Gatillon

Milton Theatre, US, 2003. d: Harry Pearce

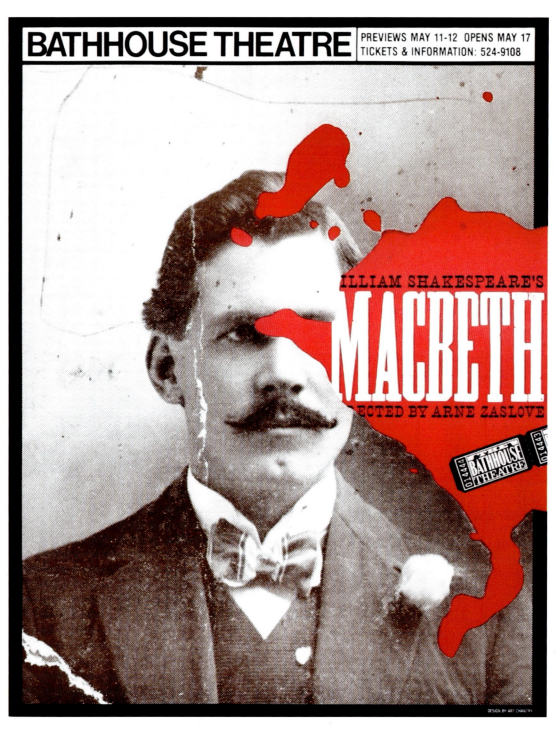

Bathhouse Theatre, US, 1983. d: Art Chantry

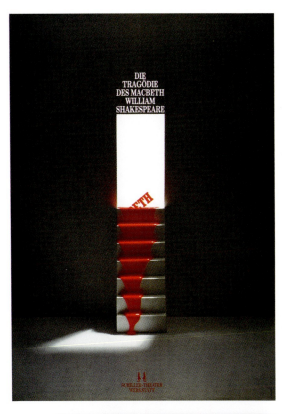
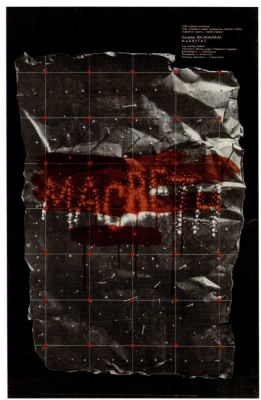
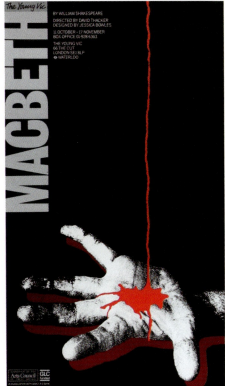
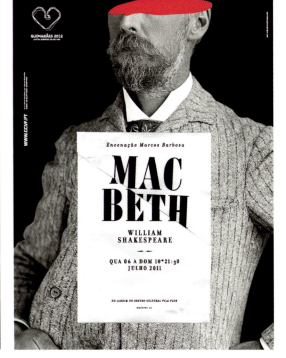

**Schiller Theater Werkstatt**, DE, 1988. **d:** Holger Matthies w(Museum Folkwang, Deutsches Plakat Museum)

**Young Vic Theatre**, UK, 1984. **ad/d:** John David Lloyd, Jim Northover, Lloyd Northover

**Academic Theater of Opera and Ballet**, LT, 1989. **d:** Adomas Jacovskis

**Centro Cultural Vila Flor**, Teatro Oficina, PT, 2011. **ad/d:** Atelier Martino & Jana

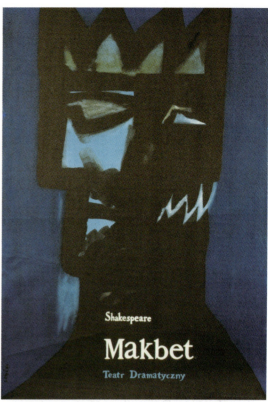

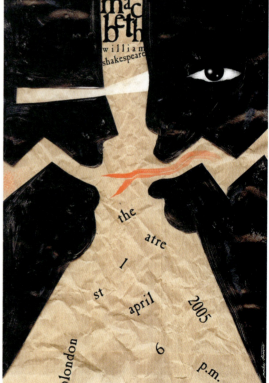

**Penn State Pavilion Theatre**, US, 1994. **ad/d:** Lanny Sommese

**Teatr Powszechny w Warszawie**, PL, 1996. **d:** Jan Lenica (Dydo Poster Collection)

**Teatr Dramatyczny**, PL, 1960. **d:** Jan Lenica (Dydo Poster Collection)

**London Theatre**, UK, 2005. **d:** Monika Starowicz

College of Marin Drama Department, US, 2012. d/ill: Roger W. Dormann

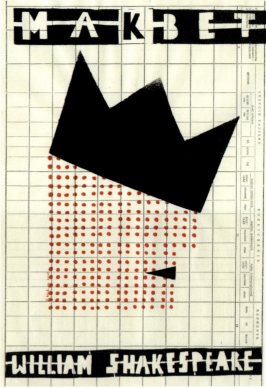
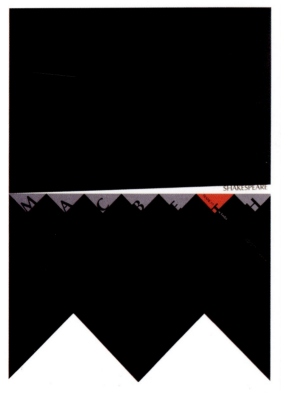
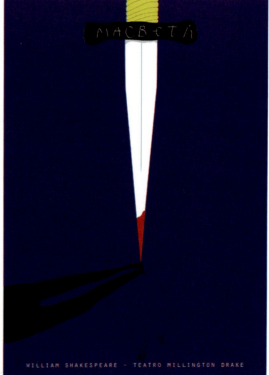

**Theatre du Soleil**, FR, 2013. **ad/d:** Francois Caspar

**Teatr 77**, PL, 1993. **d:** Tadeusz Piechura (Dydo Poster Collection)

**Theater:** n/a, PL, 2013. **d:** Sebastian Kubica (Dydo Poster Collection)

**Teatro Millington Drake**, UY, 1990. **ad/d:** Fidel Sclavo

Dramsko kazaliste Gavella, HR, 1972. d: Boris Bucan

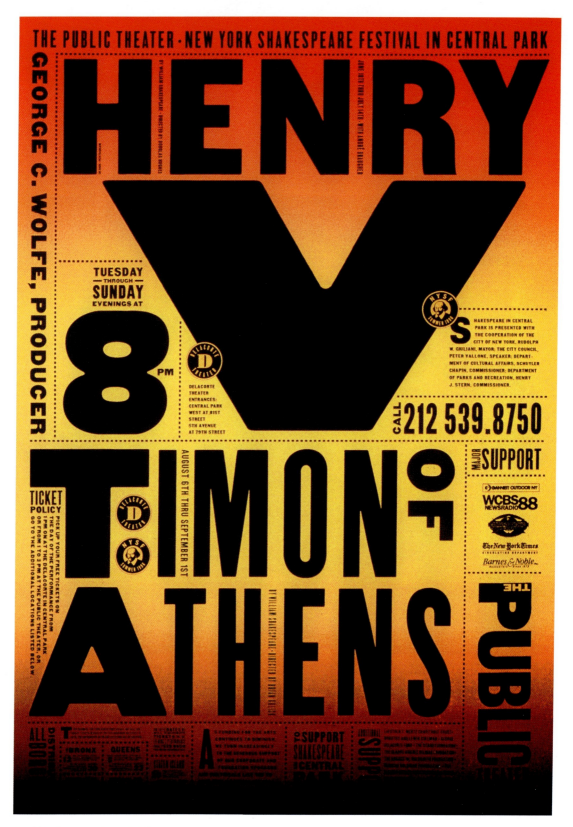

The Public Theater, US, 1996. ad/d: Paula Scher (Pentagram)

# ANTHOLOGIES

*The play's the thing wherein I'll catch the conscience of the king.*
—*Hamlet*

When director-producer Joseph Papp conceived of the New York Shakespeare Festival in 1954, he triggered popular passion for the Bard that altered the cultural and physical landscape of the city. Before 1962, when the festival moved to its permanent home in Central Park's Delacourt Theater, its plays were performed in churches, parks, and a mobile theater unit; free tickets are still distributed every summer to anyone willing to wait in line. Not all Shakespeare festival producers are so generous, but there is no paucity of plays to share with an adoring public. This section contains posters promoting pairings and anthologies of works. From the anonymous theater bills of nineteenth-century London to Paula Scher's notices for New York's Public Theater, posters joyfully celebrate the the Bard's wares.

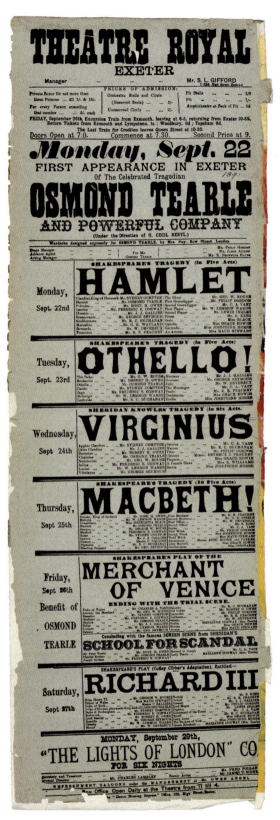
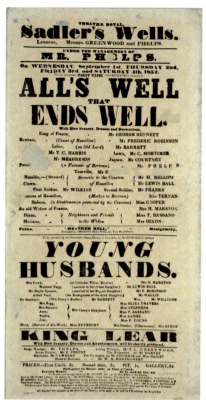
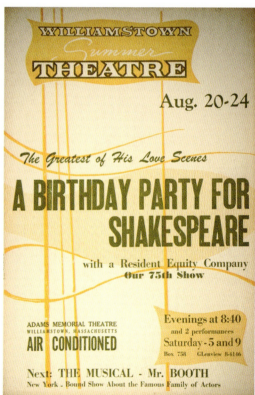

Theatre Royal, UK, 1891. d: n/a

Theatre Royal, UK, 1892. d: n/a

Williamstown Theatre Festival, US, 1963. d: n/a

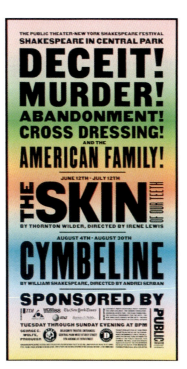
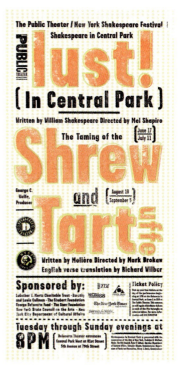
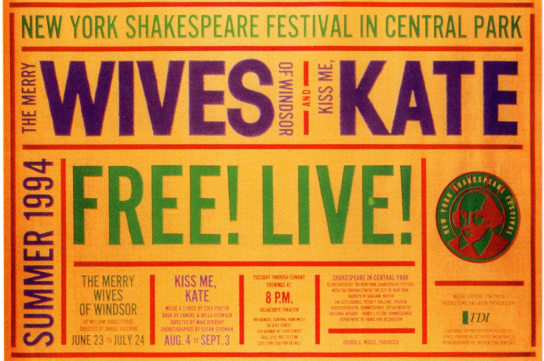

The Public Theater, US, 1995.
ad/d: Paula Scher (Pentagram)

The Public Theater, US, 1998.
ad/d: Paula Scher (Pentagram)

The Public Theater, US, 1999.
ad/d: Paula Scher (Pentagram)

The Public Theater, US, 1994. ad/d: Paula Scher (Pentagram)

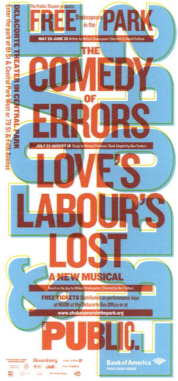
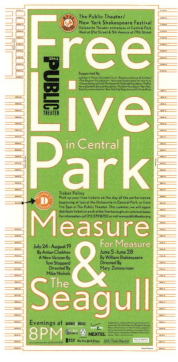
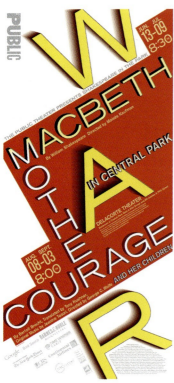
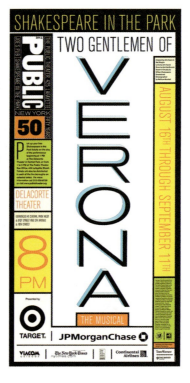
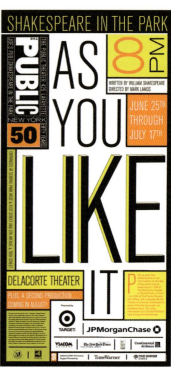

The Public Theater, US, 2000.
ad/d: Paula Scher (Pentagram)

The Public Theater, US, 2013.
ad/d: Paula Scher (Pentagram)

The Public Theater, US, 2001.
ad/d: Paula Scher (Pentagram)

The Public Theater, US, 2006.
ad/d: Paula Scher (Pentagram)

The Public Theater, US, 2005.
ad/d: Paula Scher (Pentagram)

The Public Theater, US, 2005.
ad/d: Paula Scher (Pentagram)

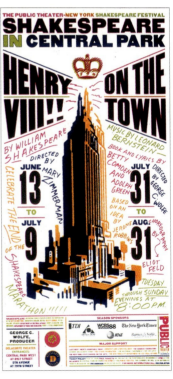

The Public Theater, US, 2012.
ad/d: Paula Scher (Pentagram)

The Public Theater, US, 2010.
ad/d: Paula Scher (Pentagram)

The Public Theater, US, 2009.
ad/d: Paula Scher (Pentagram)

The Public Theater, US, 2011.
ad/d: Paula Scher (Pentagram)

The Public Theater, US, 2014.
ad: Paula Scher (Pentagram)
d: Ludwig Janoff (Pentagram),
Kristin Huber (The Public Theater)

The Public Theater, US, 1997.
ad/d: Paula Scher (Pentagram)

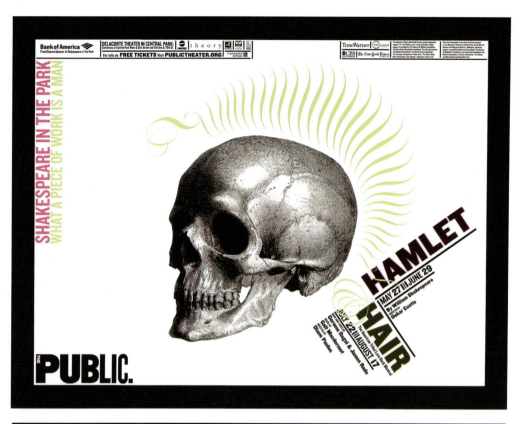

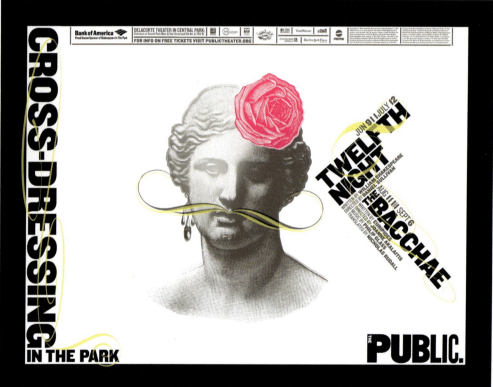

The Public Theater, US, 2007. ad/d: Paula Scher (Pentagram)

The Public Theater, US, 2008. ad/d: Paula Scher (Pentagram)

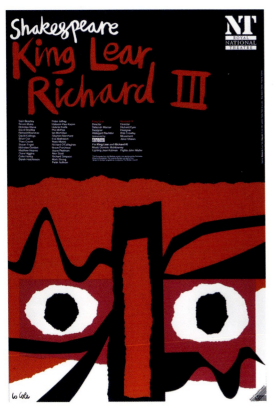

National Theatre, Lyttelton Theatre, UK, 1990. ad: Richard Eyre, cd: Michael Mayhew, d: Lo Cole

Owl Spot, JP, 2012. ad: Kiyoaki Ichikawa, d: Kaori Sato, ill: 100% Orange

Schauspiel Haus Zuerich, CH, 1964. d/ill: Platti
(Collection of Chisholm Larsson Gallery, NYC)

24 Hour Play Festival, Queen City Collective, US, 2012.
ad/d: Daniel Zender

Anthologies 307

**Federal Theatre Playhouse**, US, 1940. d: n/a

**Deutsche Shakespeare-Gesellschaft West**, DE, 1964. d: HAP Grieshaber (Museum Folkwang, Deutsches Plakat Museum)

**An Evening with Shakespeare**, Stary Teatr, PL, 1964. d: Jerzy Napieracz (Dydo Poster Collection)

**Royal Shakespeare Company**, World Class Classical Theatre, UK, 1995. ad: Sian Stirling, d: Royal Shakespeare Company, p: Nick Higgins

**California Shakespeare Festival**, University of Santa Clara, Lifeboat Theater, US, 1966. d: Earl Newman
(Collection of Chisholm Larsson Gallery, NYC)

**Shakespeare & Company**, Shakespeare Outside The Ordinary, Theatre at the Mount, US, 1997. d/ill: R. Frisina
(Collection of Chisholm Larsson Gallery, NYC)

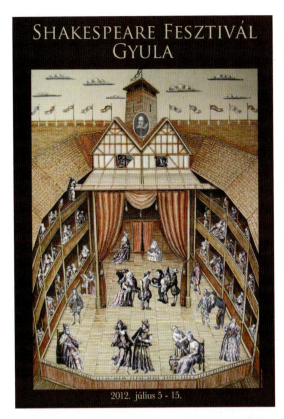
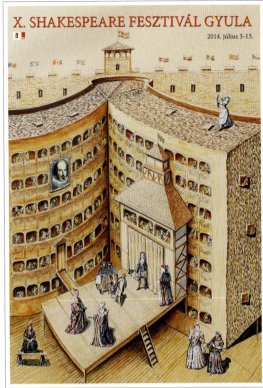
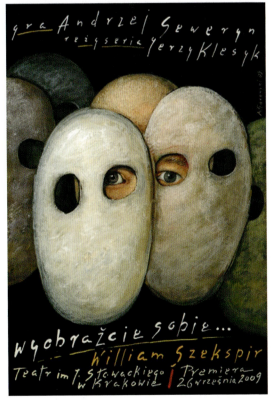

Gyula Castle Theatre, HU, 2012. **ad:** Jozef Gedeou, **d:** Onisim Colta

Gyula Castle Theatre, HU, 2014. **ad:** Jozef Gedeou, **d:** Onisim Colta

Teatr im. J. Slowackiego w Krakowie, PL, 2009. **d:** Mieczyslaw Gorowski
(Dydo Poster Collection)

The Shakespeare Theatre of New Jersey, US, 2014.
**ad/d/ill:** Scott McKowen

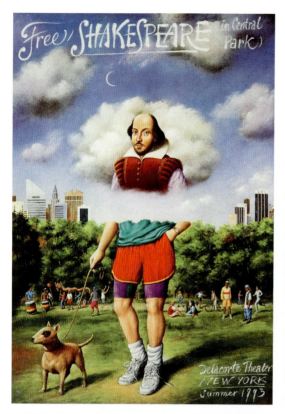

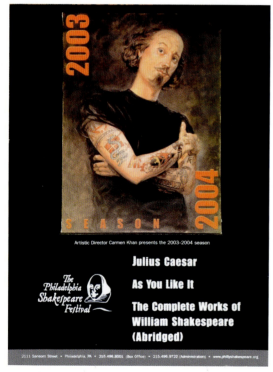
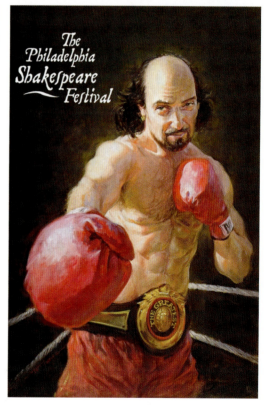

Free Shakespeare in Central Park, The Public Theater, Delacorte Theater, US, 1993. ad: Jim Russek, d: Rafal Olbinski

The Philadelphia Shakespeare Festival, The Philadelphia Shakespeare Festival, US, 2003. d: Mathew McFarren

The Philadelphia Shakespeare Festival, The Philadelphia Shakespeare Theatre, US, 2008. d: Mathew McFarren

The Philadelphia Shakespeare Festival, The Philadelphia Shakespeare Theatre, US, 2007. d: Mathew McFarren

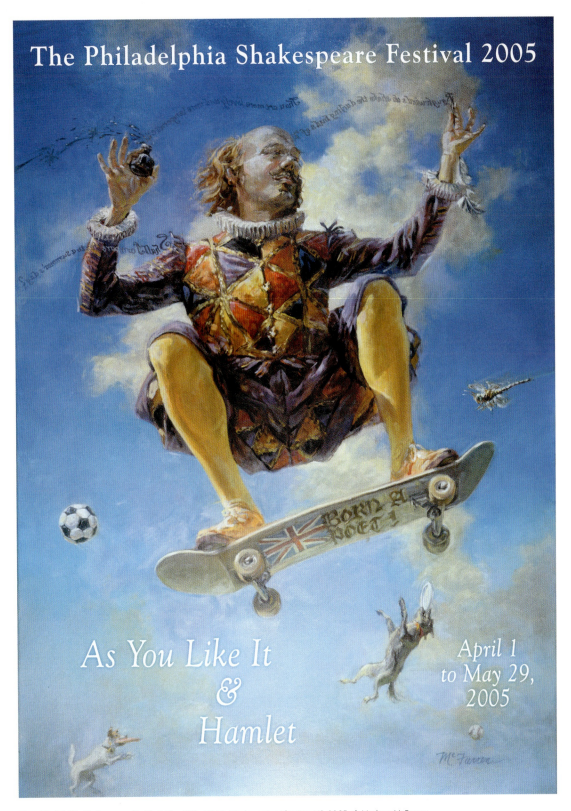

The Philadelphia Shakespeare Festival, The Philadelphia Shakespeare Theatre, US, 2005. d: Mathew McFarren

 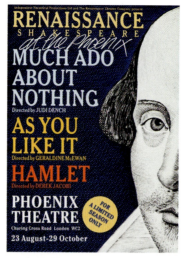 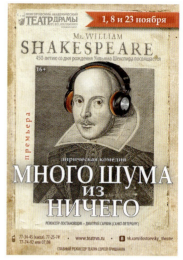

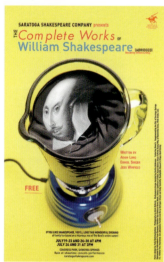 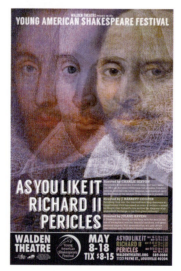 

  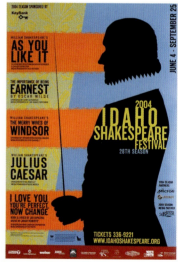

Shakespeare's Globe, UK, 2013. ad/d: Embrace

Saratoga Shakespeare Company, US, 2005. ad: Nicholas Parslow, Tom Rothermel, d: Analia Del Giorgio, Mirek Janczor, p: Mark McCarty

Cockpit Theatre, City of Westminister College, UK, 2009. ad/d: Pravin Dewdhory

The Renaissance Theatre Company, Phoenix Theatre, UK, 1988. ad/d: Shaun Webb Design

Young American Shakespeare Festival, Walden Theatre, US, 2014. ad/d: Isaac Spradlin

*Uncle Will Wants You*, Florence English Speaking Theatre Artists, IT, 2013. ad/d: David Ballerini

Dostoevsky Drama Theatre, RU, 2014. ad: Chubenko Vsevolod, d: Dmitry Sarvin, Alexandra Kashirina

Polish Shakespeare Company, PL, 1998. (Collection of Chisholm Larsson Gallery, NYC)

Idaho Shakespeare Festival, US, 2004. ad/d: Kristy Weyhrich

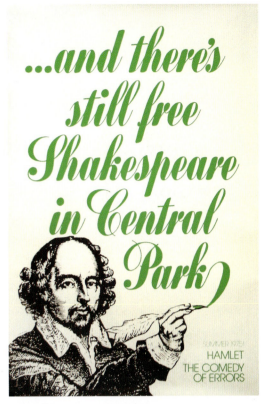

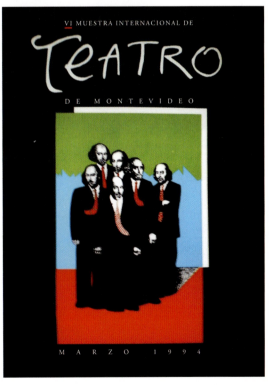

And There's Still Free Shakespeare in Central Park, The Public Theater, Delacorte Theater, US, 1972. d: Susan Frank
(Collection of Chisholm Larsson Gallery, NYC)

And There's Still Free Shakespeare in Central Park, The Public Theater, Delacorte Theater, US, 1975. d: n/a
(Collection of Chisholm Larsson Gallery, NYC)

New City Theater, US, 1989.
d: Art Chantry

New City Theater, US, 1990.
d: Art Chantry

VI International Theater Encounter, UY, 1994.
ad/d: Fidel Sclavo

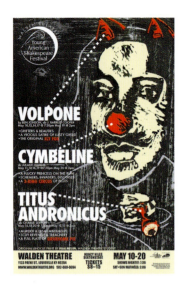

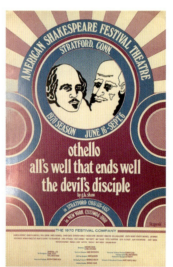
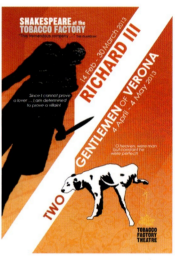

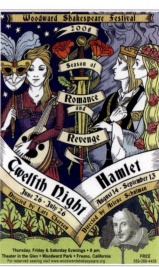

Young American Shakespeare Festival, Walden Theatre, US, 2012. ad/d: Isaac Spradlin, art: Julia Meller

Itaka Art Center, RS, 2014. ad: Slavisa Savic

Woodward Shakespeare Festival, US, 2007. d/ill: Doug Hansen

Shakespeare at Traquair Theatre, UK, 2013. ad/d: Michal Stachowiak

American Shakespeare Festival Theatre, US, 1970. d: University of Kansas, ad: Moses Gunn

Nashville Shakespeare Festival, Centennial Park Bandshell, US, 2007. ad/d: Tracy Leigh Ratliff

Lit Moon World Shakespeare Festival, US, 2006. ad/d: Yevgenia Nayberg

Shakespeare at the Tobacco Factory, UK, 2013. d: Alpha Charlie Design

Woodward Shakespeare Festival, US, 2008. d/ill: Doug Hansen

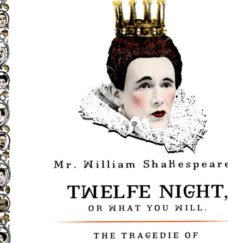

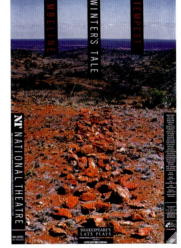

**Penn State Pavilion Theatre**, US, 1997.
**ad/d:** Lanny Sommese

**The Philadelphia Shakespeare Theatre**, US, 2011. **d:** n/a

**The English Shakespeare Company, De Stadsschouwburg**, NL, 1988. **d:** n/a

**Belasco Theatre**, US, 2013. **ad:** Stacey Lieberman Prince (SpotCo), **d:** Jacob Cooper (SpotCo)

**Shakespeare's Globe**, UK, 2006.
**ad/d:** Huw Morgan, **p:** Nick Higgins (Graphic Thought Facility)

**National Theatre, Cottesloe Theatre**, UK, 1988. **cd:** Richard Bird, **ad:** Peter Hall, **d:** Alison Chitty, **p:** Richard Long

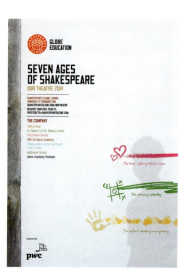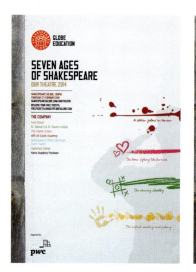

*Seven Ages of Shakespeare*, Shakespeare's Globe, UK, 2014. **d:** Embrace

...*And There's Still Free Shakespeare in Central Park*, The Public Theater, Delacorte Theater, US, 1974. **d**: Susan Frank
(Collection of Chisholm Larsson Gallery, NYC)

CREDITS

**Bakhrushin Museum** Ⓞ Federal State Budget Institution of Culture "A.A. Bakhrushin State Central Theatre Museum," Moscow.
(pgs. 27, 30, 96, 135, 152, 208, 254, 269)

Courtesy of the Budapest Poster Gallery
(pgs. 30, 134, 209)

Courtesy of Georgian State Museum of Theatre, Music, Cinema, and Choreography (pgs. 27, 73, 83, 116, 140, 152, 155, 193)

Courtesy of Naomi Games © Estate of Abram Games. (pg. 13)

**National Theatre** posters have been sourced from the NT Archive, which holds material on every NT production from 1963 up to present day. Prints of National Theatre posters can be purchased from http://posters.nationaltheatre.org.uk/
(pgs. 125, 132, 141, 164, 170, 225, 240, 255, 307, 315)

Courtesy of National Theatre of Scotland & Albert Watson (pg. 272)

Courtesy of Pentagram (pgs. 49, 63, 82, 145, 189, 196, 264, 267, 279, 300, 303, 304, 305, 306)

Courtesy of Philadelphia Shakespeare Theatre (pgs. 9, 88, 100, 110, 183, 194, 212, 256, 290, 310, 311, 315)

Courtesy of Royal Shakespeare Company
(pgs. 40, 47, 48, 49, 55, 68, 77, 82, 107, 117, 118, 124, 136, 138, 139, 141, 145, 146, 158, 160, 162, 163, 167, 170, 172, 173, 178, 180, 182, 186, 187, 198, 215, 216, 220, 223, 226, 228, 231, 232, 239, 240, 248, 250, 251, 256, 257, 258, 264, 265, 270, 283, 288)

Courtesy of Susan Homar, Laura Damm, and the Colección Museo de Historia, Antropología y Arte Universidad de Puerto Rico (pg. 259)

Courtesy of Victoria and Albert Museum
(pgs. 14, 16, 18, 20, 26, 151, 274, 302)

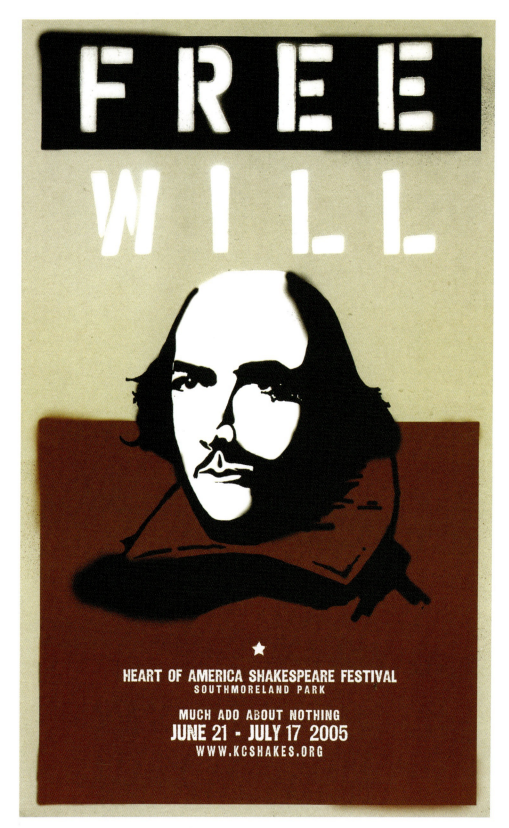

*Free Will*, Heart of America Shakespeare Festival, US, 2005. **d:** Nathaniel Cooper